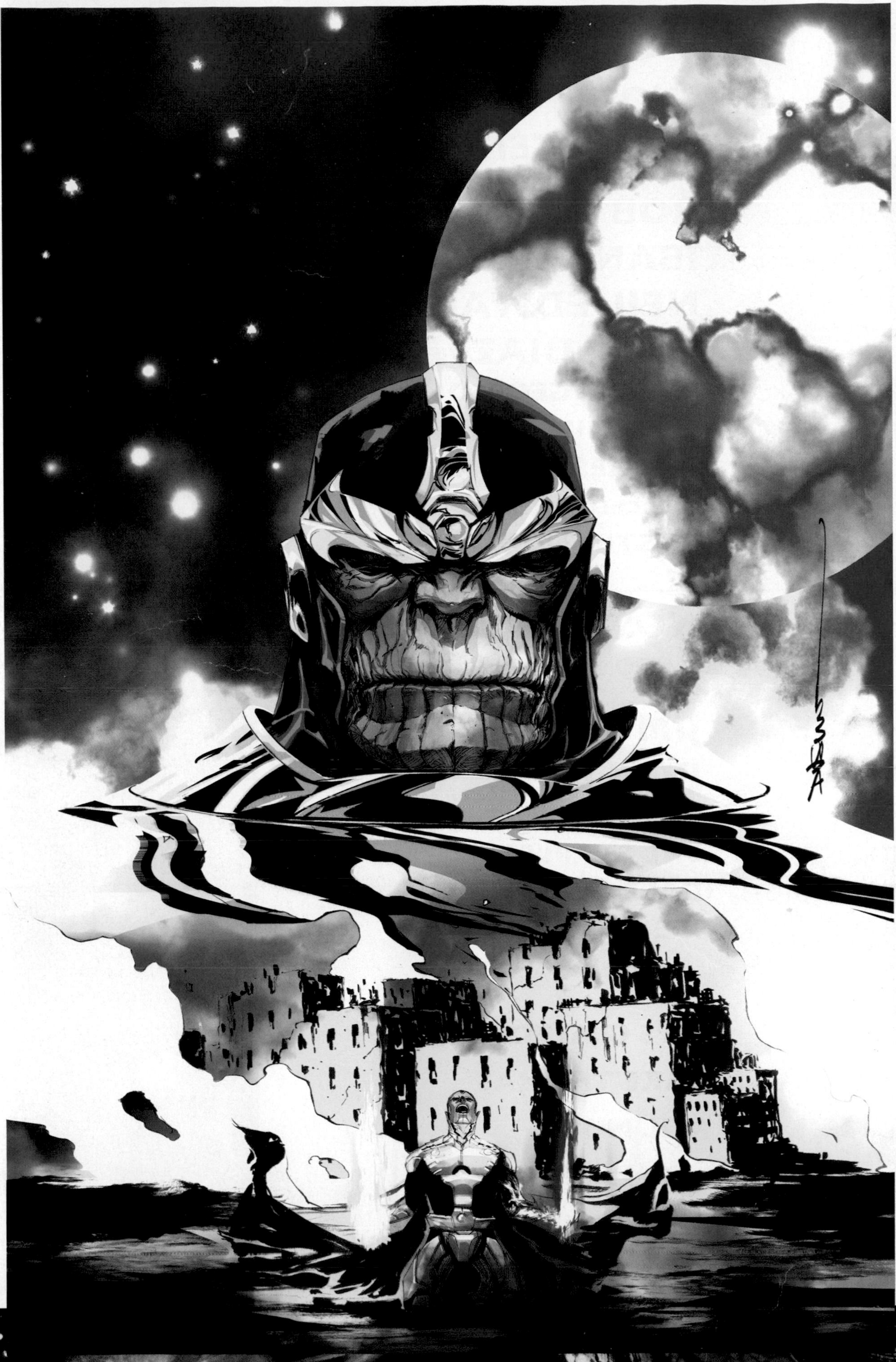

ONE

THANOS: A GOD UP THERE LISTENING

WRITER **ROB WILLIAMS**
PENCILERS/INKERS **IBAN COELLO** (#1 & 3),
NEIL EDWARDS (#2-3) &
ARTISTS **PACO DIAZ** (#2 & 4)
STORYBOARDS **MAST & GEOFFO**
AND **DANIEL GOVAR**
COLORIST **ANDRES MOSSA** WITH
SOTOCOLOR'S L. MOLINAR (#4)
COVER ARTIST **DUSTIN NGUYEN**

THANOS ANNUAL #1

"DAMNATION & REDEMPTION"

WRITER **JIM STARLIN**
PENCILER **RON LIM**
INKER **ANDY SMITH**
COLORIST **VAL STAPLES**
COVER ARTISTS **DALE KEOWN** &
IVE SVORCINA

LETTERER **VC'S CLAYTON COWLES**
ASSISTANT EDITOR **JAKE THOMAS**
EDITOR **WIL MOSS**
EXECUTIVE EDITOR **TOM BREVOORT**

HANOS: A GOD UP THERE LISTENING. Contains material originally published in magazine form as THANOS: A GOD UP THERE LISTENING #1-4 and THANOS ANNUAL #1. First rinting 2014. ISBN# 978-0-7851-9158-2. Published by MARVEL WORLDWIDE, INC., a subsidiary of MARVEL ENTERTAINMENT, LLC. OFFICE OF PUBLICATION: 135 West 50th treet, New York, NY 10020. **Printed in the U.S.A.** ALAN FINE, EVP - Office of the President, larvel Worldwide, Inc. and EVP & CMO Marvel Characters B.V.; DAN BUCKLEY, Publisher & President - Print, Animation & Digital Divisions; JOE QUESADA, Chief Creative Officer; OM BREVOORT, SVP of Publishing; DAVID BOGART, SVP of Operations & Procurement, Publishing; C.B. CEBULSKI, SVP of Creator & Content Development; DAVID GABRIEL, SVP rint, Sales & Marketing; JIM O'KEEFE, VP of Operations & Logistics; DAN CARR, Executive Director of Publishing Technology; SUSAN CRESPI, Editorial Operations Manager; ALEX IORALES, Publishing Operations Manager; STAN LEE, Chairman Emeritus. For information regarding advertising in Marvel Comics or on Marvel.com, please contact Niza Disla, irector of Marvel Partnerships, at ndisla@marvel.com. For Marvel subscription inquiries, please call 800-217-9158. **Manufactured between 10/3/2014 and 11/17/2014 by VORZALLA PUBLISHING CO., STEVENS POINT, WI, USA.**

0987654321

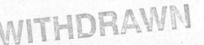

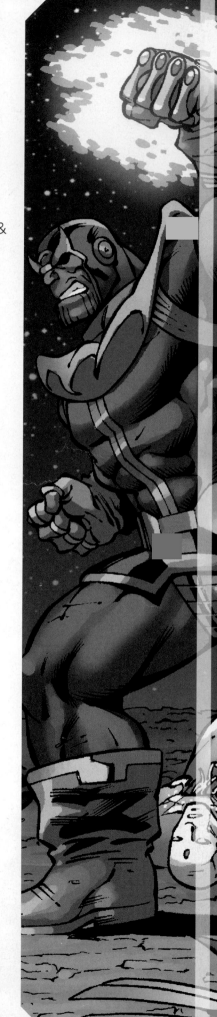

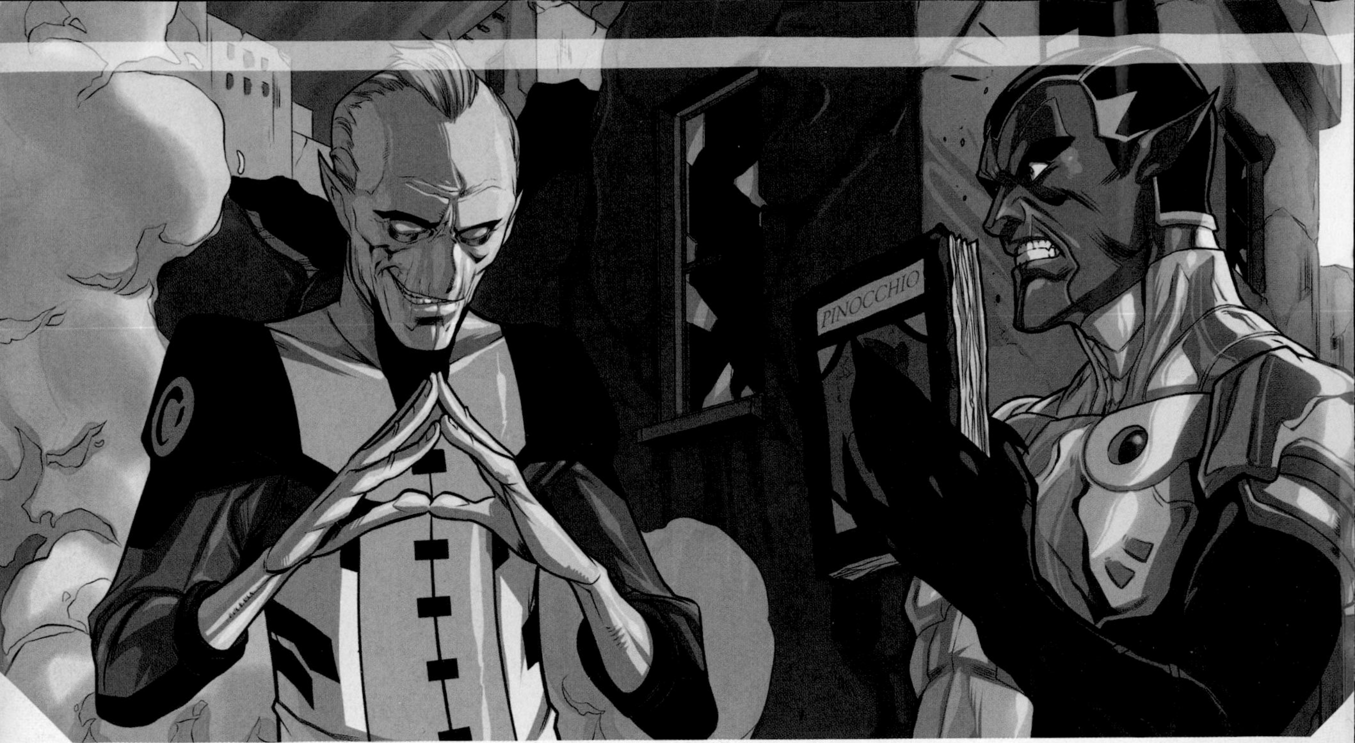

PINOCCHIO

COLLECTION EDITOR
MARK D. BEAZLEY
DIGITAL TRAFFIC COORDINATOR
JOE HOCHSTEIN
ASSOCIATE MANAGING EDITOR
ALEX STARBUCK
EDITOR, SPECIAL PROJECTS
JENNIFER GRÜNWALD
SENIOR EDITOR, SPECIAL PROJECTS
JEFF YOUNGQUIST
SVP PRINT, SALES & MARKETING
DAVID GABRIEL

PRODUCTION MANAGER
TIM SMITH 3
PRODUCTION
LARISSA LOUIS & **ARLIN ORTIZ**

EDITOR IN CHIEF
AXEL ALONSO
CHIEF CREATIVE OFFICER
JOE QUESADA
PUBLISHER
DAN BUCKLEY
EXECUTIVE PRODUCER
ALAN FINE

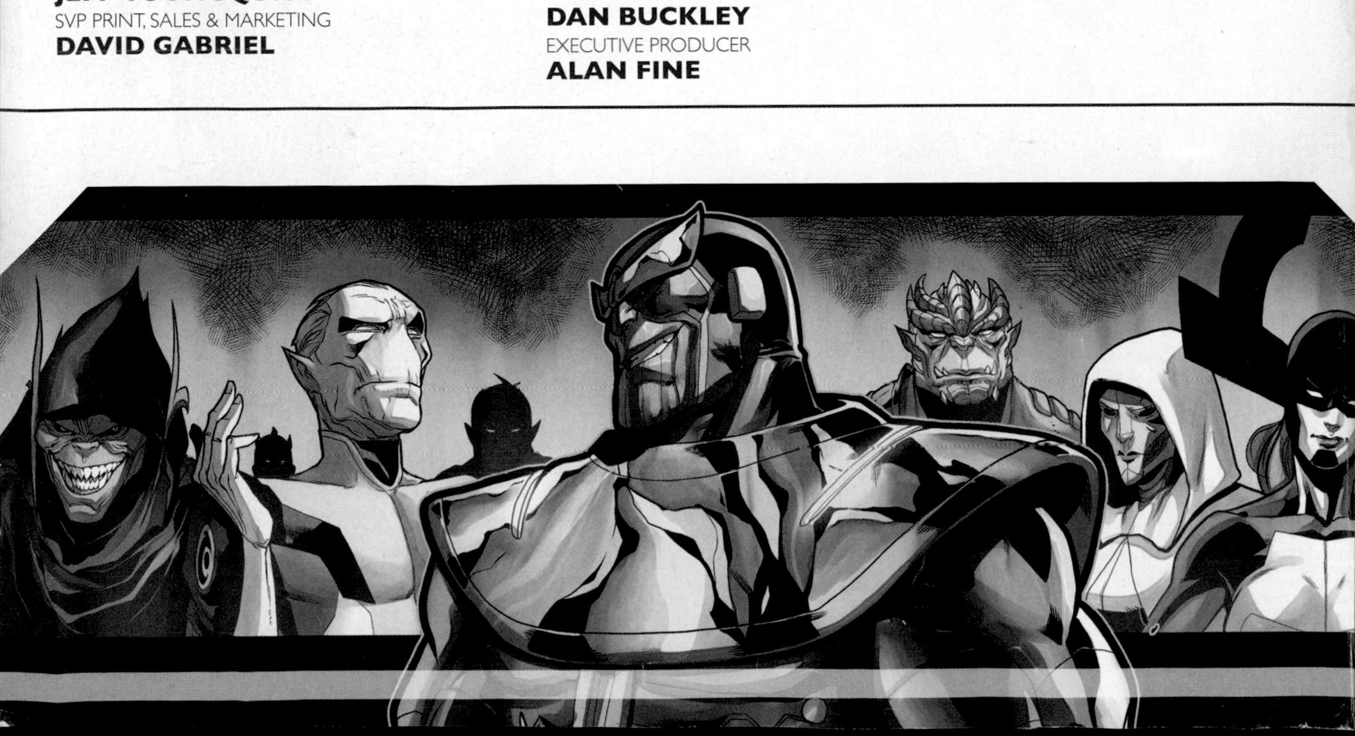

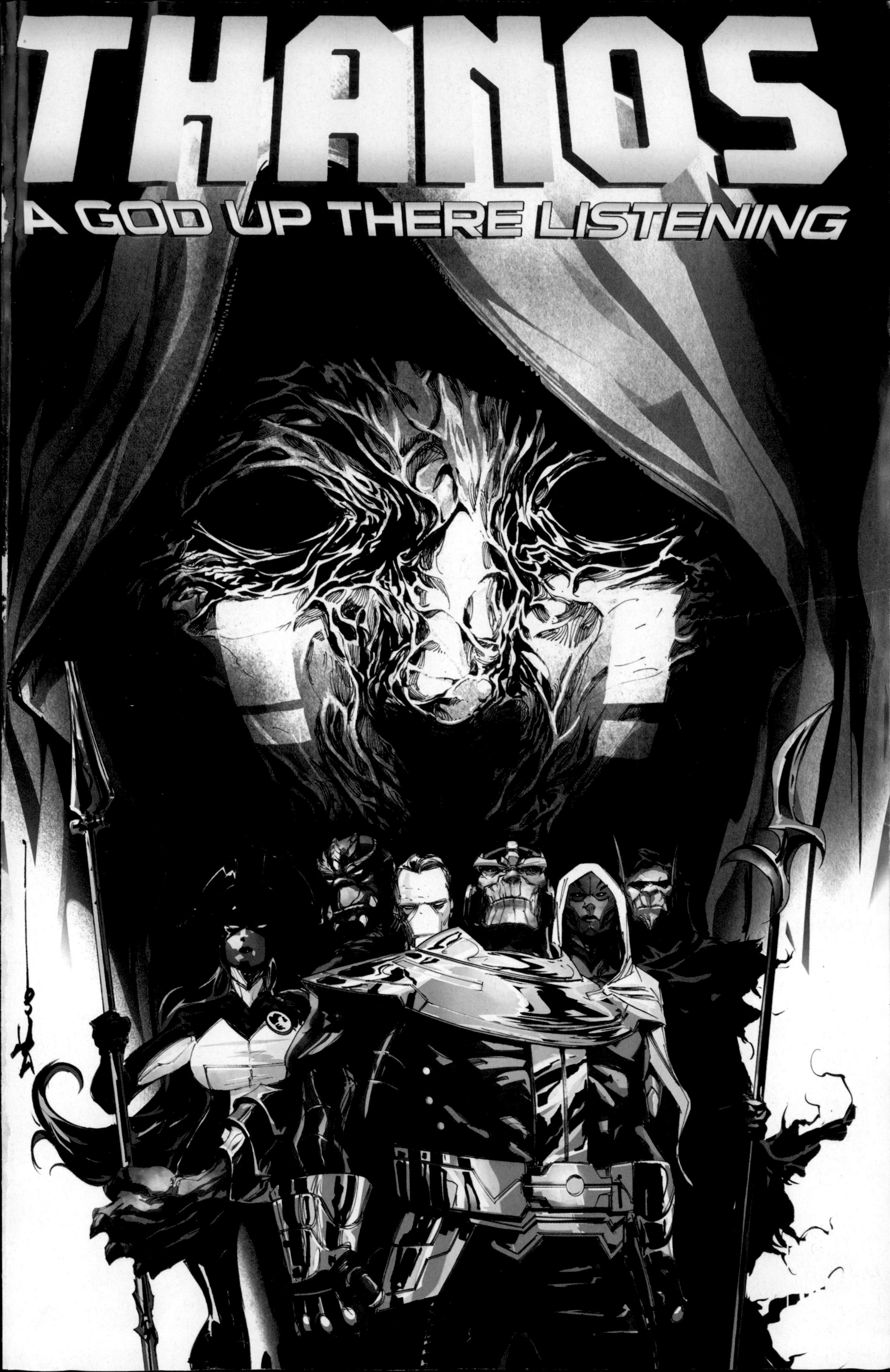
THANOS
A GOD UP THERE LISTENING

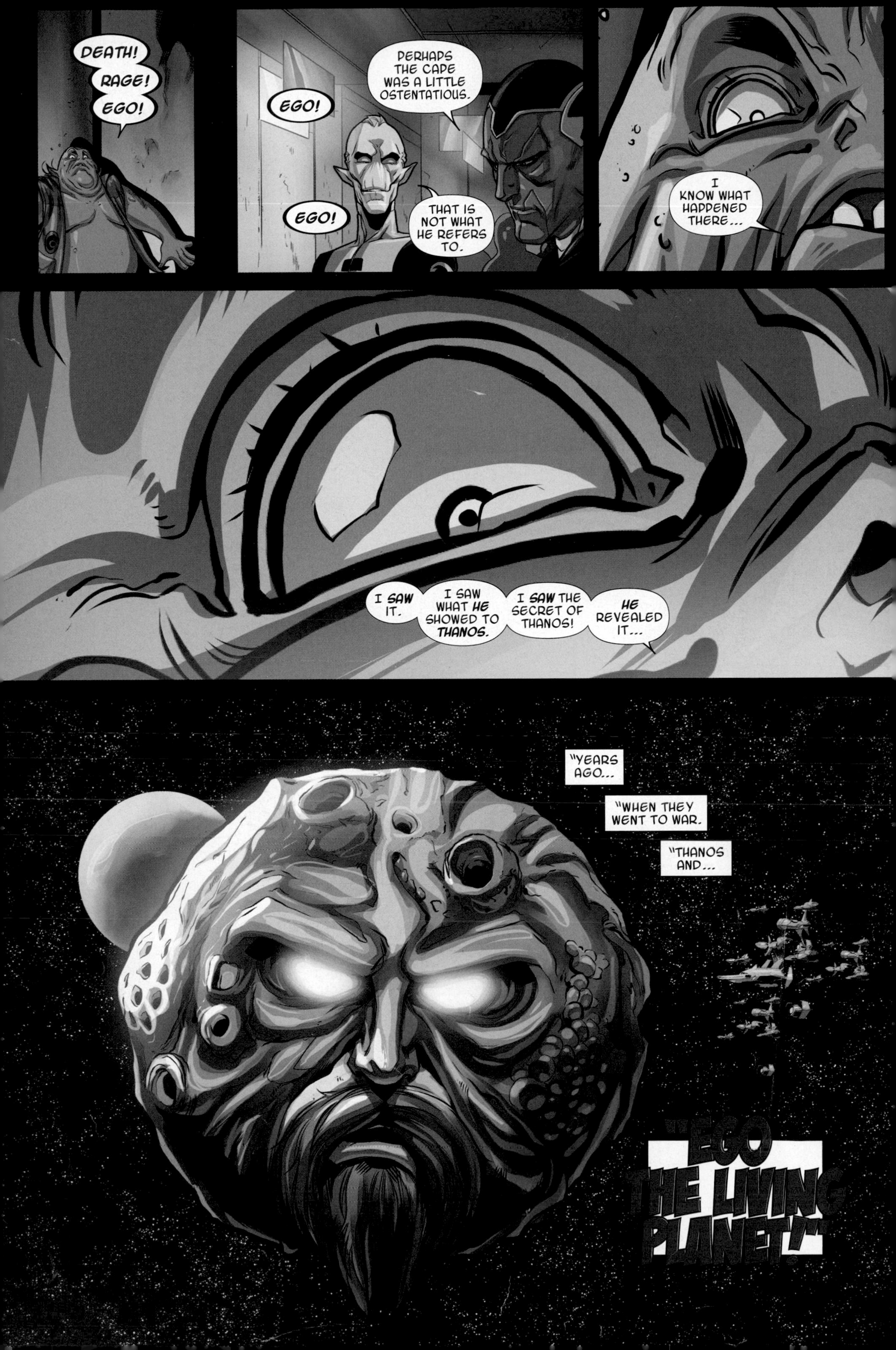
DEATH!
RAGE!
EGO!
EGO!
PERHAPS THE CAPE WAS A LITTLE OSTENTATIOUS.
EGO!
THAT IS NOT WHAT HE REFERS TO.
I KNOW WHAT HAPPENED THERE...
I SAW IT.
I SAW WHAT HE SHOWED TO THANOS.
I SAW THE SECRET OF THANOS!
HE REVEALED IT...
"YEARS AGO...
"WHEN THEY WENT TO WAR.
"THANOS AND...
"EGO THE LIVING PLANET!"

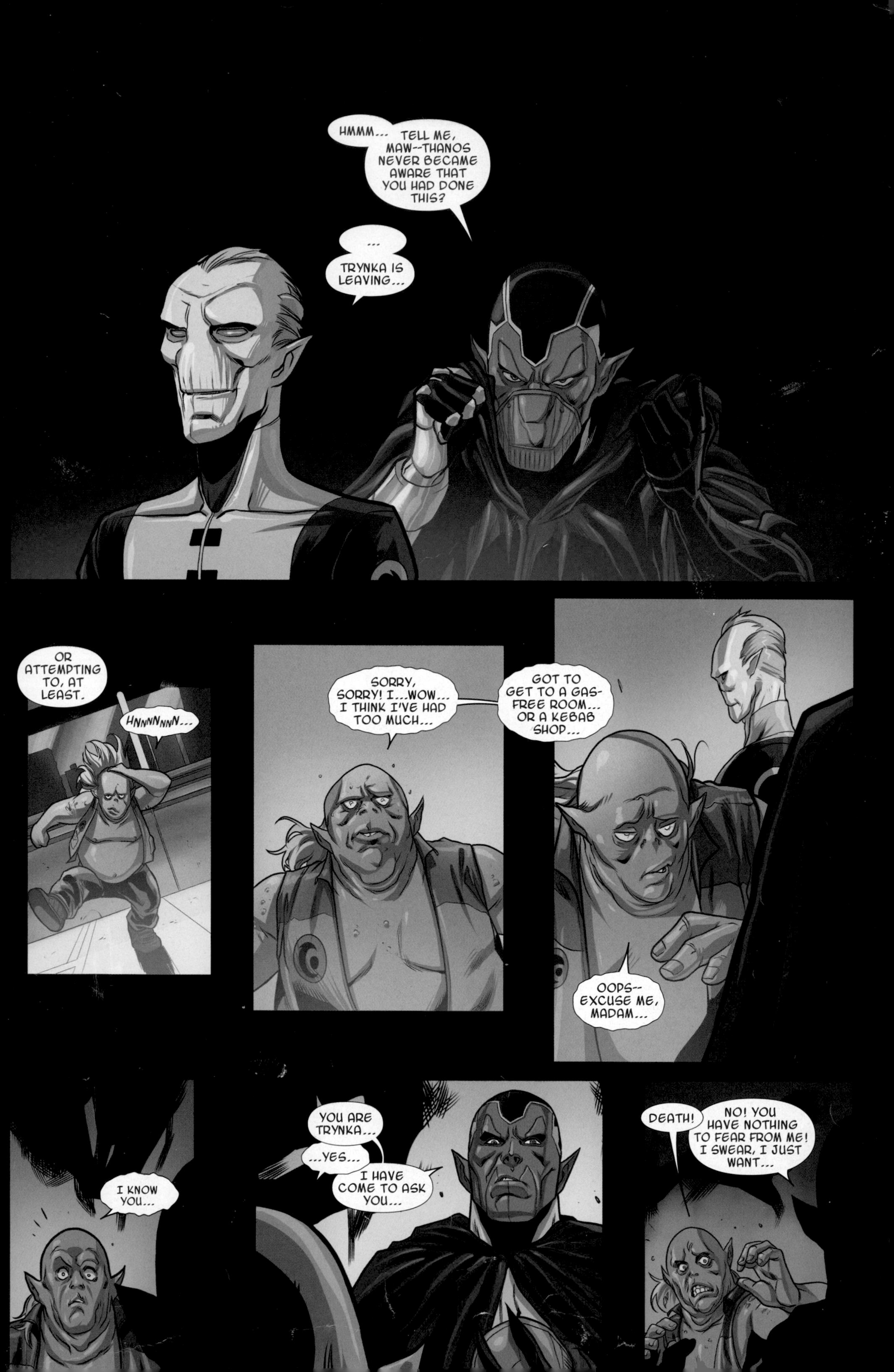
HMMM...
TELL ME, MAW--THANOS NEVER BECAME AWARE THAT YOU HAD DONE THIS?
...
TRYNKA IS LEAVING...
OR ATTEMPTING TO, AT LEAST.
HNNNNNNN...
SORRY, SORRY! I...WOW... I THINK I'VE HAD TOO MUCH...
GOT TO GET TO A GAS-FREE ROOM... OR A KEBAB SHOP...
OOPS-- EXCUSE ME, MADAM...
I KNOW YOU...
YOU ARE TRYNKA...
...YES...
I HAVE COME TO ASK YOU...
DEATH!
NO! YOU HAVE NOTHING TO FEAR FROM ME! I SWEAR, I JUST WANT...

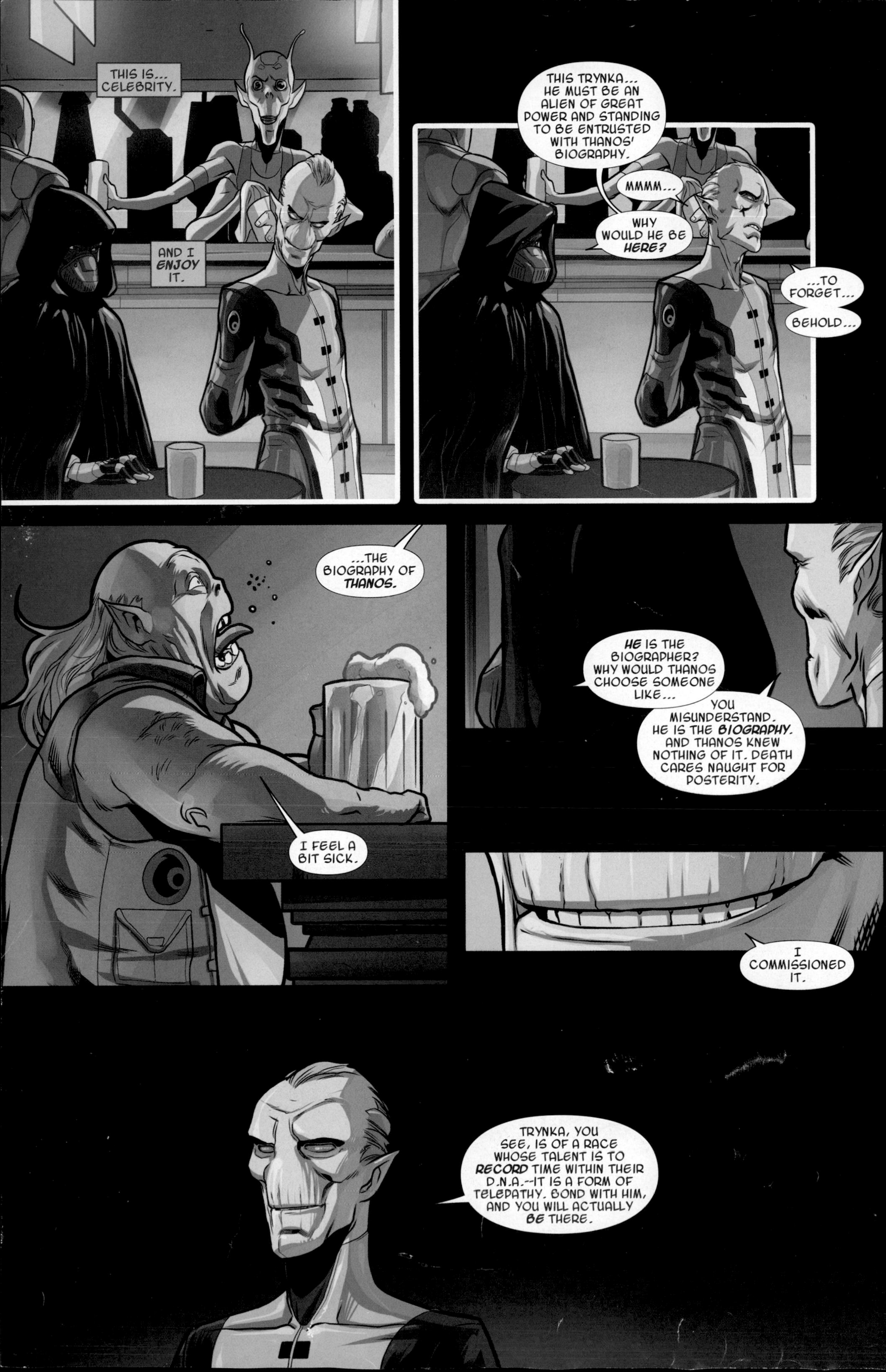
THIS IS... CELEBRITY.
AND I ENJOY IT.
THIS TRYNKA... HE MUST BE AN ALIEN OF GREAT POWER AND STANDING TO BE ENTRUSTED WITH THANOS' BIOGRAPHY.
MMMM...
WHY WOULD HE BE HERE?
...TO FORGET...
BEHOLD...
...THE BIOGRAPHY OF THANOS.
I FEEL A BIT SICK.
HE IS THE BIOGRAPHER? WHY WOULD THANOS CHOOSE SOMEONE LIKE...
YOU MISUNDERSTAND. HE IS THE BIOGRAPHY. AND THANOS KNEW NOTHING OF IT. DEATH CARES NAUGHT FOR POSTERITY.
I COMMISSIONED IT.
TRYNKA, YOU SEE, IS OF A RACE WHOSE TALENT IS TO RECORD TIME WITHIN THEIR D.N.A.--IT IS A FORM OF TELEPATHY. BOND WITH HIM, AND YOU WILL ACTUALLY BE THERE.

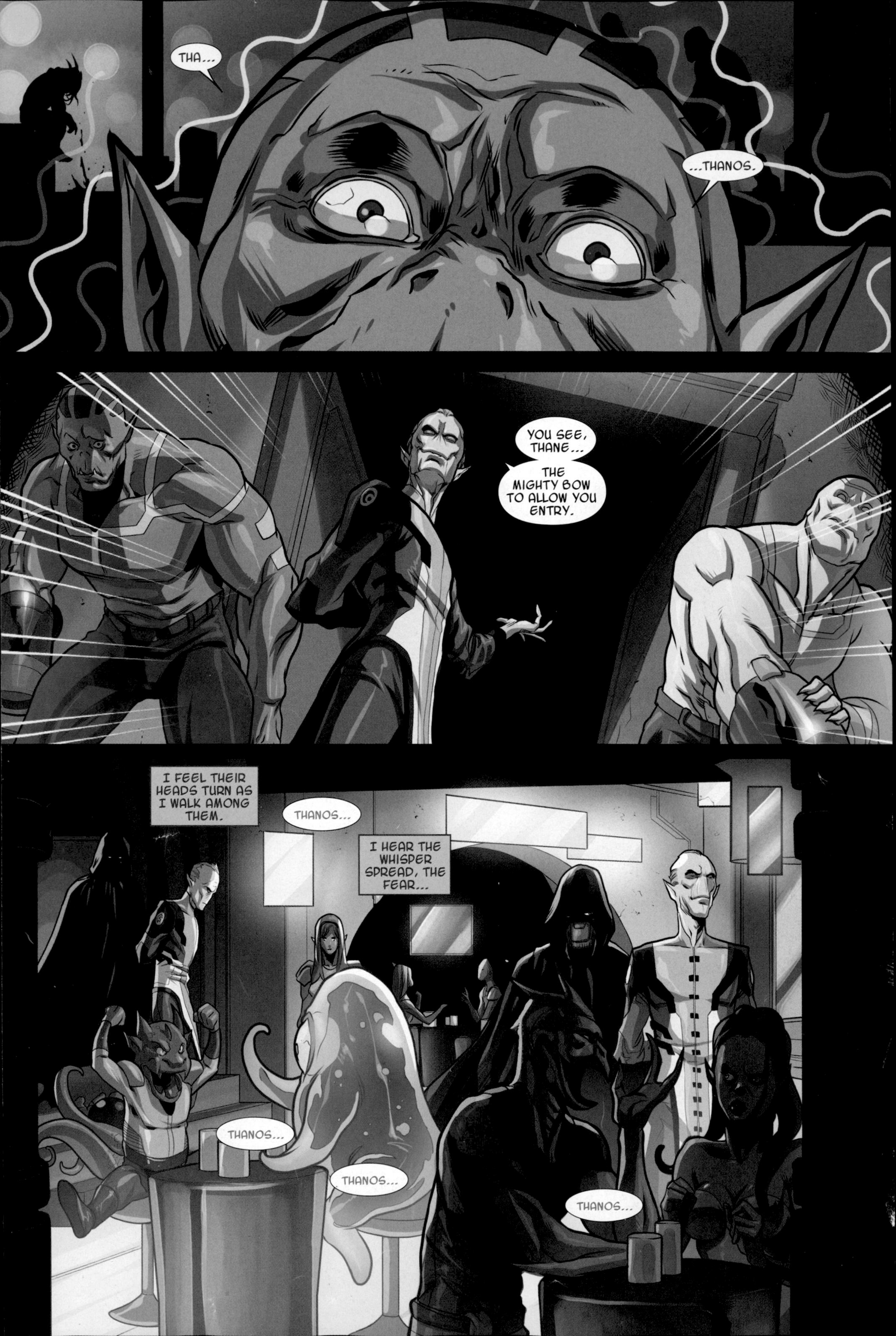
THA...
...THANOS.
YOU SEE, THANE...
THE MIGHTY BOW TO ALLOW YOU ENTRY.
I FEEL THEIR HEADS TURN AS I WALK AMONG THEM.
THANOS...
I HEAR THE WHISPER SPREAD, THE FEAR...
THANOS...
THANOS...
THANOS...

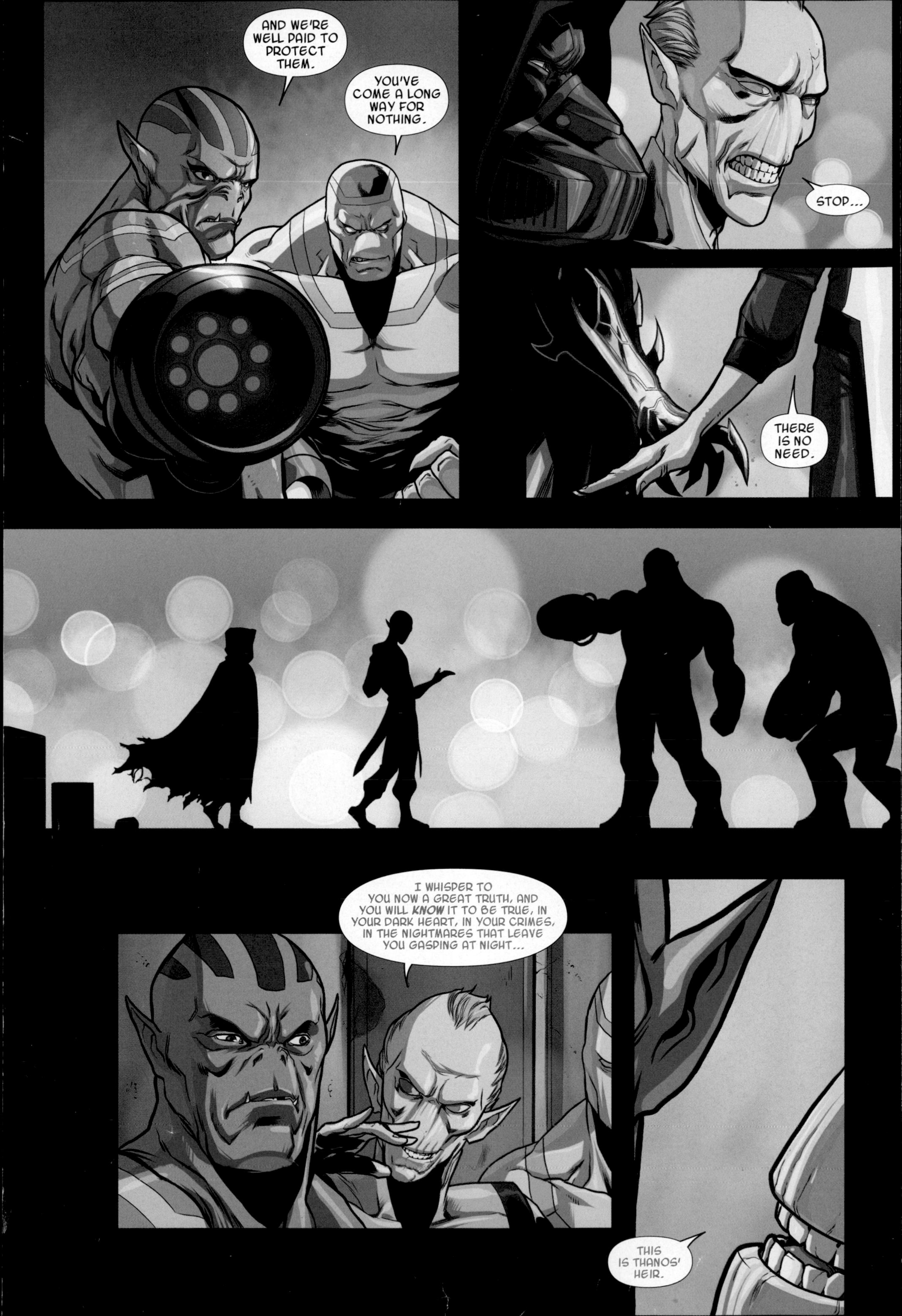
AND WE'RE WELL PAID TO PROTECT THEM.
YOU'VE COME A LONG WAY FOR NOTHING.
STOP...
THERE IS NO NEED.
I WHISPER TO YOU NOW A GREAT TRUTH, AND YOU WILL KNOW IT TO BE TRUE, IN YOUR DARK HEART, IN YOUR CRIMES, IN THE NIGHTMARES THAT LEAVE YOU GASPING AT NIGHT...
THIS IS THANOS' HEIR.

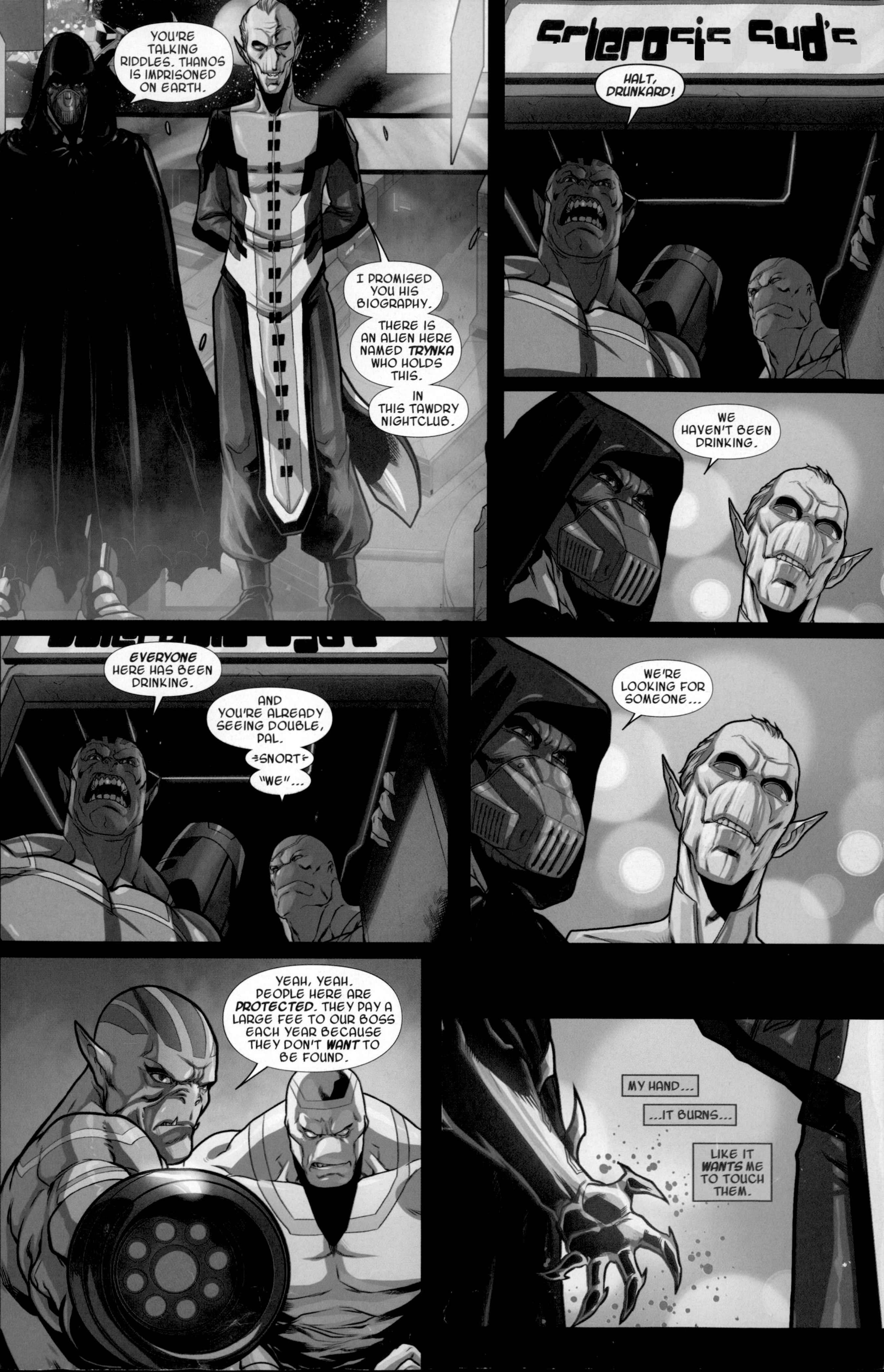
YOU'RE TALKING RIDDLES. THANOS IS IMPRISONED ON EARTH.
I PROMISED YOU HIS BIOGRAPHY.
THERE IS AN ALIEN HERE NAMED TRYNKA WHO HOLDS THIS.
IN THIS TAWDRY NIGHTCLUB.
Sclerosis Sud's
HALT, DRUNKARD!
WE HAVEN'T BEEN DRINKING.
EVERYONE HERE HAS BEEN DRINKING.
AND YOU'RE ALREADY SEEING DOUBLE, PAL.
SNORT
"WE"...
WE'RE LOOKING FOR SOMEONE...
YEAH, YEAH. PEOPLE HERE ARE PROTECTED. THEY PAY A LARGE FEE TO OUR BOSS EACH YEAR BECAUSE THEY DON'T WANT TO BE FOUND.
MY HAND...
...IT BURNS...
LIKE IT WANTS ME TO TOUCH THEM.

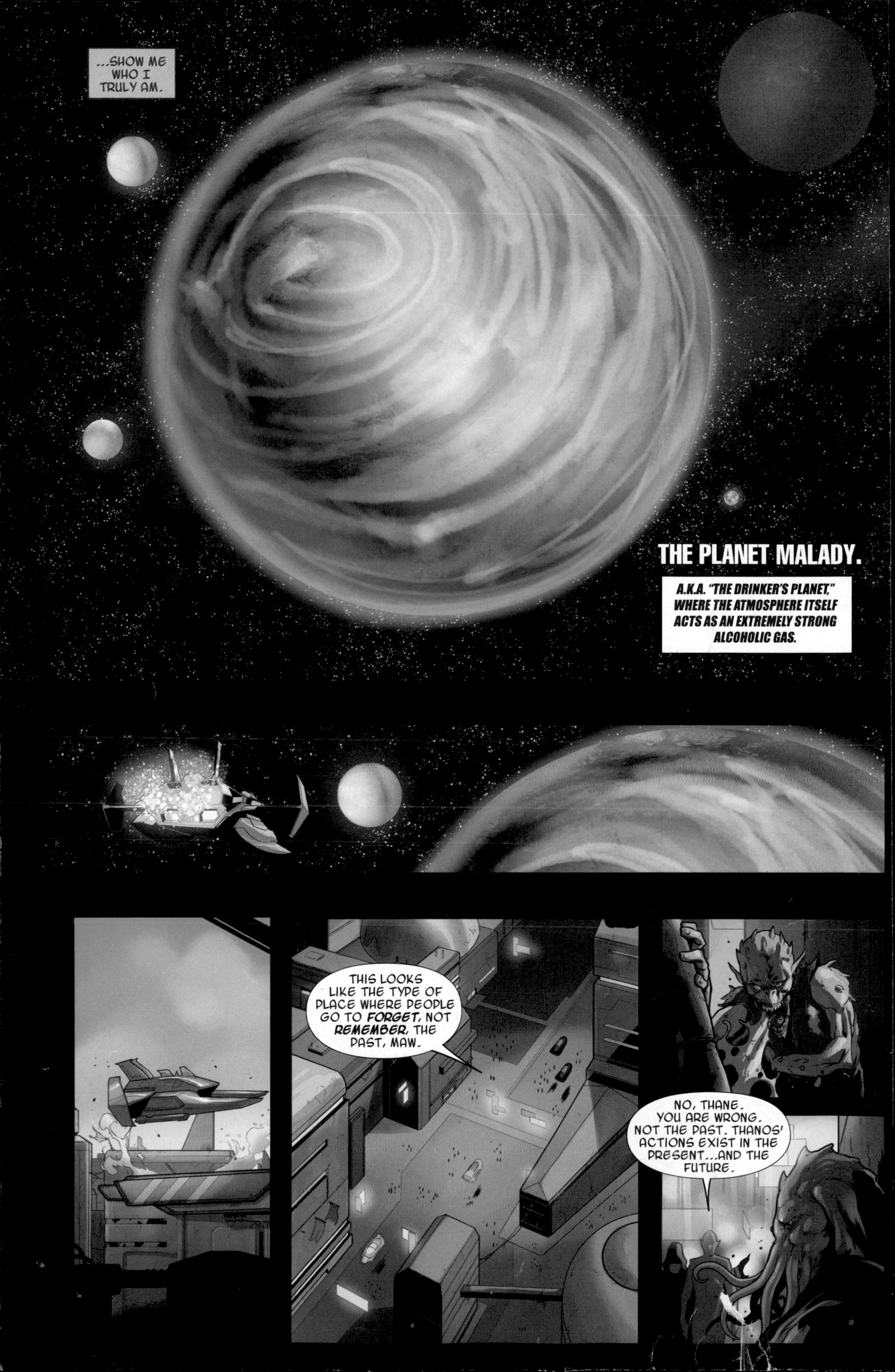

...SHOW ME WHO I TRULY AM.
THE PLANET MALADY.
A.K.A. "THE DRINKER'S PLANET," WHERE THE ATMOSPHERE ITSELF ACTS AS AN EXTREMELY STRONG ALCOHOLIC GAS.
THIS LOOKS LIKE THE TYPE OF PLACE WHERE PEOPLE GO TO FORGET, NOT REMEMBER, THE PAST, MAW.
NO, THANE. YOU ARE WRONG. NOT THE PAST. THANOS' ACTIONS EXIST IN THE PRESENT...AND THE FUTURE.

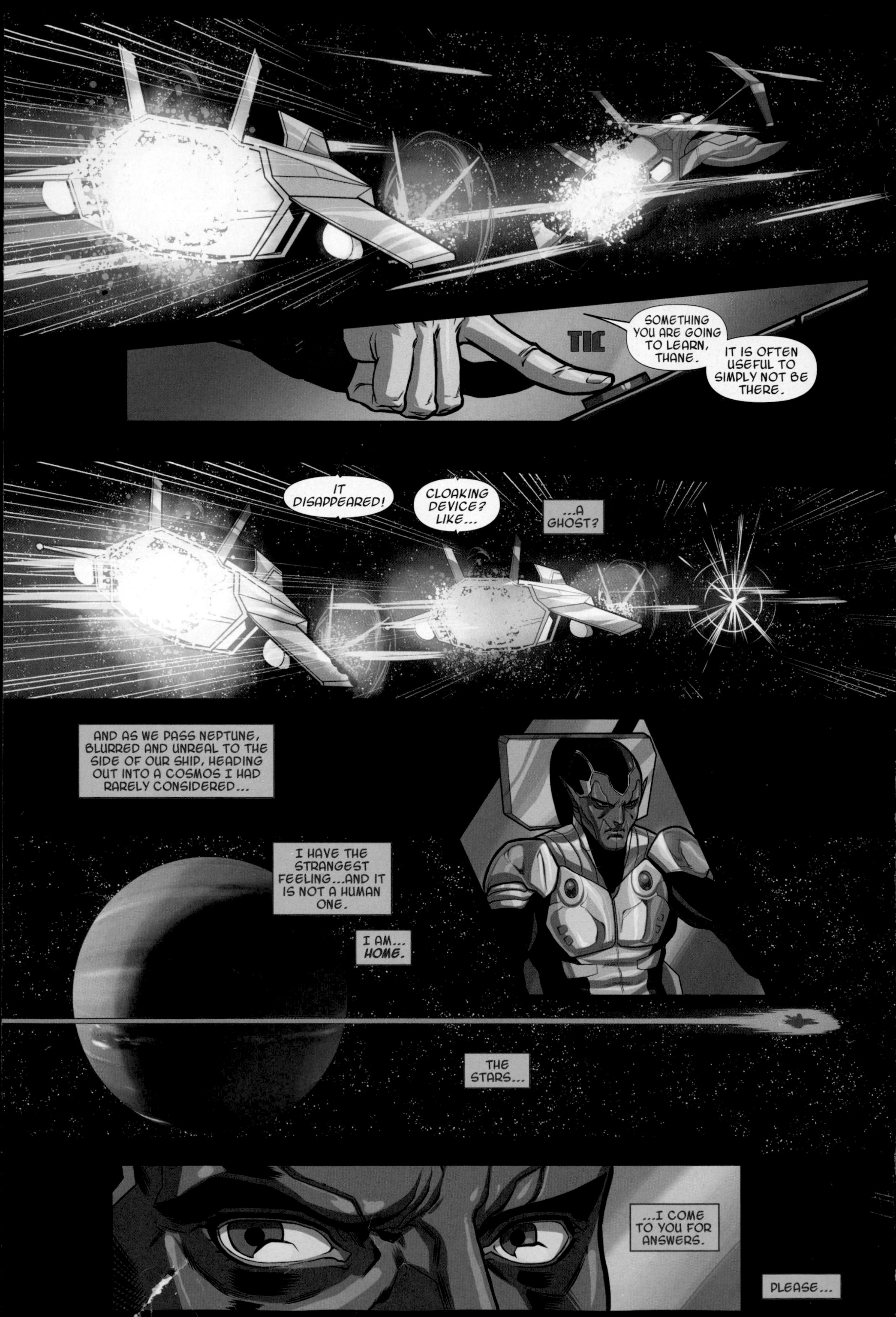
TIC
SOMETHING YOU ARE GOING TO LEARN, THANE.
IT IS OFTEN USEFUL TO SIMPLY NOT BE THERE.
IT DISAPPEARED!
CLOAKING DEVICE? LIKE...
...A GHOST?
AND AS WE PASS NEPTUNE, BLURRED AND UNREAL TO THE SIDE OF OUR SHIP, HEADING OUT INTO A COSMOS I HAD RARELY CONSIDERED...
I HAVE THE STRANGEST FEELING...AND IT IS NOT A HUMAN ONE.
I AM... HOME.
THE STARS...
...I COME TO YOU FOR ANSWERS.
PLEASE...

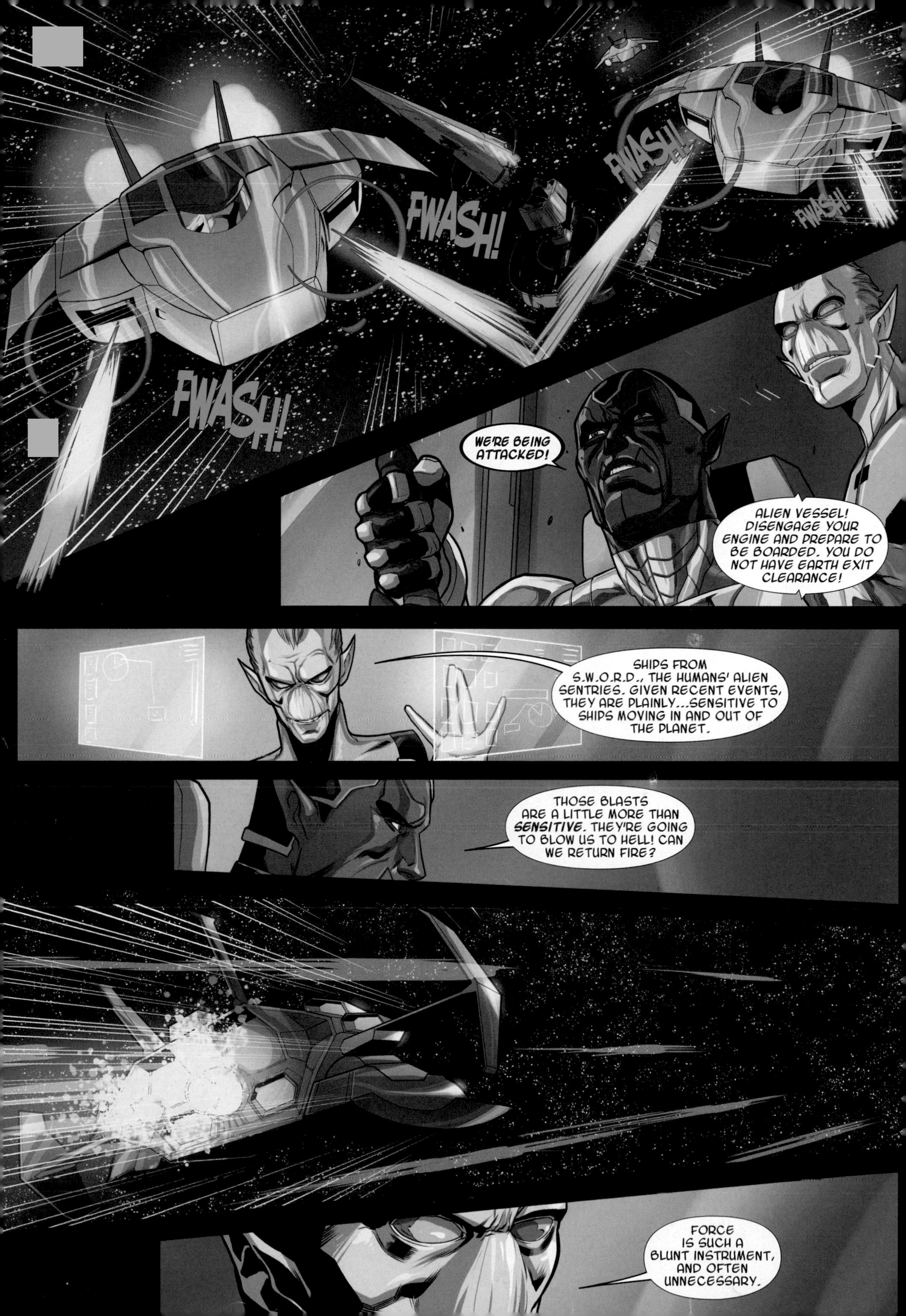
FWASH!
FWASH!
FWASH!
FWASH!
WE'RE BEING ATTACKED!
ALIEN VESSEL! DISENGAGE YOUR ENGINE AND PREPARE TO BE BOARDED. YOU DO NOT HAVE EARTH EXIT CLEARANCE!
SHIPS FROM S.W.O.R.D., THE HUMANS' ALIEN SENTRIES. GIVEN RECENT EVENTS, THEY ARE PLAINLY...SENSITIVE TO SHIPS MOVING IN AND OUT OF THE PLANET.
THOSE BLASTS ARE A LITTLE MORE THAN SENSITIVE. THEY'RE GOING TO BLOW US TO HELL! CAN WE RETURN FIRE?
FORCE IS SUCH A BLUNT INSTRUMENT, AND OFTEN UNNECESSARY.

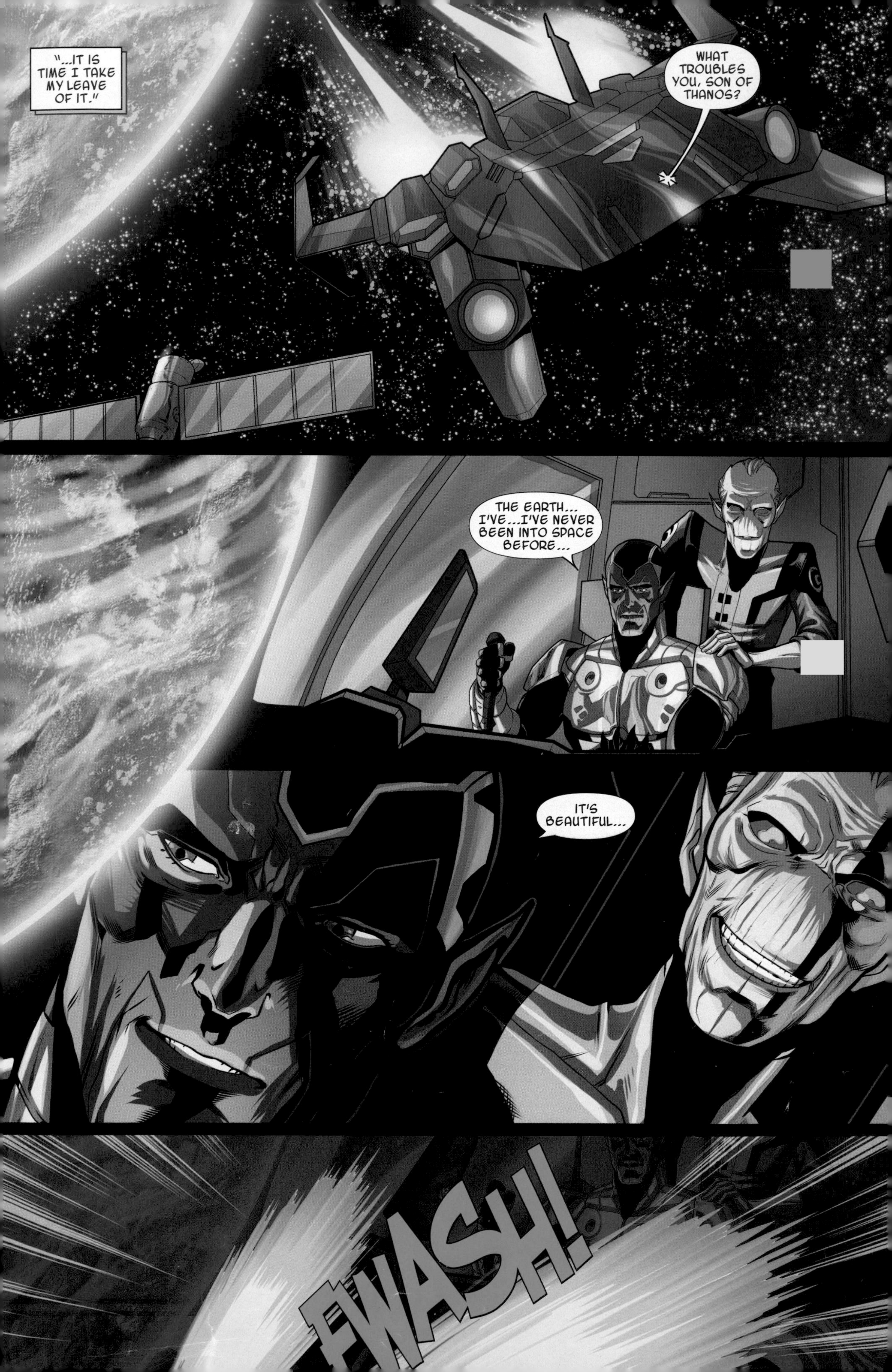
"...IT IS TIME I TAKE MY LEAVE OF IT."
WHAT TROUBLES YOU, SON OF THANOS?
THE EARTH... I'VE...I'VE NEVER BEEN INTO SPACE BEFORE...
IT'S BEAUTIFUL...
FWASH!

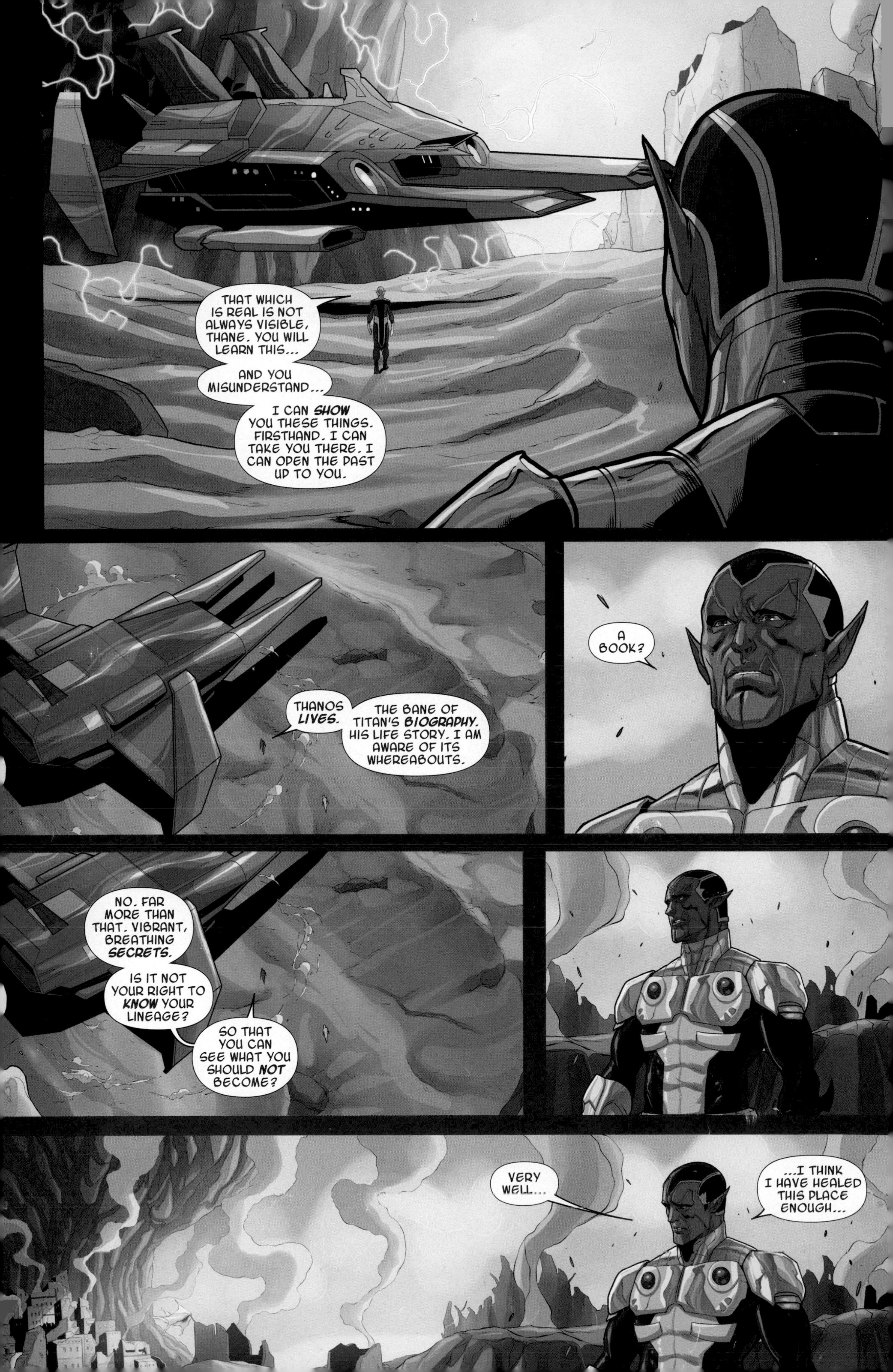
THAT WHICH IS REAL IS NOT ALWAYS VISIBLE, THANE. YOU WILL LEARN THIS...
AND YOU MISUNDERSTAND...
I CAN SHOW YOU THESE THINGS. FIRSTHAND. I CAN TAKE YOU THERE. I CAN OPEN THE PAST UP TO YOU.
THANOS LIVES.
THE BANE OF TITAN'S BIOGRAPHY. HIS LIFE STORY. I AM AWARE OF ITS WHEREABOUTS.
A BOOK?
NO. FAR MORE THAN THAT. VIBRANT, BREATHING SECRETS.
IS IT NOT YOUR RIGHT TO KNOW YOUR LINEAGE?
SO THAT YOU CAN SEE WHAT YOU SHOULD NOT BECOME?
VERY WELL...
...I THINK I HAVE HEALED THIS PLACE ENOUGH...

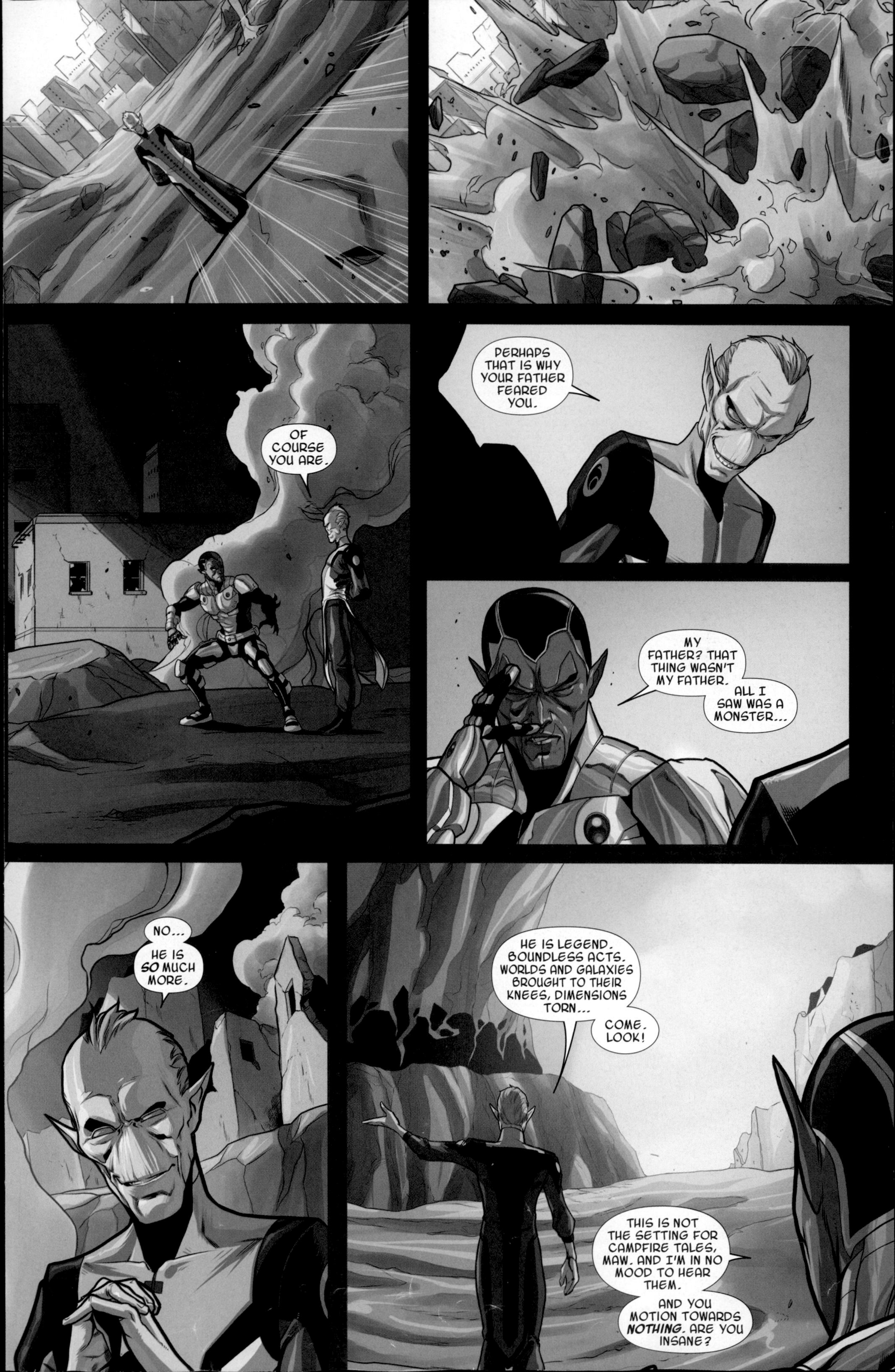
OF COURSE YOU ARE.
PERHAPS THAT IS WHY YOUR FATHER FEARED YOU.
MY FATHER? THAT THING WASN'T MY FATHER.
ALL I SAW WAS A MONSTER...
NO... HE IS **SO** MUCH MORE.
HE IS LEGEND. BOUNDLESS ACTS. WORLDS AND GALAXIES BROUGHT TO THEIR KNEES, DIMENSIONS TORN...
COME. LOOK!
THIS IS NOT THE SETTING FOR CAMPFIRE TALES, MAW. AND I'M IN NO MOOD TO HEAR THEM.
AND YOU MOTION TOWARDS ***NOTHING***. ARE YOU INSANE?

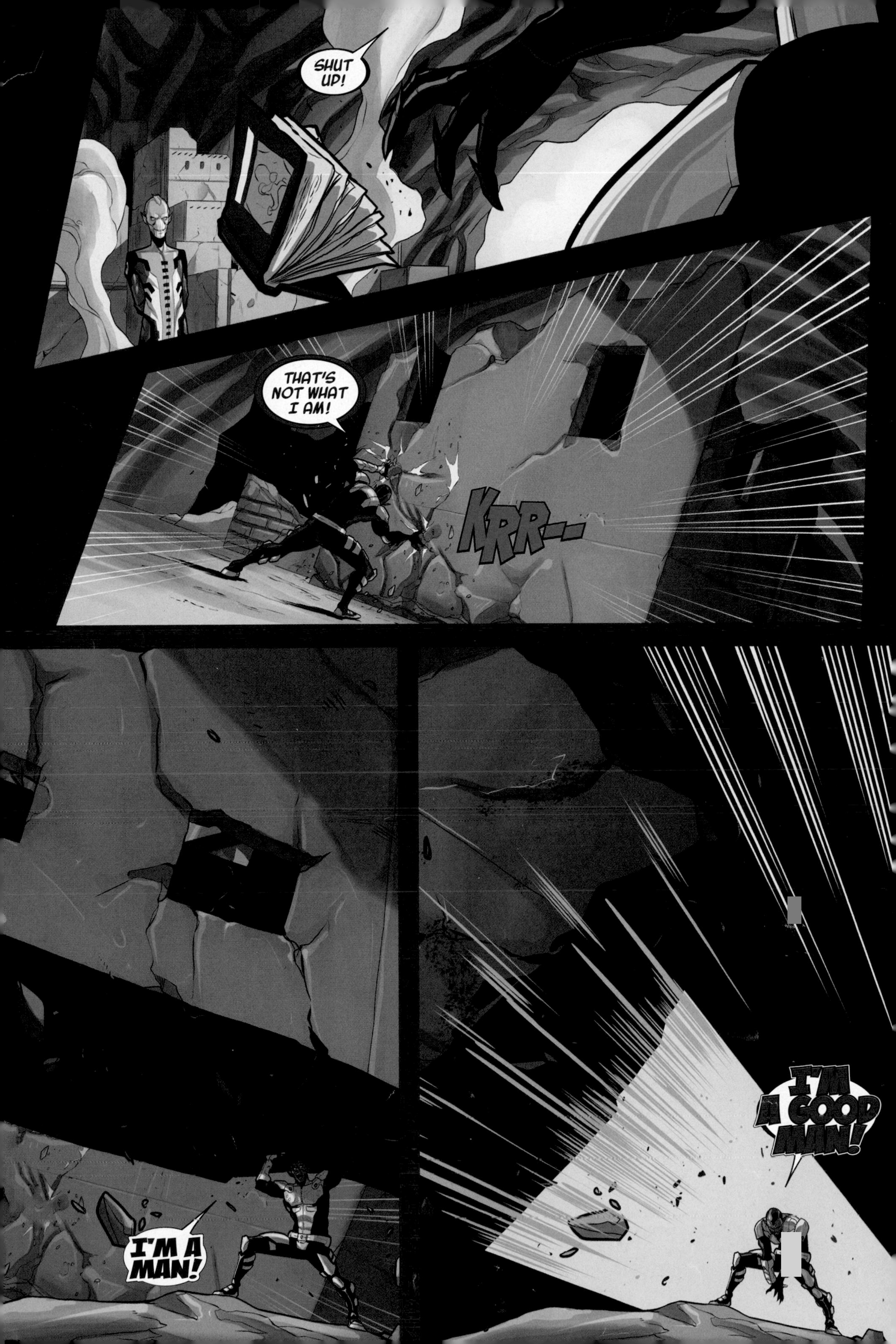
SHUT UP!
THAT'S NOT WHAT I AM!
KRR--
I'M A MAN!
I'M A GOOD MAN!

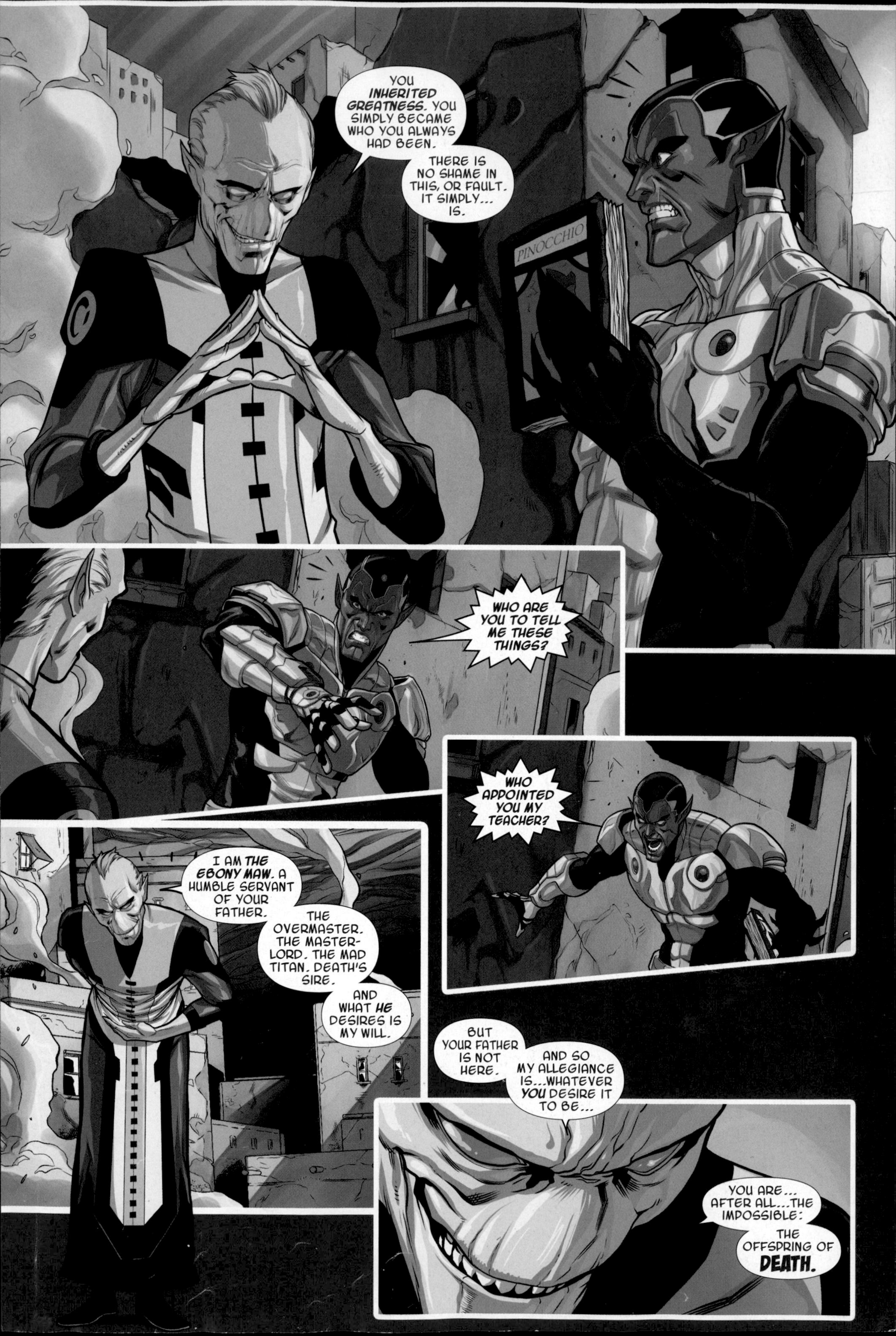
YOU INHERITED GREATNESS. YOU SIMPLY BECAME WHO YOU ALWAYS HAD BEEN.
THERE IS NO SHAME IN THIS, OR FAULT. IT SIMPLY... IS.
PINOCCHIO
WHO ARE YOU TO TELL ME THESE THINGS?
WHO APPOINTED YOU MY TEACHER?
I AM THE EBONY MAW. A HUMBLE SERVANT OF YOUR FATHER.
THE OVERMASTER. THE MASTER-LORD. THE MAD TITAN. DEATH'S SIRE.
AND WHAT HE DESIRES IS MY WILL.
BUT YOUR FATHER IS NOT HERE.
AND SO MY ALLEGIANCE IS...WHATEVER YOU DESIRE IT TO BE...
YOU ARE... AFTER ALL... THE IMPOSSIBLE:
THE OFFSPRING OF DEATH.

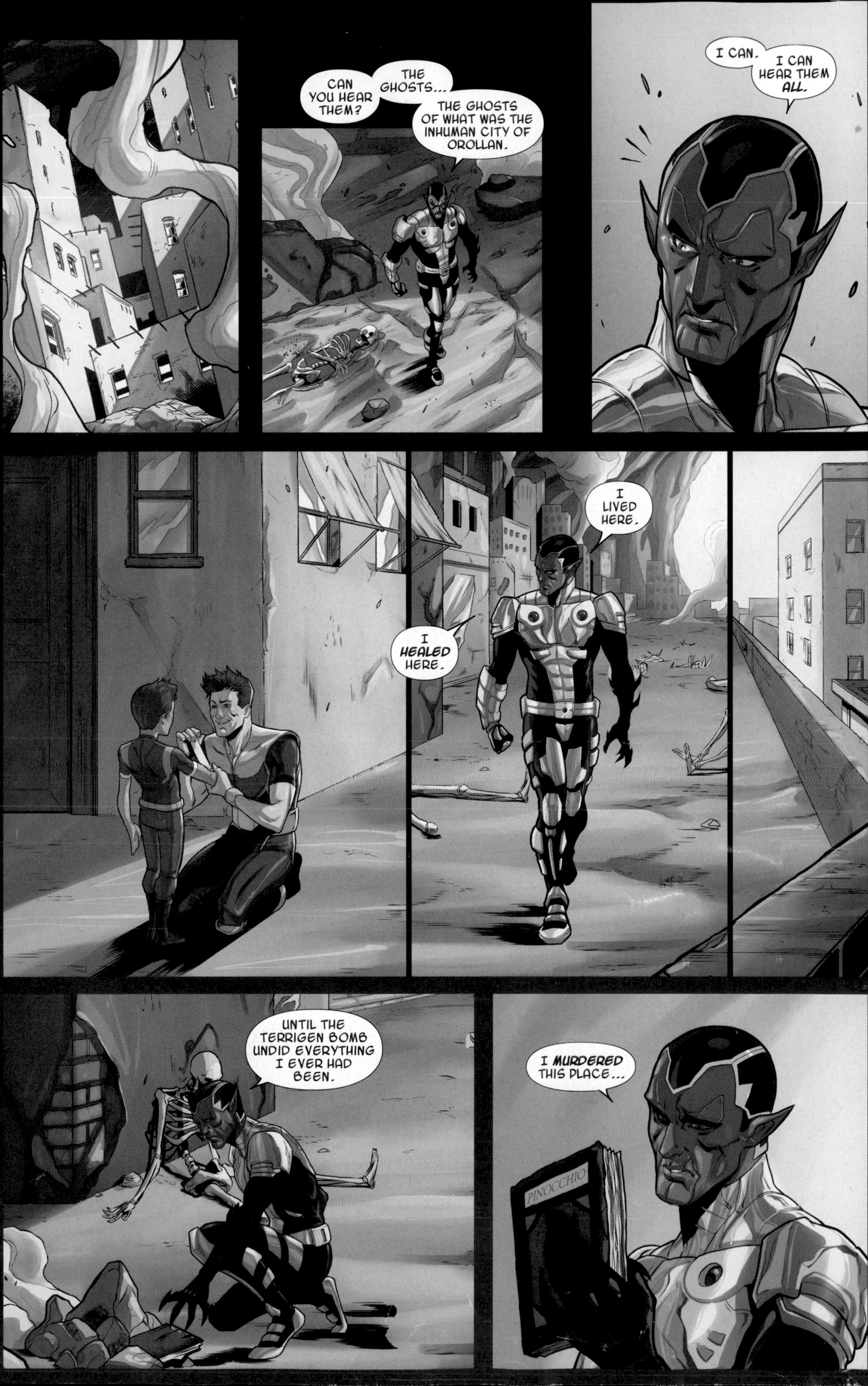
CAN YOU HEAR THEM?
THE GHOSTS...
THE GHOSTS OF WHAT WAS THE INHUMAN CITY OF OROLLAN.
I CAN.
I CAN HEAR THEM ALL.
I LIVED HERE.
I HEALED HERE.
UNTIL THE TERRIGEN BOMB UNDID EVERYTHING I EVER HAD BEEN.
I MURDERED THIS PLACE...
PINOCCHIO

THANOS
A GOD UP THERE LISTENING

In his youth, the dreaded Thanos cut a violent swath throughout the cosmos, leaving behind him chaos, carnage...and a number of progeny. To show his fealty to Death, Thanos decided to murder all of his children. One of those children was on Earth—a half-Inhuman named Thane, living as a healer in the hidden Inhuman city of Orollan.

Exposure to the Inhumans' transformative Terrigen Mists unlocked Thane's true birthright: ending any and all life that's in his presence. A member of Thanos' crew, the Ebony Maw, gave Thane a suit of armor that allows him to control his new abilities, but not before Thane accidentally destroyed all of Orollan.

With the armor on, Thane's left hand brings about death, and his right brings about something even worse—"living death." When Thanos came to claim his life, Thane used the power of his right hand on his father, seemingly stopping Thanos once and for all.

Now Thane must come to grips with his newfound abilities and the knowledge that he is the son of the Mad Titan himself...

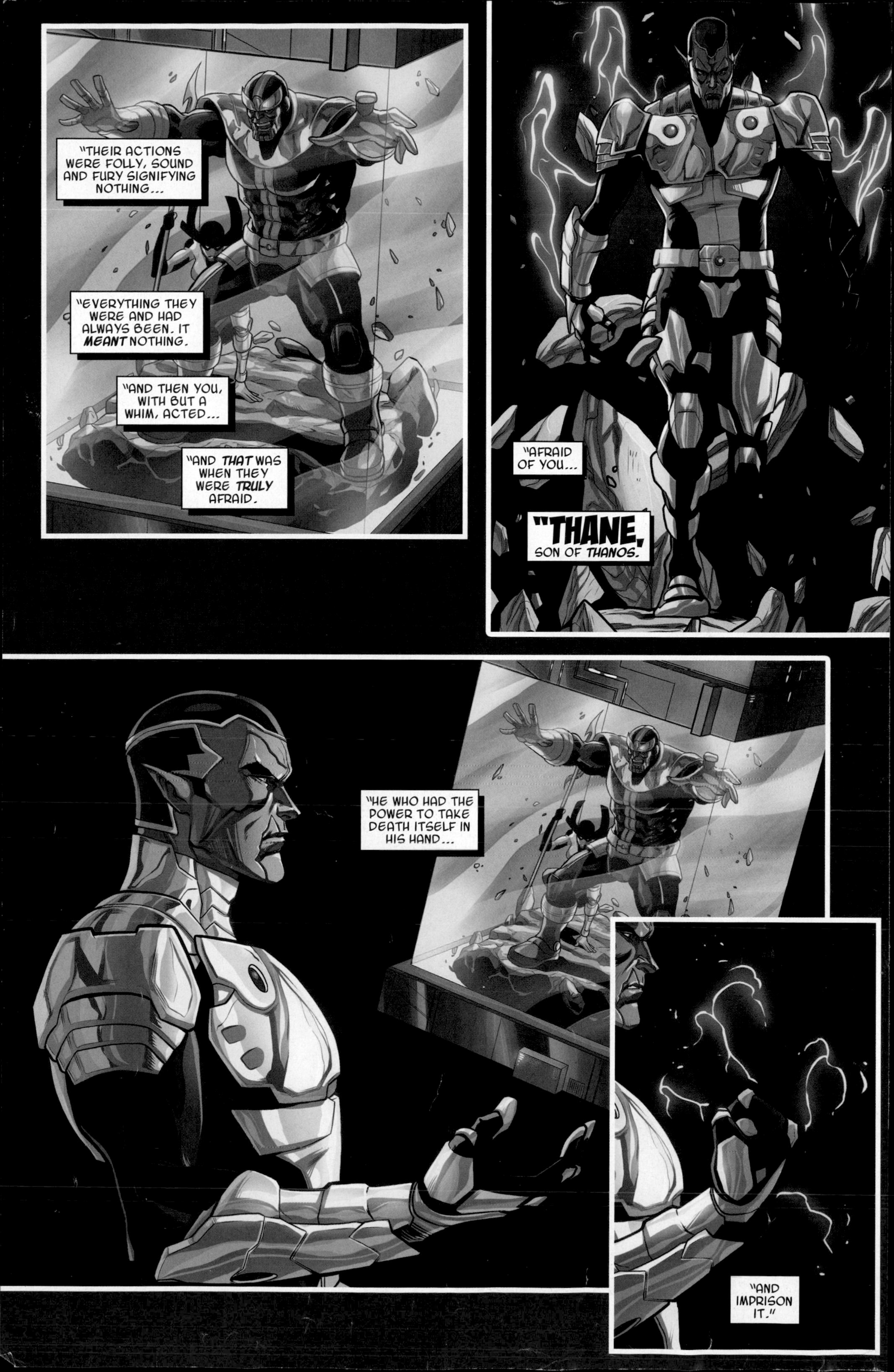
"THEIR ACTIONS WERE FOLLY, SOUND AND FURY SIGNIFYING NOTHING...
"EVERYTHING THEY WERE AND HAD ALWAYS BEEN. IT MEANT NOTHING.
"AND THEN YOU, WITH BUT A WHIM, ACTED...
"AND THAT WAS WHEN THEY WERE TRULY AFRAID.
"AFRAID OF YOU...
"THANE, SON OF THANOS.
"HE WHO HAD THE POWER TO TAKE DEATH ITSELF IN HIS HAND...
"AND IMPRISON IT."

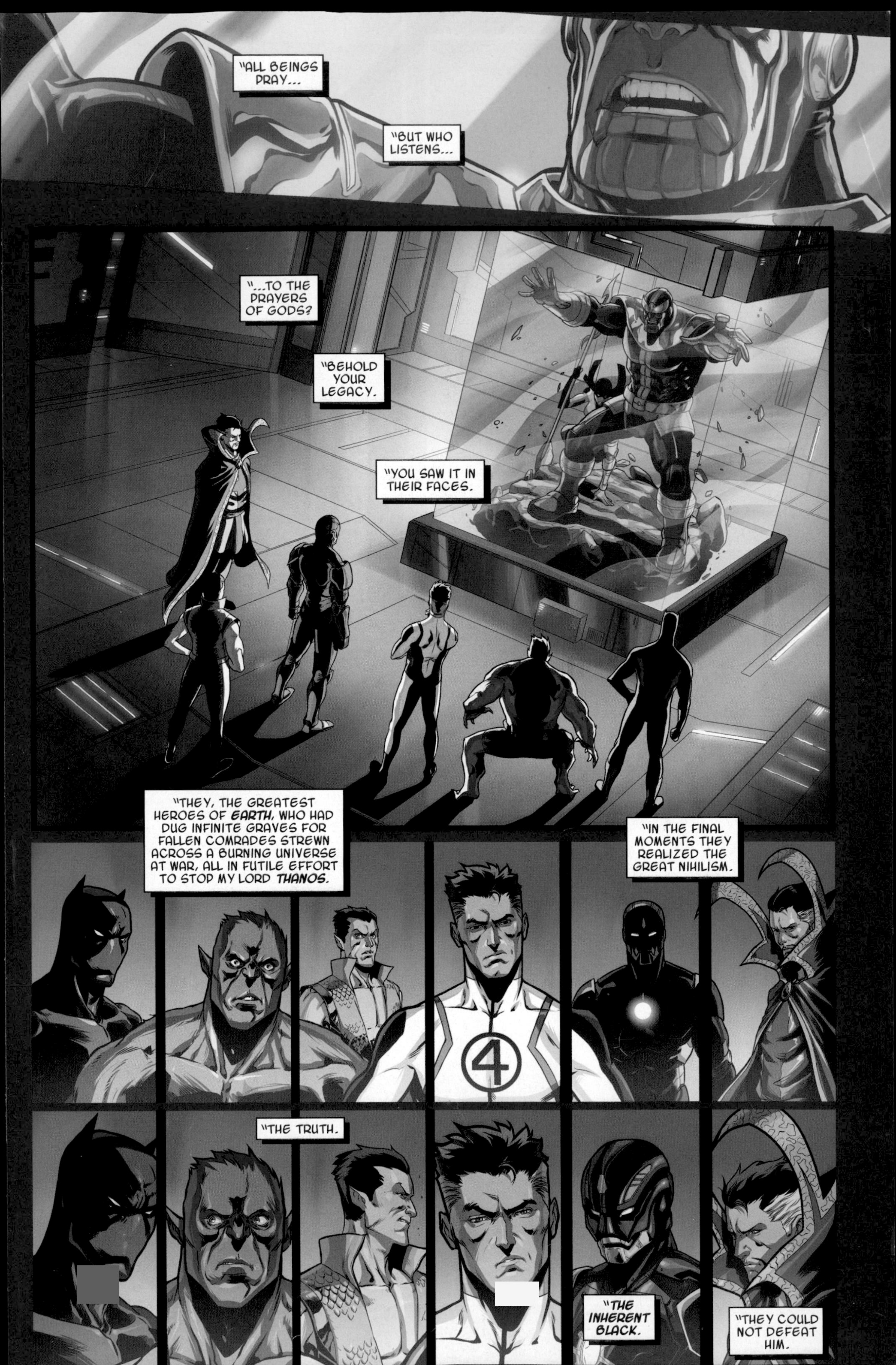
"ALL BEINGS PRAY...
"BUT WHO LISTENS...
"...TO THE PRAYERS OF GODS?
"BEHOLD YOUR LEGACY.
"YOU SAW IT IN THEIR FACES.
"THEY, THE GREATEST HEROES OF EARTH, WHO HAD DUG INFINITE GRAVES FOR FALLEN COMRADES STREWN ACROSS A BURNING UNIVERSE AT WAR, ALL IN FUTILE EFFORT TO STOP MY LORD THANOS.
"IN THE FINAL MOMENTS THEY REALIZED THE GREAT NIHILISM.
"THE TRUTH.
"THE INHERENT BLACK.
"THEY COULD NOT DEFEAT HIM.

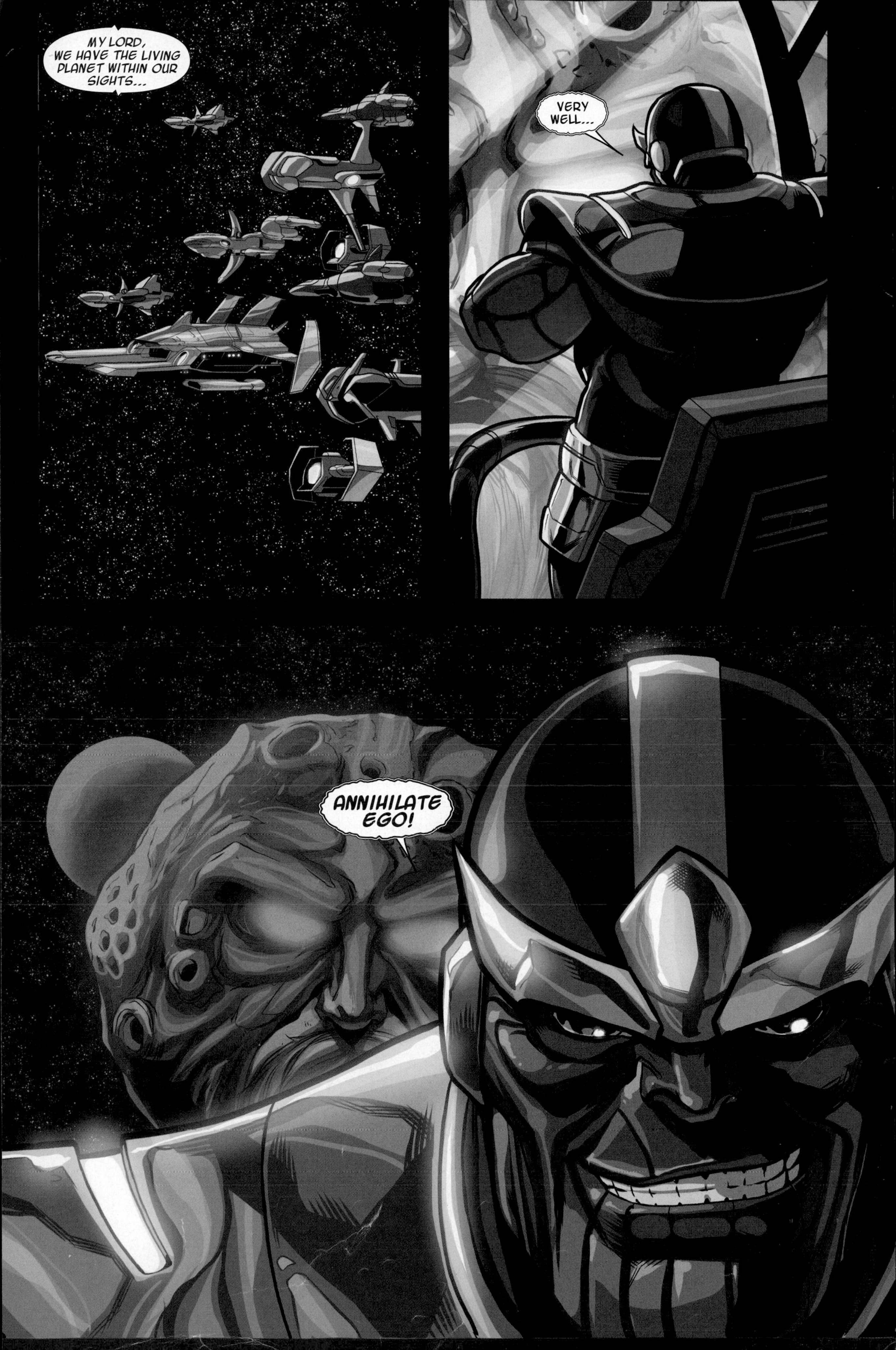
MY LORD, WE HAVE THE LIVING PLANET WITHIN OUR SIGHTS...
VERY WELL...
ANNIHILATE EGO!

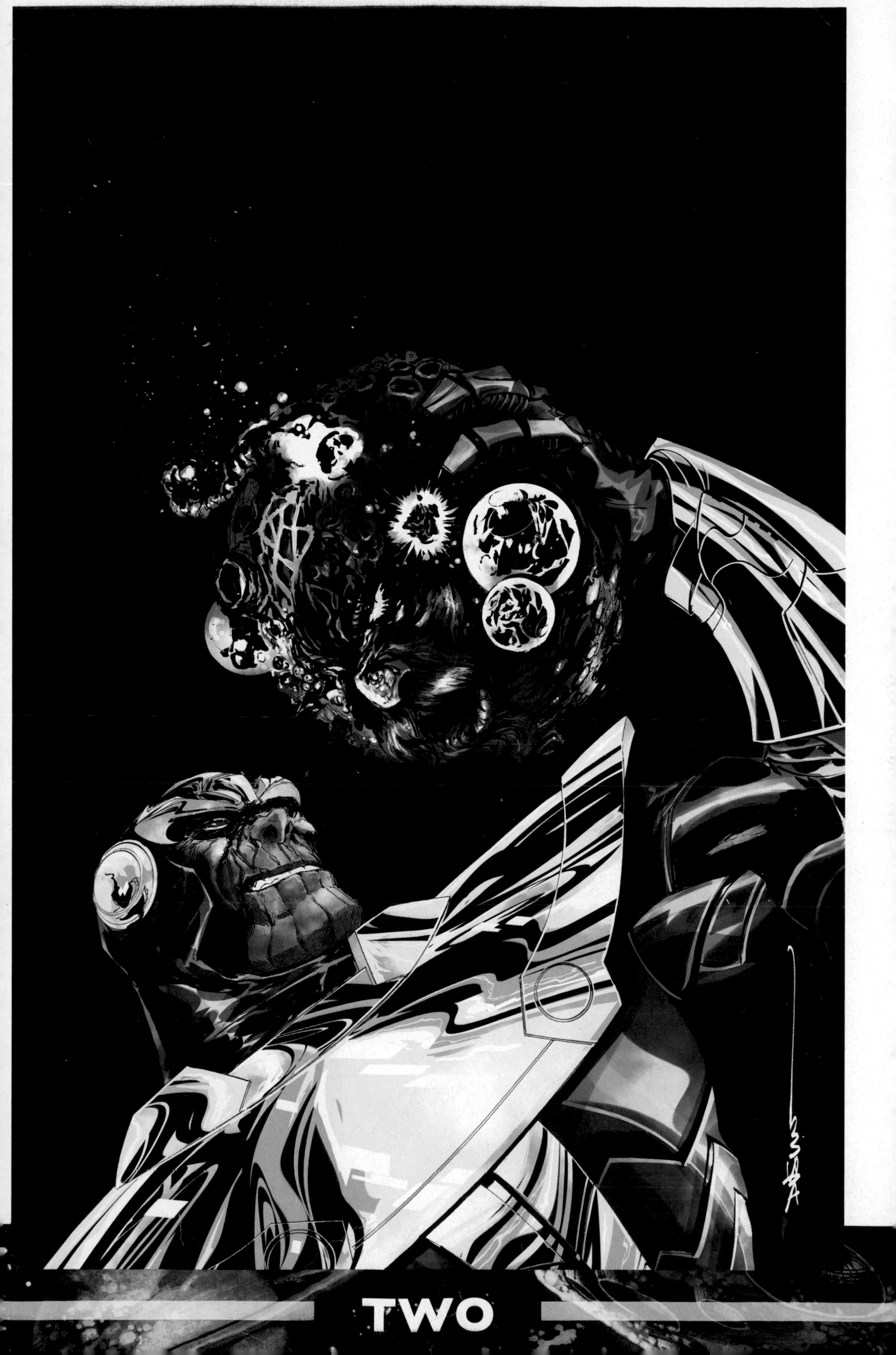

TWO

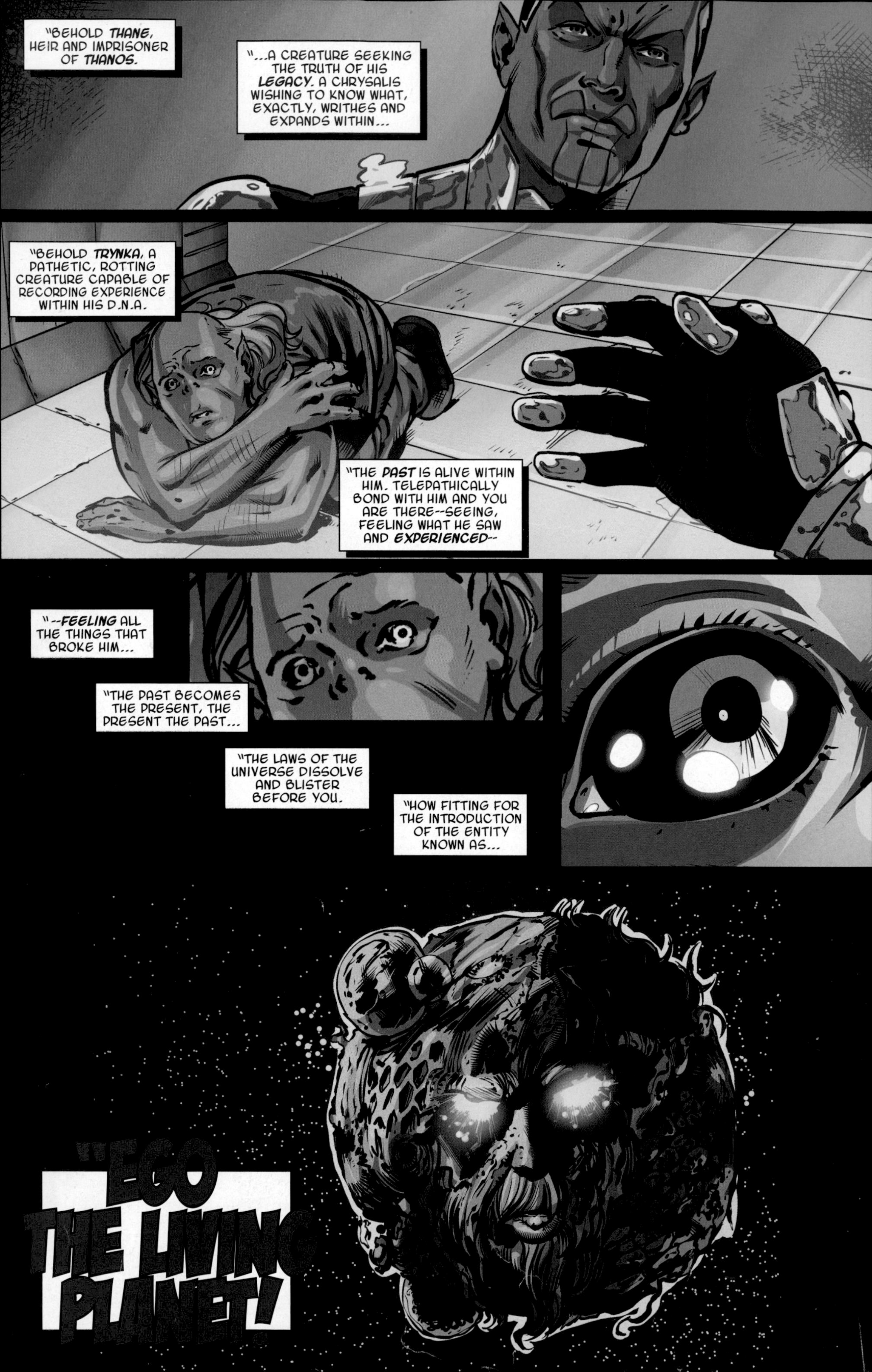
"BEHOLD THANE, HEIR AND IMPRISONER OF THANOS.
"...A CREATURE SEEKING THE TRUTH OF HIS LEGACY. A CHRYSALIS WISHING TO KNOW WHAT, EXACTLY, WRITHES AND EXPANDS WITHIN...
"BEHOLD TRYNKA, A PATHETIC, ROTTING CREATURE CAPABLE OF RECORDING EXPERIENCE WITHIN HIS D.N.A.
"THE PAST IS ALIVE WITHIN HIM. TELEPATHICALLY BOND WITH HIM AND YOU ARE THERE--SEEING, FEELING WHAT HE SAW AND EXPERIENCED--
"--FEELING ALL THE THINGS THAT BROKE HIM...
"THE PAST BECOMES THE PRESENT, THE PRESENT THE PAST...
"THE LAWS OF THE UNIVERSE DISSOLVE AND BLISTER BEFORE YOU.
"HOW FITTING FOR THE INTRODUCTION OF THE ENTITY KNOWN AS...
"EGO THE LIVING PLANET!

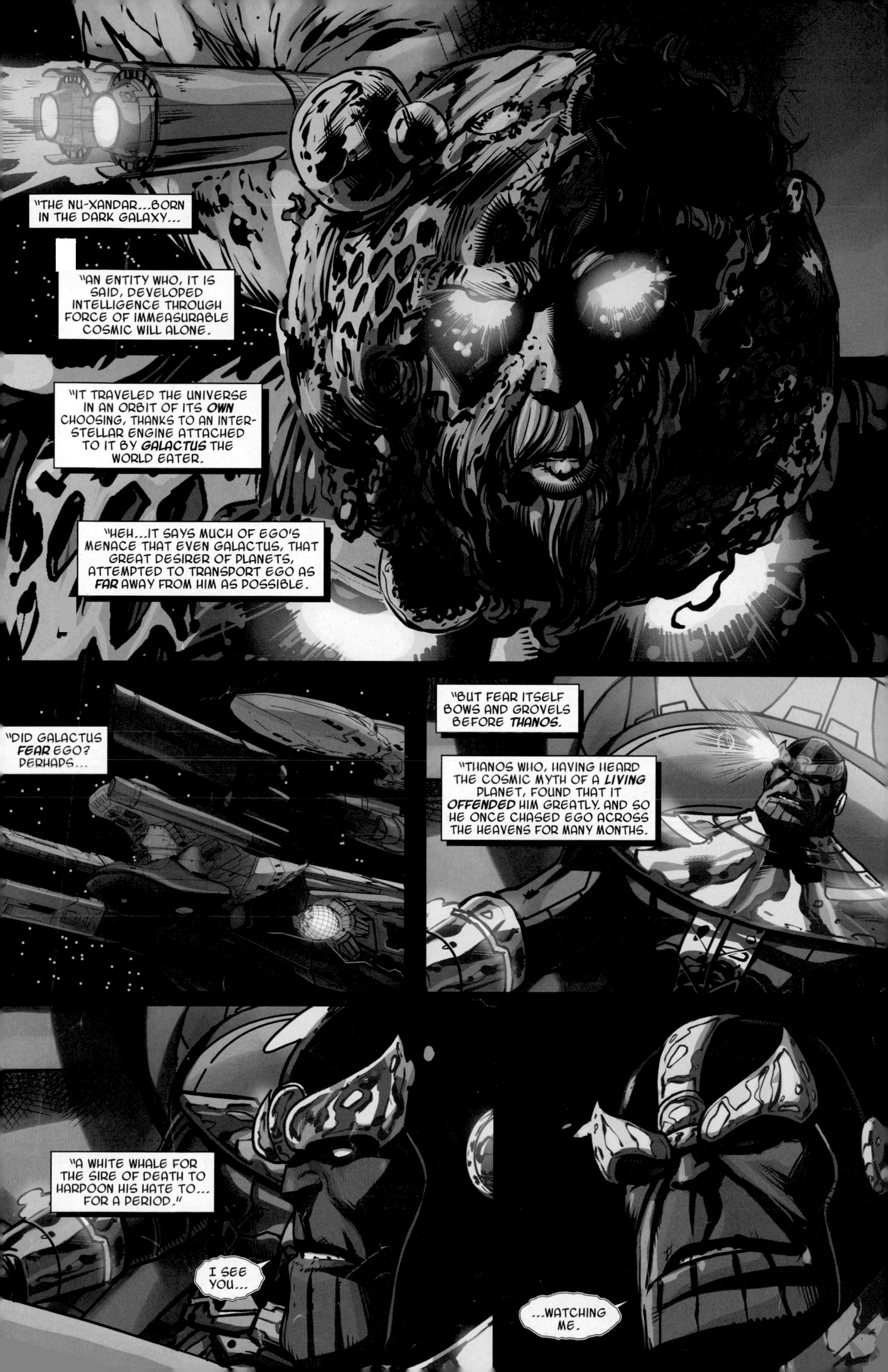
"THE NU-XANDAR...BORN IN THE DARK GALAXY...
"AN ENTITY WHO, IT IS SAID, DEVELOPED INTELLIGENCE THROUGH FORCE OF IMMEASURABLE COSMIC WILL ALONE.
"IT TRAVELED THE UNIVERSE IN AN ORBIT OF ITS OWN CHOOSING, THANKS TO AN INTER-STELLAR ENGINE ATTACHED TO IT BY GALACTUS THE WORLD EATER.
"HEH...IT SAYS MUCH OF EGO'S MENACE THAT EVEN GALACTUS, THAT GREAT DESIRER OF PLANETS, ATTEMPTED TO TRANSPORT EGO AS FAR AWAY FROM HIM AS POSSIBLE.
"DID GALACTUS FEAR EGO? PERHAPS...
"BUT FEAR ITSELF BOWS AND GROVELS BEFORE THANOS.
"THANOS WHO, HAVING HEARD THE COSMIC MYTH OF A LIVING PLANET, FOUND THAT IT OFFENDED HIM GREATLY. AND SO HE ONCE CHASED EGO ACROSS THE HEAVENS FOR MANY MONTHS.
"A WHITE WHALE FOR THE SIRE OF DEATH TO HARPOON HIS HATE TO... FOR A PERIOD."
I SEE YOU...
...WATCHING ME.

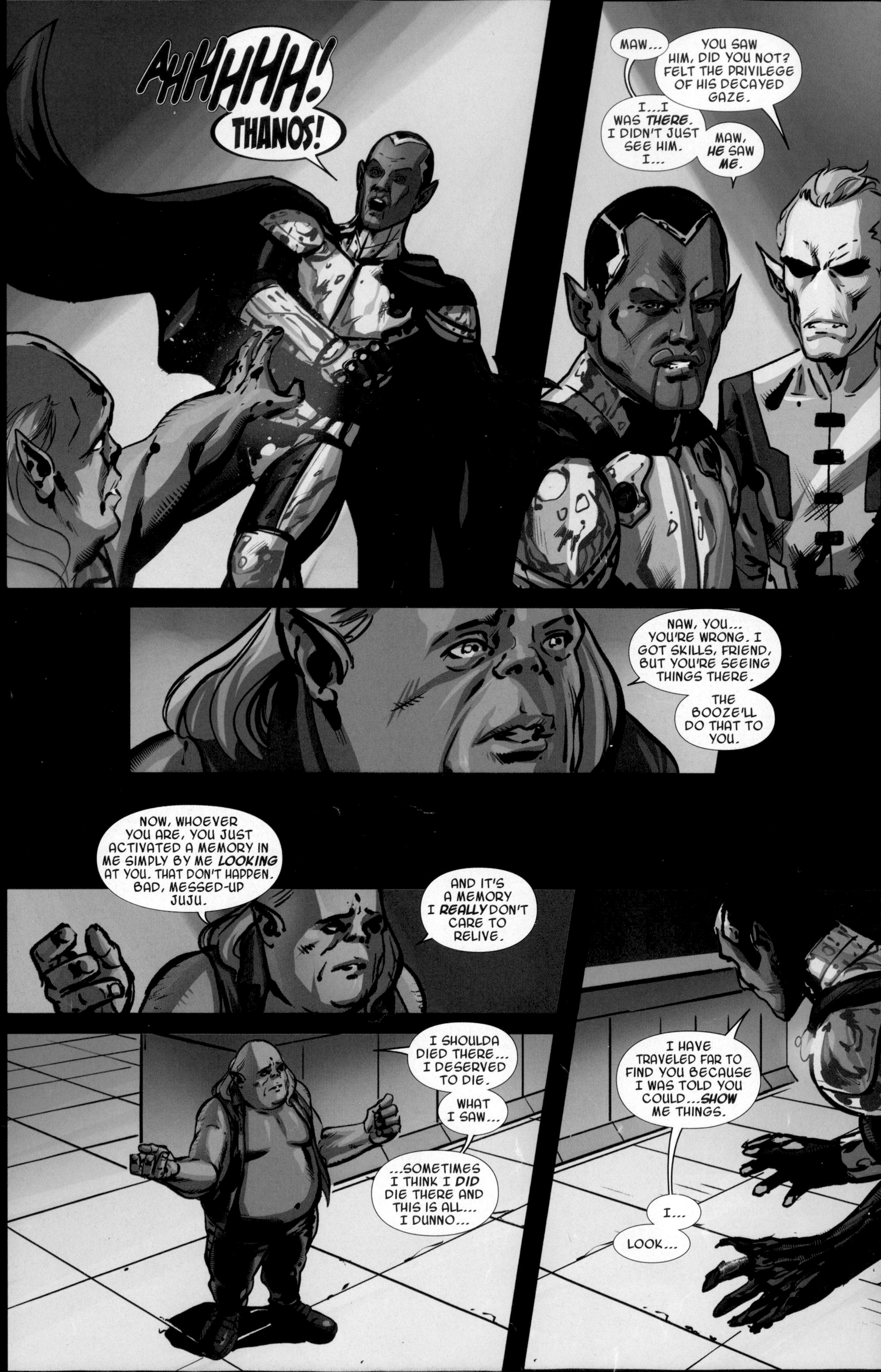
AHHHHH!
THANOS!
MAW...
YOU SAW HIM, DID YOU NOT? FELT THE PRIVILEGE OF HIS DECAYED GAZE.
I...I WAS THERE. I DIDN'T JUST SEE HIM. I...
MAW, HE SAW ME.
NAW, YOU... YOU'RE WRONG. I GOT SKILLS, FRIEND, BUT YOU'RE SEEING THINGS THERE.
THE BOOZE'LL DO THAT TO YOU.
NOW, WHOEVER YOU ARE, YOU JUST ACTIVATED A MEMORY IN ME SIMPLY BY ME LOOKING AT YOU. THAT DON'T HAPPEN. BAD, MESSED-UP JUJU.
AND IT'S A MEMORY I REALLY DON'T CARE TO RELIVE.
I SHOULDA DIED THERE... I DESERVED TO DIE.
WHAT I SAW...
...SOMETIMES I THINK I DID DIE THERE AND THIS IS ALL... I DUNNO...
I HAVE TRAVELED FAR TO FIND YOU BECAUSE I WAS TOLD YOU COULD...SHOW ME THINGS.
I...
LOOK...

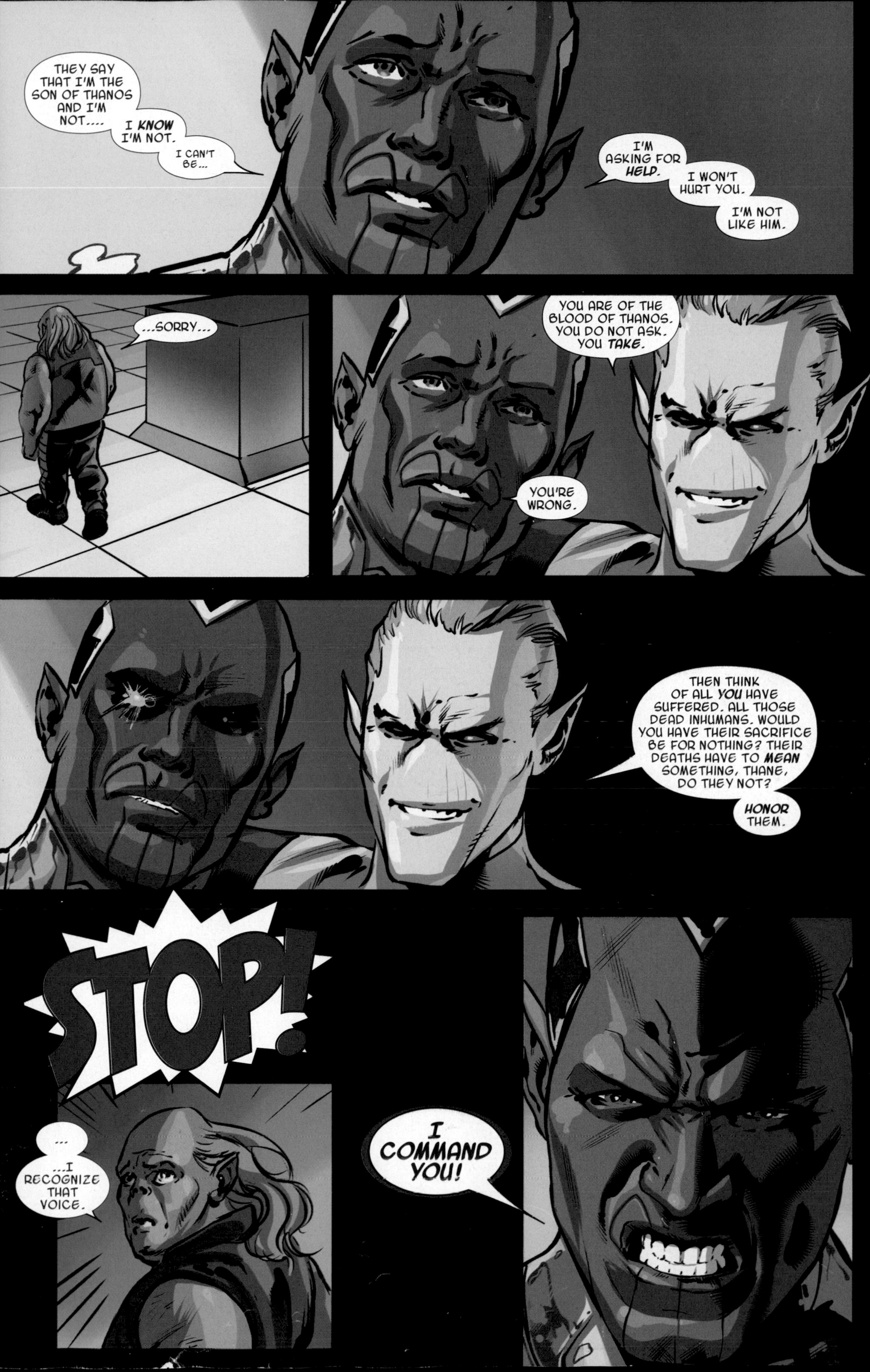
THEY SAY THAT I'M THE SON OF THANOS AND I'M NOT....
I KNOW I'M NOT.
I CAN'T BE...
I'M ASKING FOR HELP.
I WON'T HURT YOU.
I'M NOT LIKE HIM.
...SORRY...
YOU ARE OF THE BLOOD OF THANOS. YOU DO NOT ASK. YOU TAKE.
YOU'RE WRONG.
THEN THINK OF ALL YOU HAVE SUFFERED. ALL THOSE DEAD INHUMANS. WOULD YOU HAVE THEIR SACRIFICE BE FOR NOTHING? THEIR DEATHS HAVE TO MEAN SOMETHING, THANE, DO THEY NOT?
HONOR THEM.
STOP!
...
...I RECOGNIZE THAT VOICE.
I COMMAND YOU!

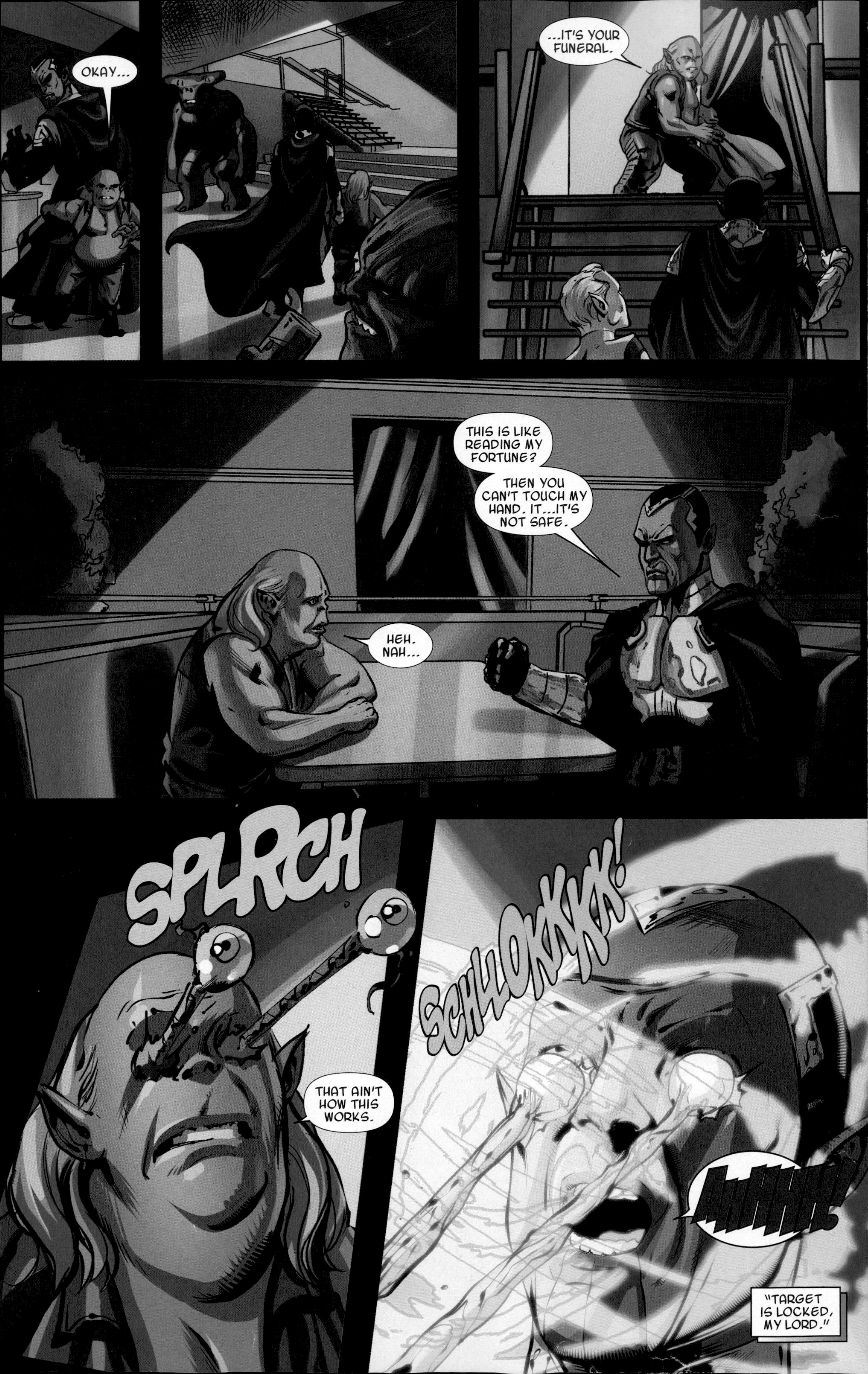
OKAY...
...IT'S YOUR FUNERAL.
THIS IS LIKE READING MY FORTUNE?
THEN YOU CAN'T TOUCH MY HAND. IT...IT'S NOT SAFE.
HEH. NAH...
SPLRCH
THAT AIN'T HOW THIS WORKS.
SCHLLOKKKK!
"TARGET IS LOCKED, MY LORD."

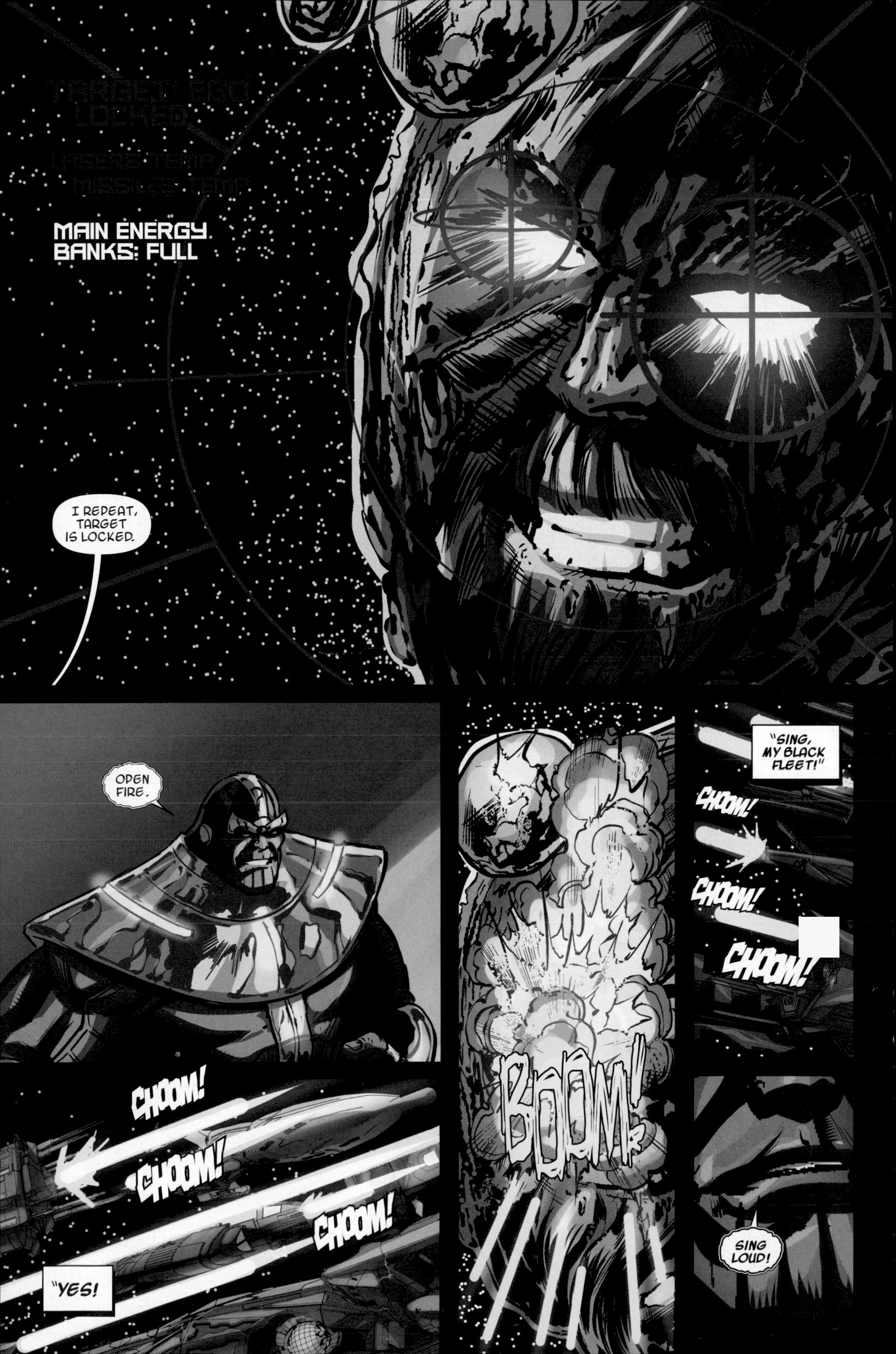
TARGET: EGO LOCKED
LASERS: TEMP
MISSILES: TEMP
MAIN ENERGY BANKS: FULL
I REPEAT, TARGET IS LOCKED.
OPEN FIRE.
CHOOM!
CHOOM!
CHOOM!
"YES!
BOOM!
"SING, MY BLACK FLEET!"
CHOOM!
CHOOM!
CHOOM!
SING LOUD!

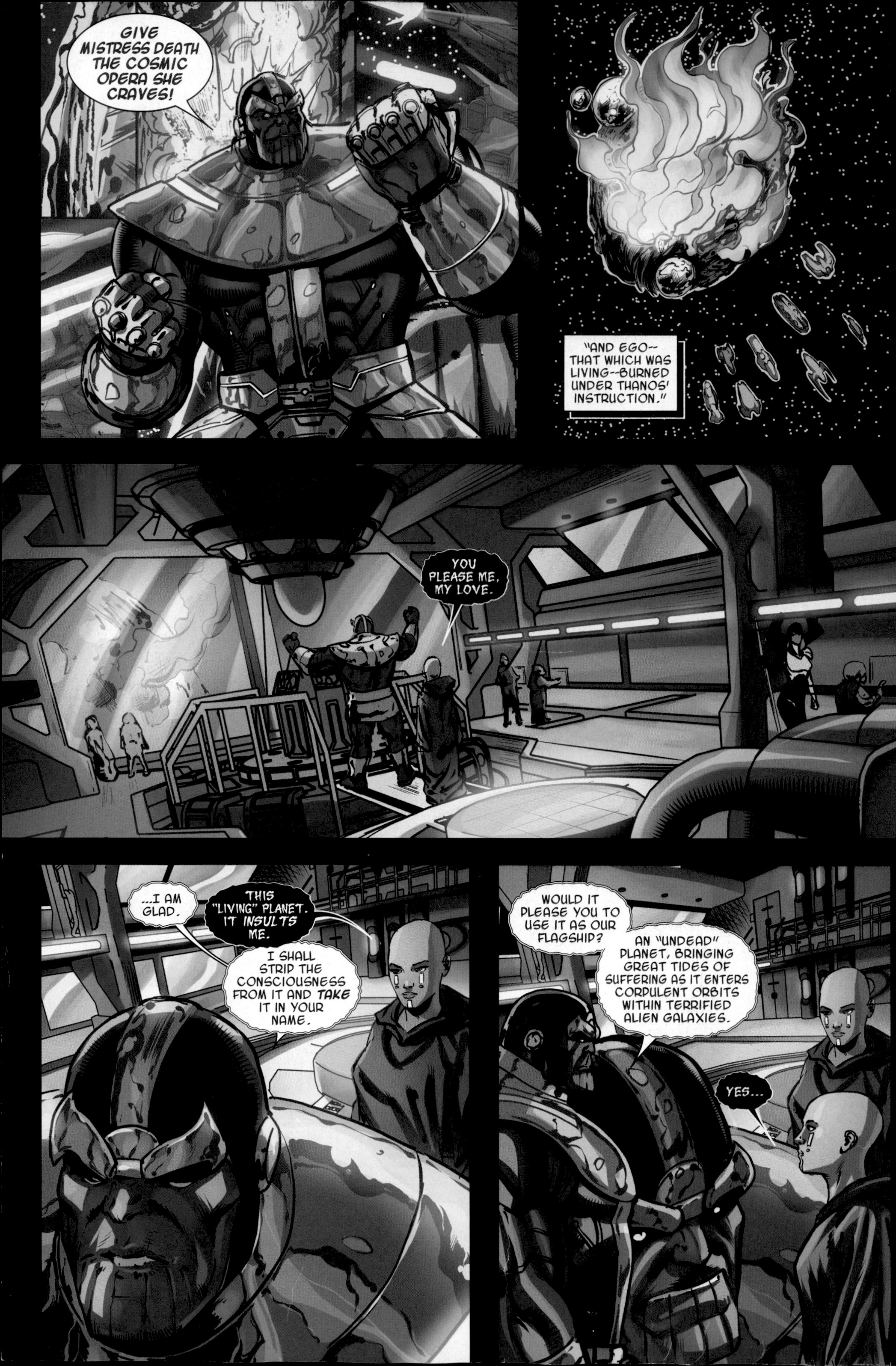
GIVE MISTRESS DEATH THE COSMIC OPERA SHE CRAVES!
"AND EGO--THAT WHICH WAS LIVING--BURNED UNDER THANOS' INSTRUCTION."
YOU PLEASE ME, MY LOVE.
...I AM GLAD.
THIS "LIVING" PLANET. IT INSULTS ME.
I SHALL STRIP THE CONSCIOUSNESS FROM IT AND TAKE IT IN YOUR NAME.
WOULD IT PLEASE YOU TO USE IT AS OUR FLAGSHIP?
AN "UNDEAD" PLANET, BRINGING GREAT TIDES OF SUFFERING AS IT ENTERS CORPULENT ORBITS WITHIN TERRIFIED ALIEN GALAXIES.
YES...

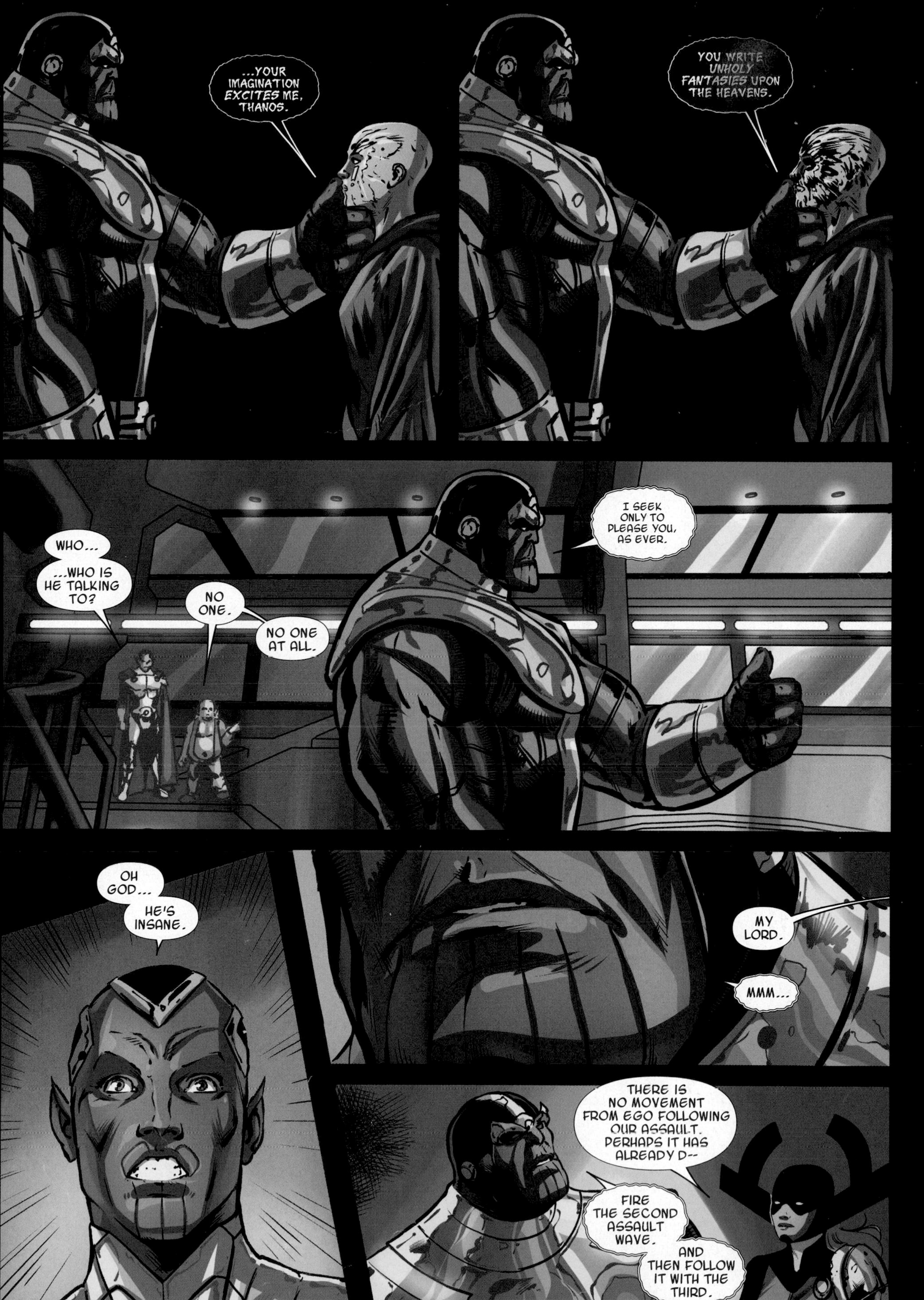
...YOUR IMAGINATION EXCITES ME, THANOS.
YOU WRITE UNHOLY FANTASIES UPON THE HEAVENS.
WHO...
...WHO IS HE TALKING TO?
NO ONE.
NO ONE AT ALL.
I SEEK ONLY TO PLEASE YOU, AS EVER.
OH GOD...
HE'S INSANE.
MY LORD.
MMM...
THERE IS NO MOVEMENT FROM EGO FOLLOWING OUR ASSAULT. PERHAPS IT HAS ALREADY D--
FIRE THE SECOND ASSAULT WAVE.
AND THEN FOLLOW IT WITH THE THIRD.

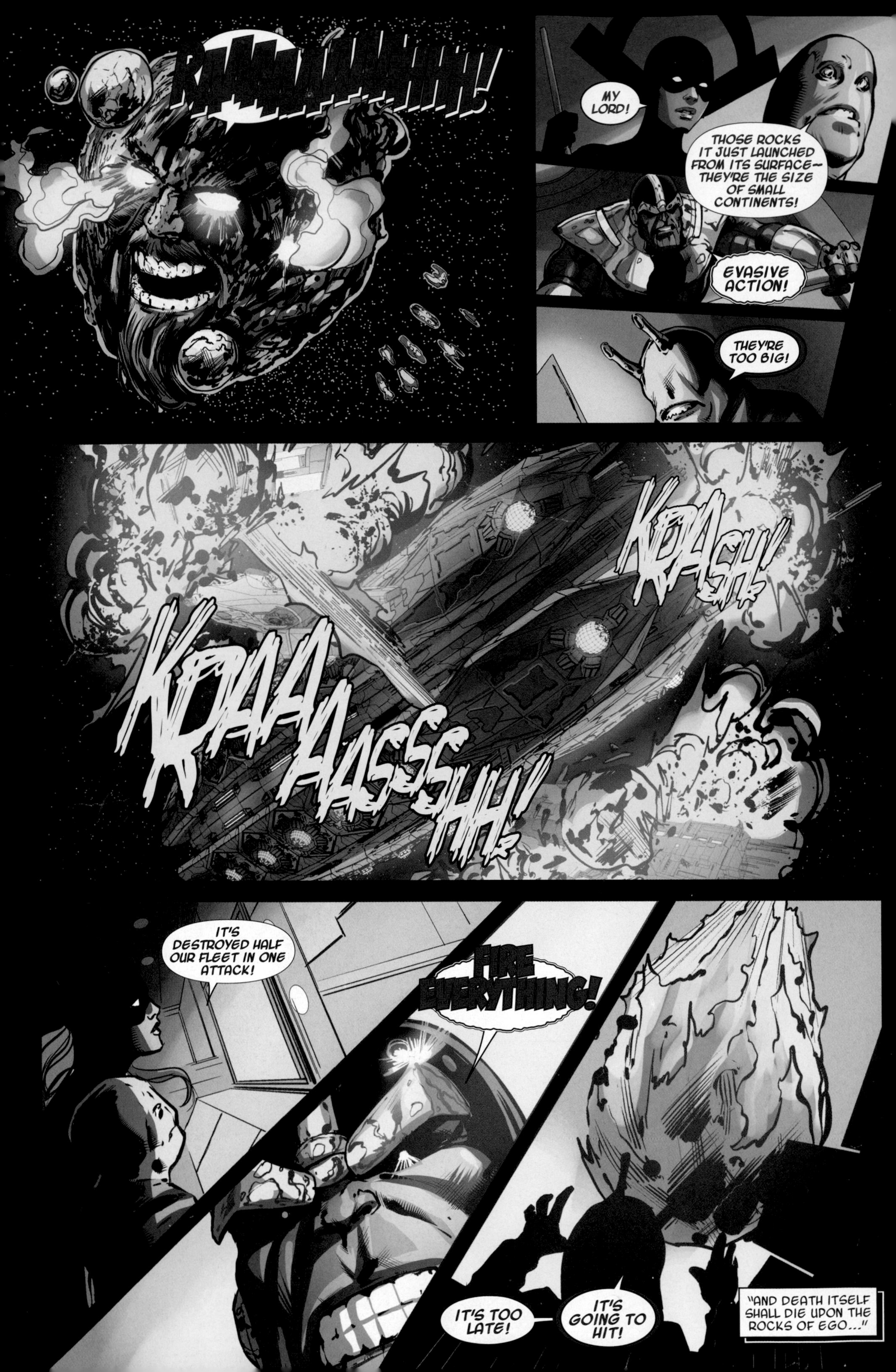
MY LORD!
THOSE ROCKS IT JUST LAUNCHED FROM ITS SURFACE-- THEY'RE THE SIZE OF SMALL CONTINENTS!
EVASIVE ACTION!
THEY'RE TOO BIG!
KRASH!
KRAAAAASSSHH!
IT'S DESTROYED HALF OUR FLEET IN ONE ATTACK!
FIRE EVERYTHING!
IT'S TOO LATE!
IT'S GOING TO HIT!
"AND DEATH ITSELF SHALL DIE UPON THE ROCKS OF EGO..."

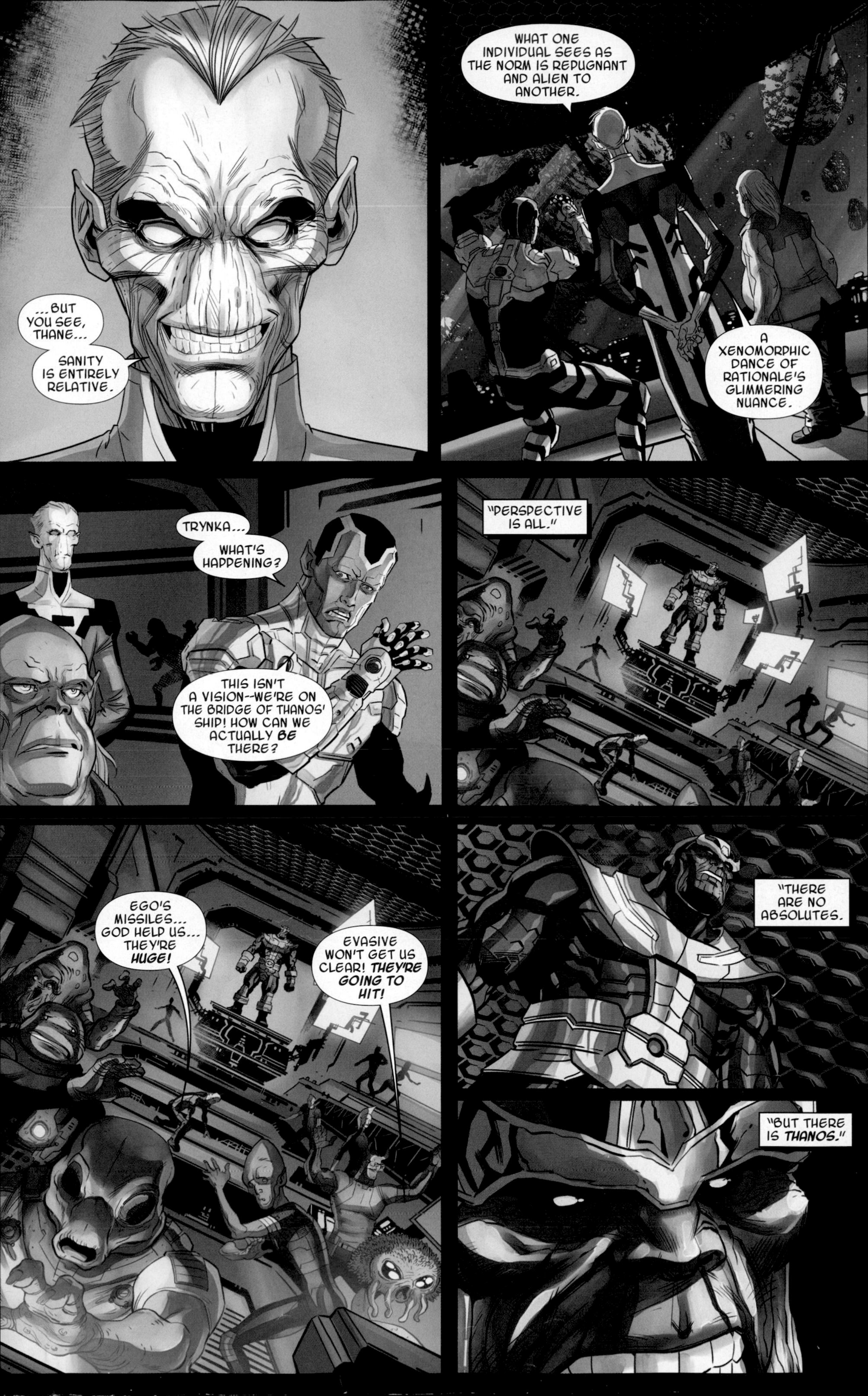
...BUT YOU SEE, THANE...
SANITY IS ENTIRELY RELATIVE.
WHAT ONE INDIVIDUAL SEES AS THE NORM IS REPUGNANT AND ALIEN TO ANOTHER.
A XENOMORPHIC DANCE OF RATIONALE'S GLIMMERING NUANCE.
TRYNKA...
WHAT'S HAPPENING?
THIS ISN'T A VISION--WE'RE ON THE BRIDGE OF THANOS' SHIP! HOW CAN WE ACTUALLY BE THERE?
"PERSPECTIVE IS ALL."
EGO'S MISSILES... GOD HELP US... THEY'RE HUGE!
EVASIVE WON'T GET US CLEAR! THEY'RE GOING TO HIT!
"THERE ARE NO ABSOLUTES.
"BUT THERE IS THANOS."

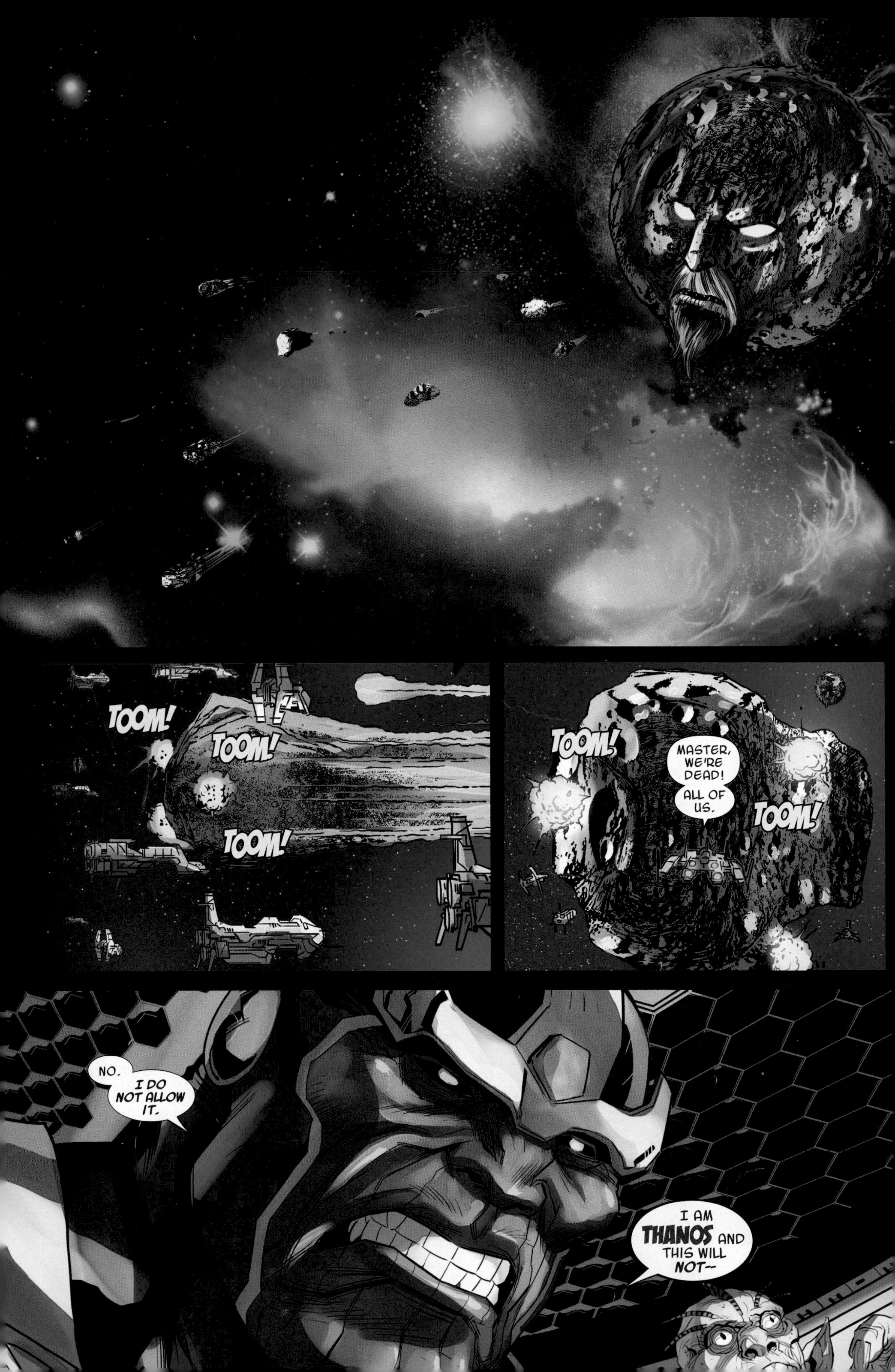
TOOM!
TOOM!
TOOM!
TOOM!
MASTER, WE'RE DEAD!
ALL OF US.
TOOM!
NO.
I DO NOT ALLOW IT.
I AM THANOS AND THIS WILL NOT--

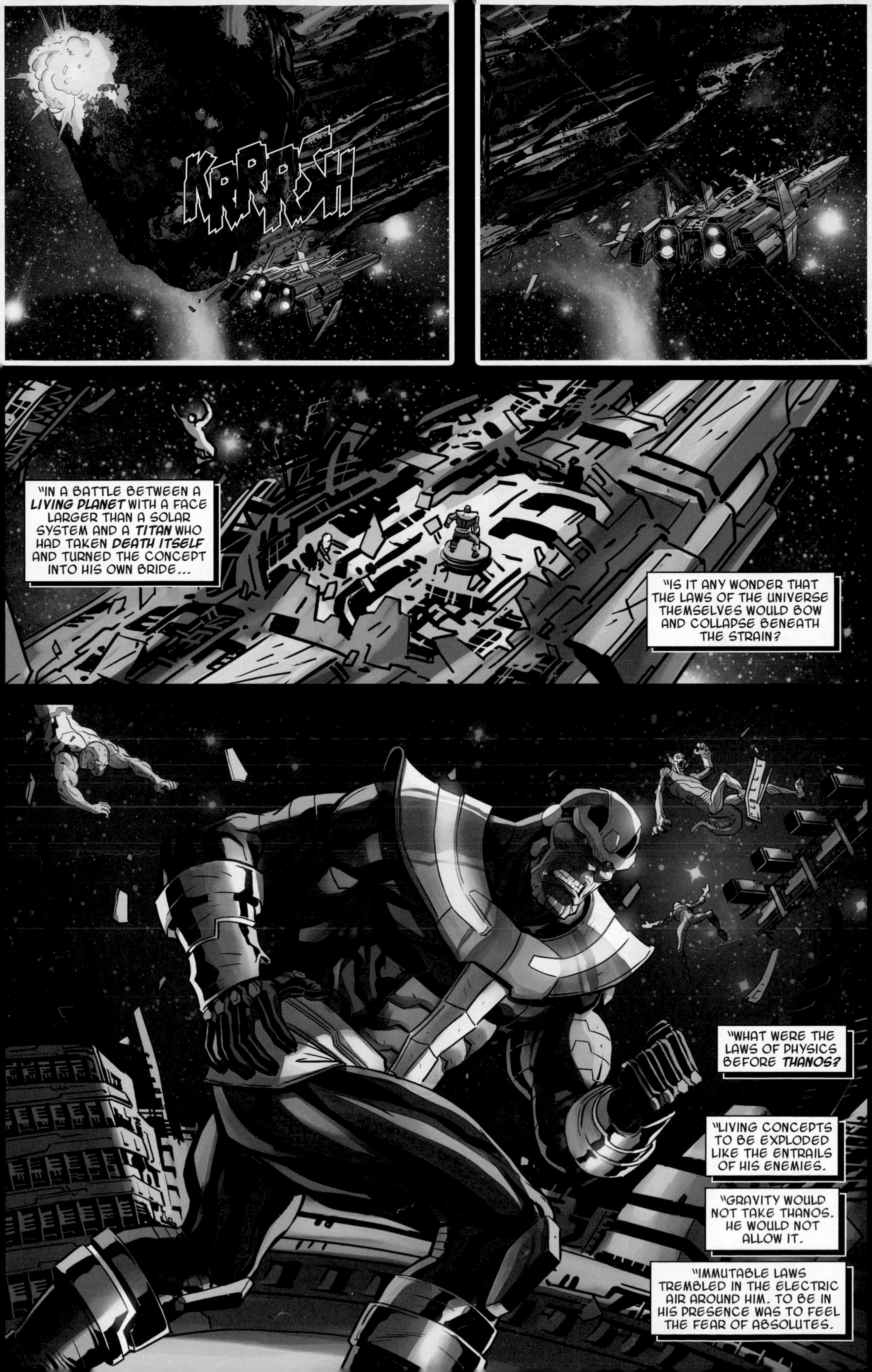
KRRASH
"IN A BATTLE BETWEEN A *LIVING PLANET* WITH A FACE LARGER THAN A SOLAR SYSTEM AND A *TITAN* WHO HAD TAKEN *DEATH ITSELF* AND TURNED THE CONCEPT INTO HIS OWN BRIDE...
"IS IT ANY WONDER THAT THE LAWS OF THE UNIVERSE THEMSELVES WOULD BOW AND COLLAPSE BENEATH THE STRAIN?
"WHAT WERE THE LAWS OF PHYSICS BEFORE *THANOS?*
"LIVING CONCEPTS TO BE EXPLODED LIKE THE ENTRAILS OF HIS ENEMIES.
"GRAVITY WOULD NOT TAKE THANOS. HE WOULD NOT ALLOW IT.
"IMMUTABLE LAWS TREMBLED IN THE ELECTRIC AIR AROUND HIM. TO BE IN HIS PRESENCE WAS TO FEEL THE FEAR OF ABSOLUTES.

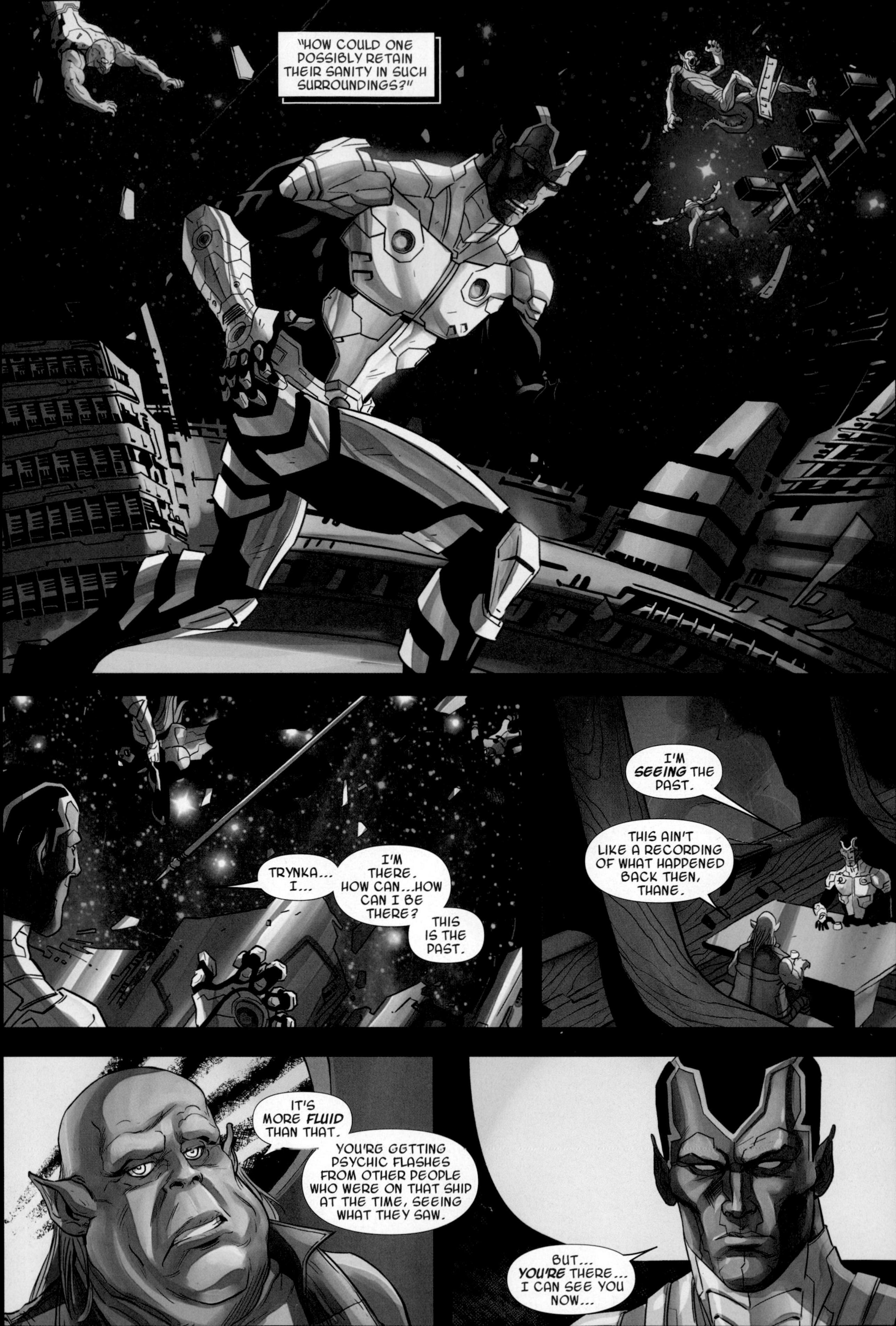
"HOW COULD ONE POSSIBLY RETAIN THEIR SANITY IN SUCH SURROUNDINGS?"
TRYNKA... I...
I'M THERE. HOW CAN...HOW CAN I BE THERE?
THIS IS THE PAST.
I'M SEEING THE PAST.
THIS AIN'T LIKE A RECORDING OF WHAT HAPPENED BACK THEN, THANE.
IT'S MORE FLUID THAN THAT.
YOU'RE GETTING PSYCHIC FLASHES FROM OTHER PEOPLE WHO WERE ON THAT SHIP AT THE TIME, SEEING WHAT THEY SAW.
BUT... YOU'RE THERE... I CAN SEE YOU NOW...

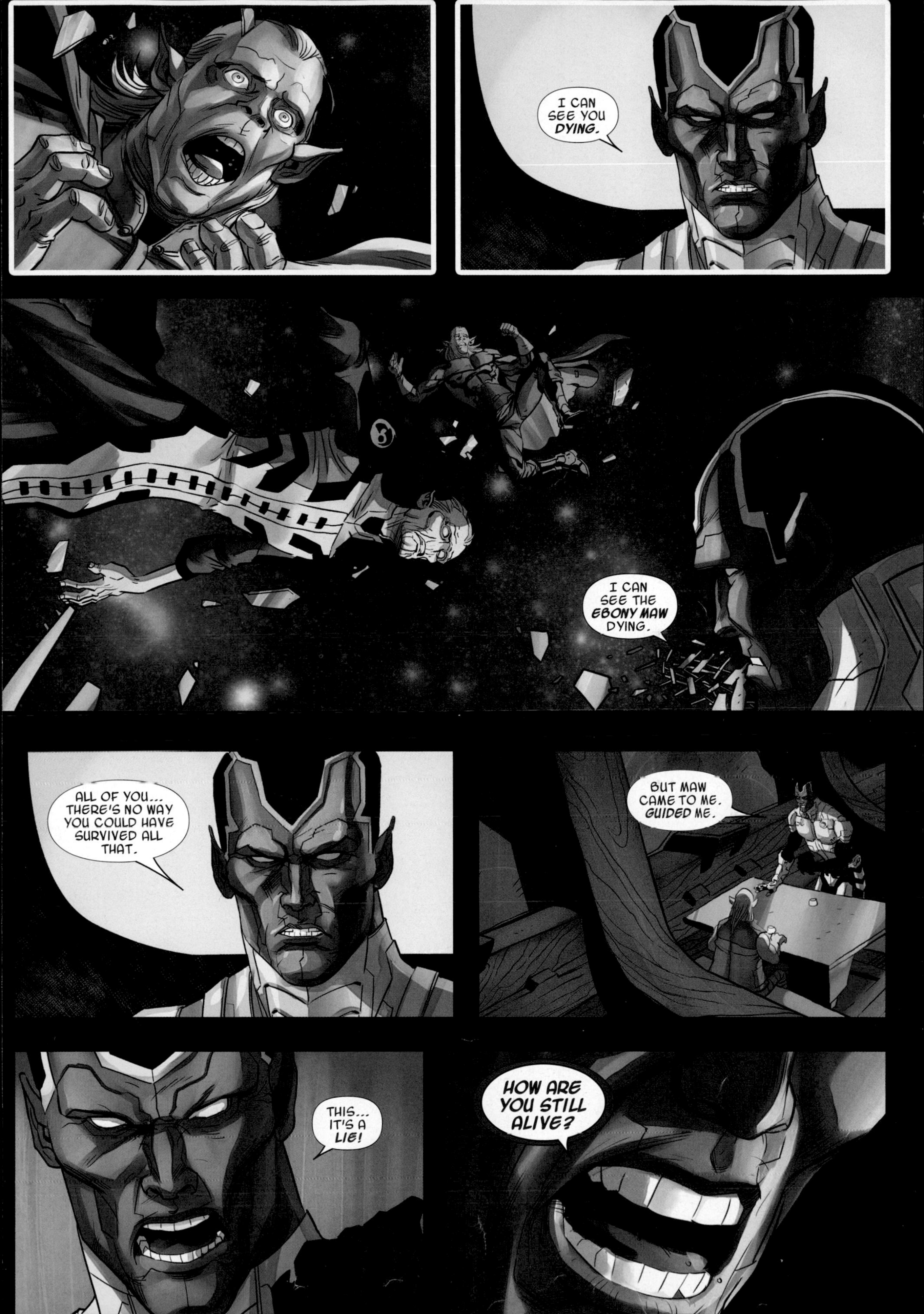
I CAN SEE YOU DYING.
I CAN SEE THE EBONY MAW DYING.
ALL OF YOU... THERE'S NO WAY YOU COULD HAVE SURVIVED ALL THAT.
BUT MAW CAME TO ME. GUIDED ME.
THIS... IT'S A LIE!
HOW ARE YOU STILL ALIVE?

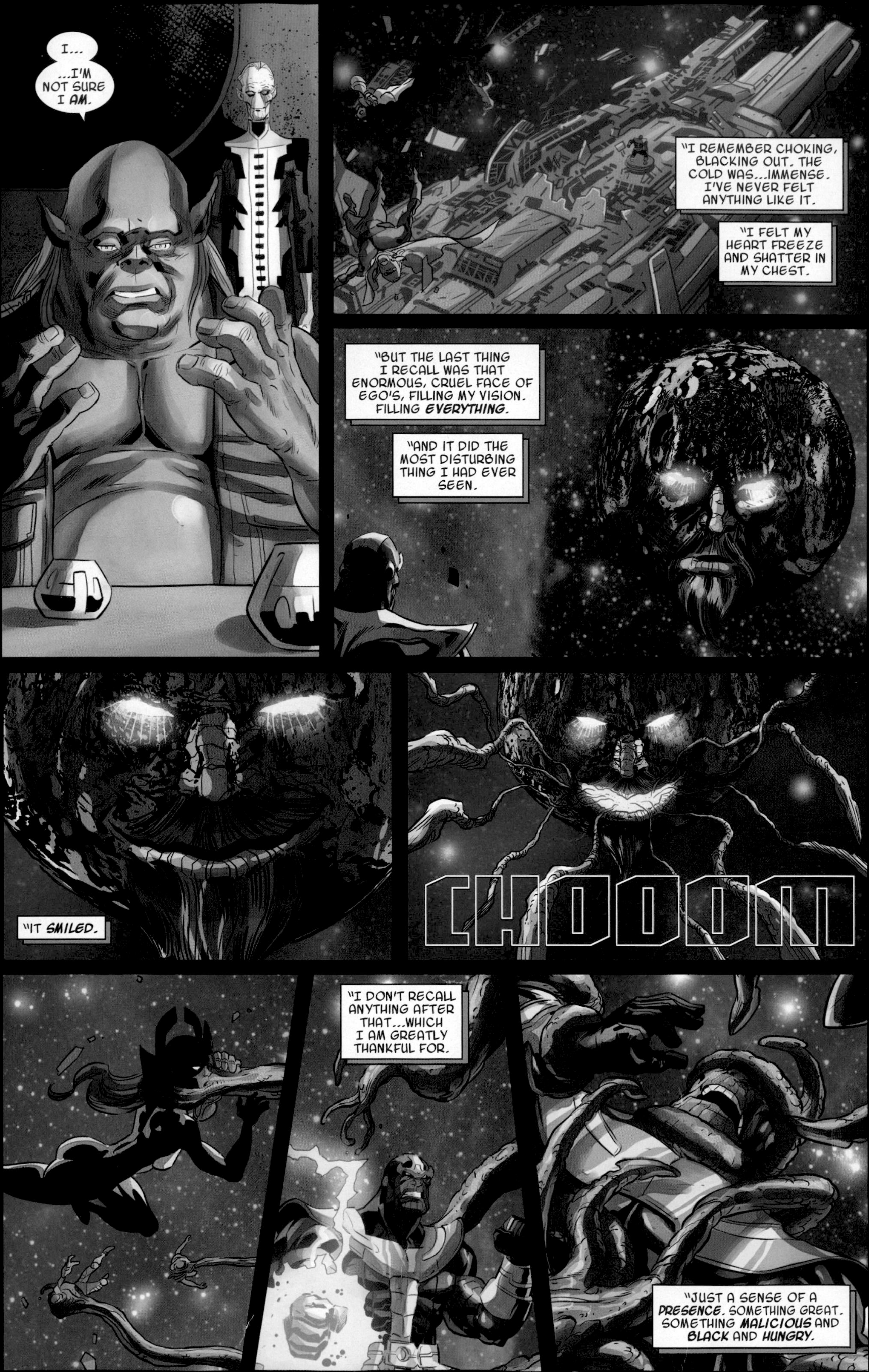
I...
...I'M NOT SURE I AM.
"I REMEMBER CHOKING, BLACKING OUT. THE COLD WAS...IMMENSE. I'VE NEVER FELT ANYTHING LIKE IT.
"I FELT MY HEART FREEZE AND SHATTER IN MY CHEST.
"BUT THE LAST THING I RECALL WAS THAT ENORMOUS, CRUEL FACE OF EGO'S, FILLING MY VISION. FILLING EVERYTHING.
"AND IT DID THE MOST DISTURBING THING I HAD EVER SEEN.
"IT SMILED.
CHOOOM
"I DON'T RECALL ANYTHING AFTER THAT...WHICH I AM GREATLY THANKFUL FOR.
"JUST A SENSE OF A PRESENCE. SOMETHING GREAT. SOMETHING MALICIOUS AND BLACK AND HUNGRY.

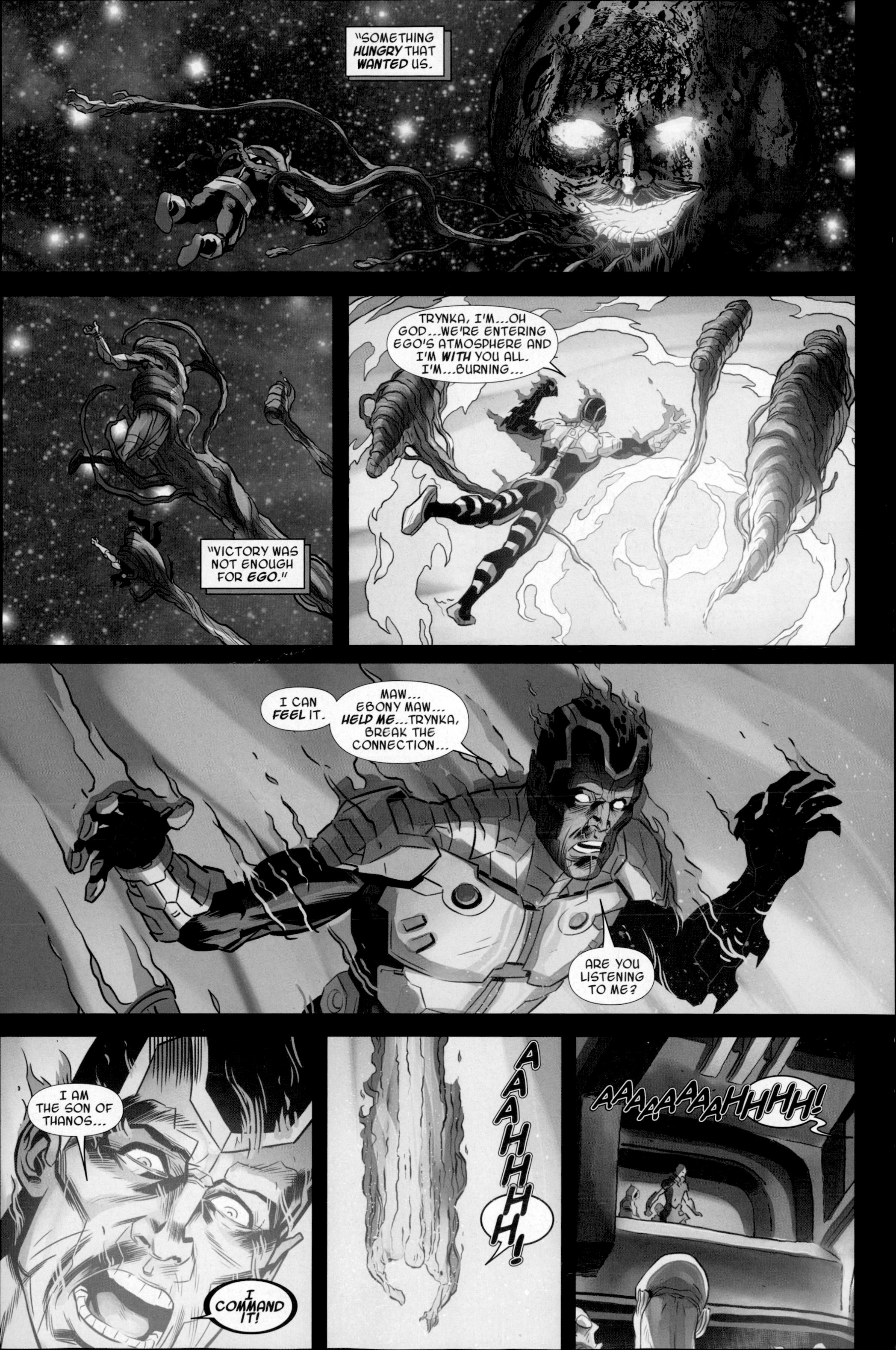
"SOMETHING HUNGRY THAT WANTED US.
"VICTORY WAS NOT ENOUGH FOR EGO."
TRYNKA, I'M...OH GOD...WE'RE ENTERING EGO'S ATMOSPHERE AND I'M WITH YOU ALL. I'M...BURNING...
I CAN FEEL IT.
MAW... EBONY MAW... HELP ME...TRYNKA, BREAK THE CONNECTION...
ARE YOU LISTENING TO ME?
I AM THE SON OF THANOS...
I COMMAND IT!
AAAHHHHH!
AAAAAAAAHHHH!

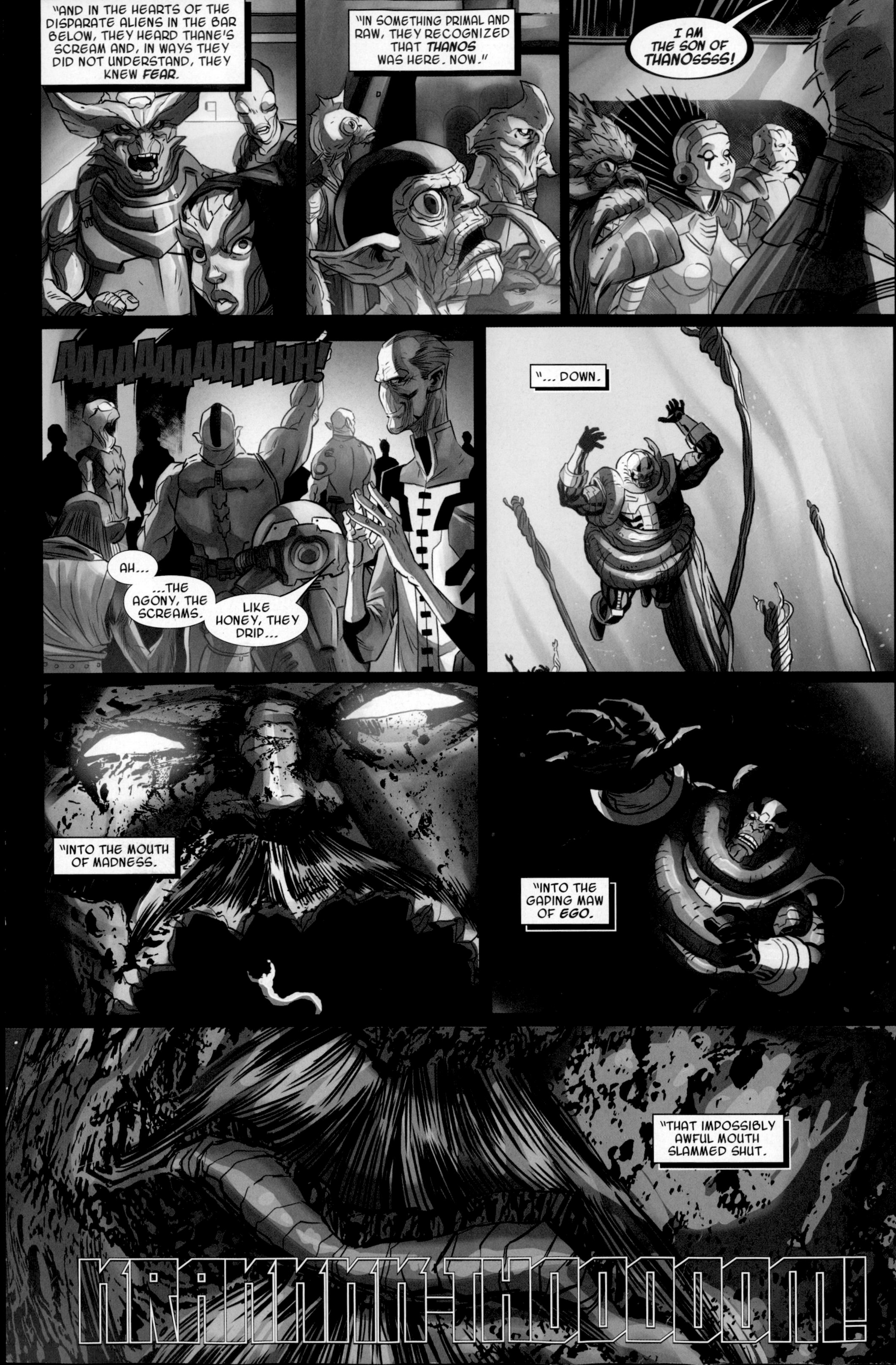
"AND IN THE HEARTS OF THE DISPARATE ALIENS IN THE BAR BELOW, THEY HEARD THANE'S SCREAM AND, IN WAYS THEY DID NOT UNDERSTAND, THEY KNEW FEAR.
"IN SOMETHING PRIMAL AND RAW, THEY RECOGNIZED THAT THANOS WAS HERE. NOW."
I AM THE SON OF THANOSSSS!
AAAAAAAAAHHHH!
AH...
...THE AGONY, THE SCREAMS.
LIKE HONEY, THEY DRIP...
"... DOWN.
"INTO THE MOUTH OF MADNESS.
"INTO THE GAPING MAW OF EGO.
"THAT IMPOSSIBLY AWFUL MOUTH SLAMMED SHUT.
KRAKKKKK-THOOOOOM!

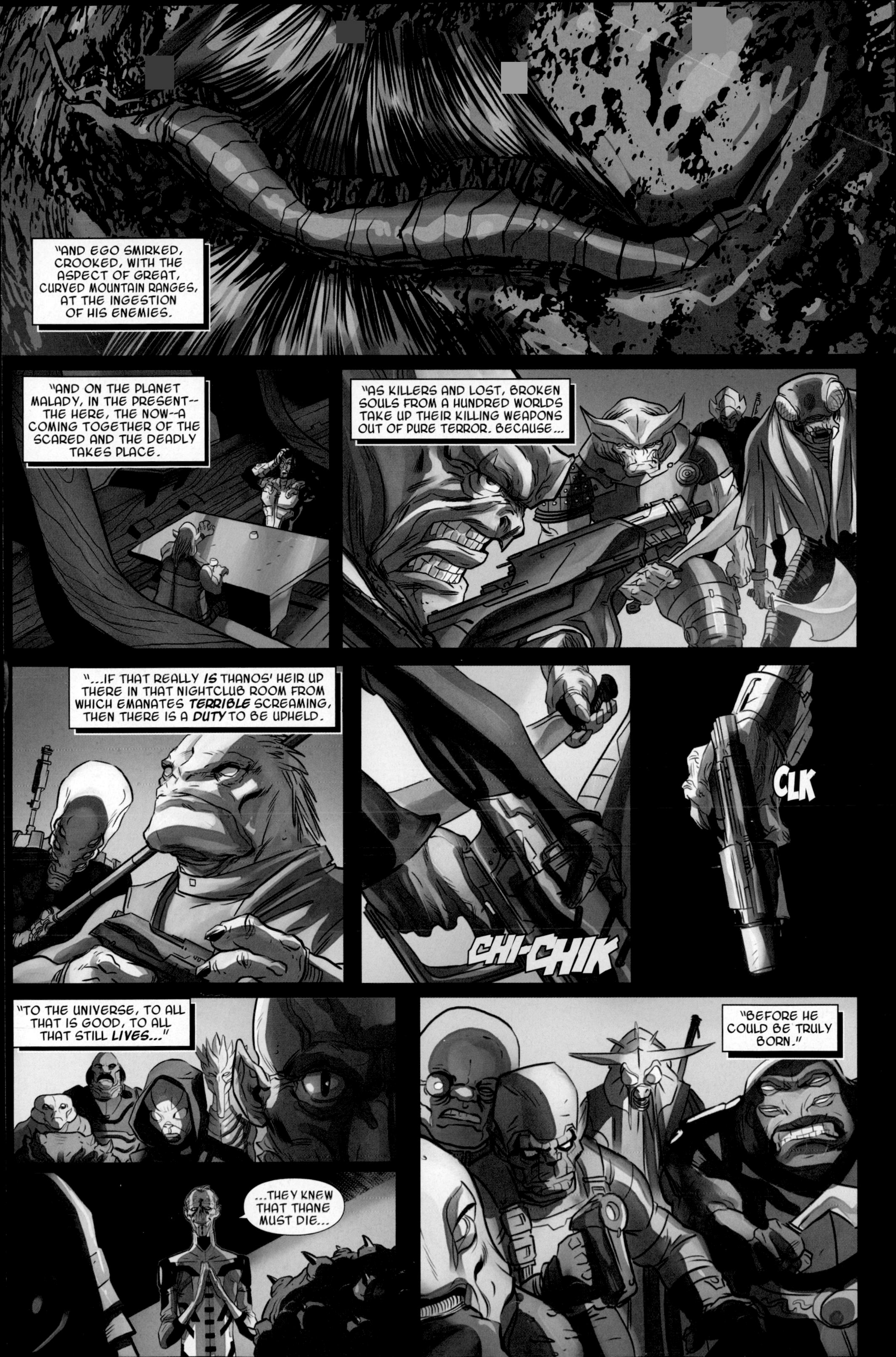
"AND EGO SMIRKED, CROOKED, WITH THE ASPECT OF GREAT, CURVED MOUNTAIN RANGES, AT THE INGESTION OF HIS ENEMIES.
"AND ON THE PLANET MALADY, IN THE PRESENT-- THE HERE, THE NOW--A COMING TOGETHER OF THE SCARED AND THE DEADLY TAKES PLACE.
"AS KILLERS AND LOST, BROKEN SOULS FROM A HUNDRED WORLDS TAKE UP THEIR KILLING WEAPONS OUT OF PURE TERROR. BECAUSE...
"...IF THAT REALLY IS THANOS' HEIR UP THERE IN THAT NIGHTCLUB ROOM FROM WHICH EMANATES TERRIBLE SCREAMING, THEN THERE IS A DUTY TO BE UPHELD.
CHI-CHIK
CLK
"TO THE UNIVERSE, TO ALL THAT IS GOOD, TO ALL THAT STILL LIVES..."
...THEY KNEW THAT THANE MUST DIE...
"BEFORE HE COULD BE TRULY BORN."

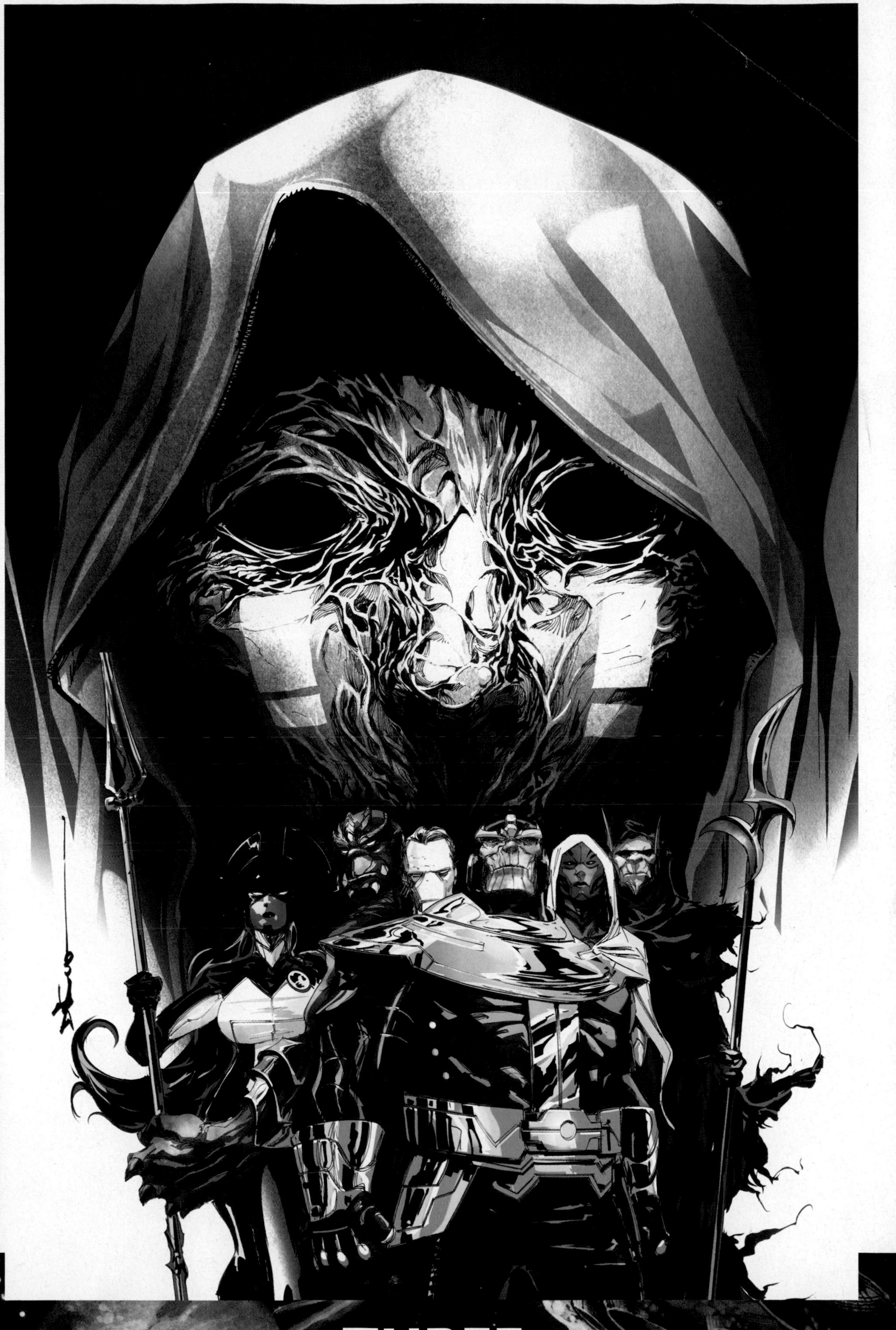

THREE

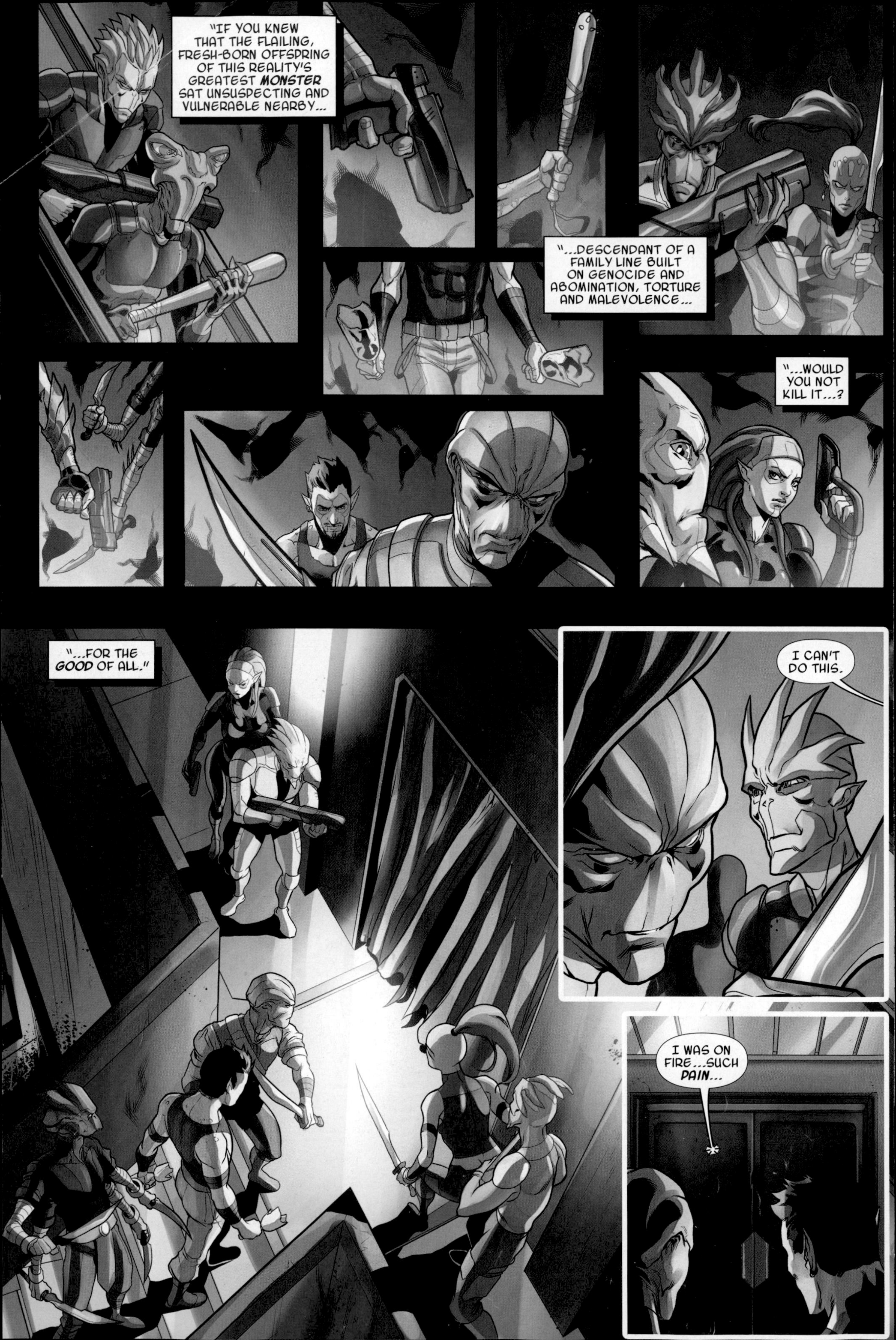

"IF YOU KNEW THAT THE FLAILING, FRESH-BORN OFFSPRING OF THIS REALITY'S GREATEST MONSTER SAT UNSUSPECTING AND VULNERABLE NEARBY...
"...DESCENDANT OF A FAMILY LINE BUILT ON GENOCIDE AND ABOMINATION, TORTURE AND MALEVOLENCE...
"...WOULD YOU NOT KILL IT...?
"...FOR THE GOOD OF ALL."
I CAN'T DO THIS.
I WAS ON FIRE...SUCH PAIN...

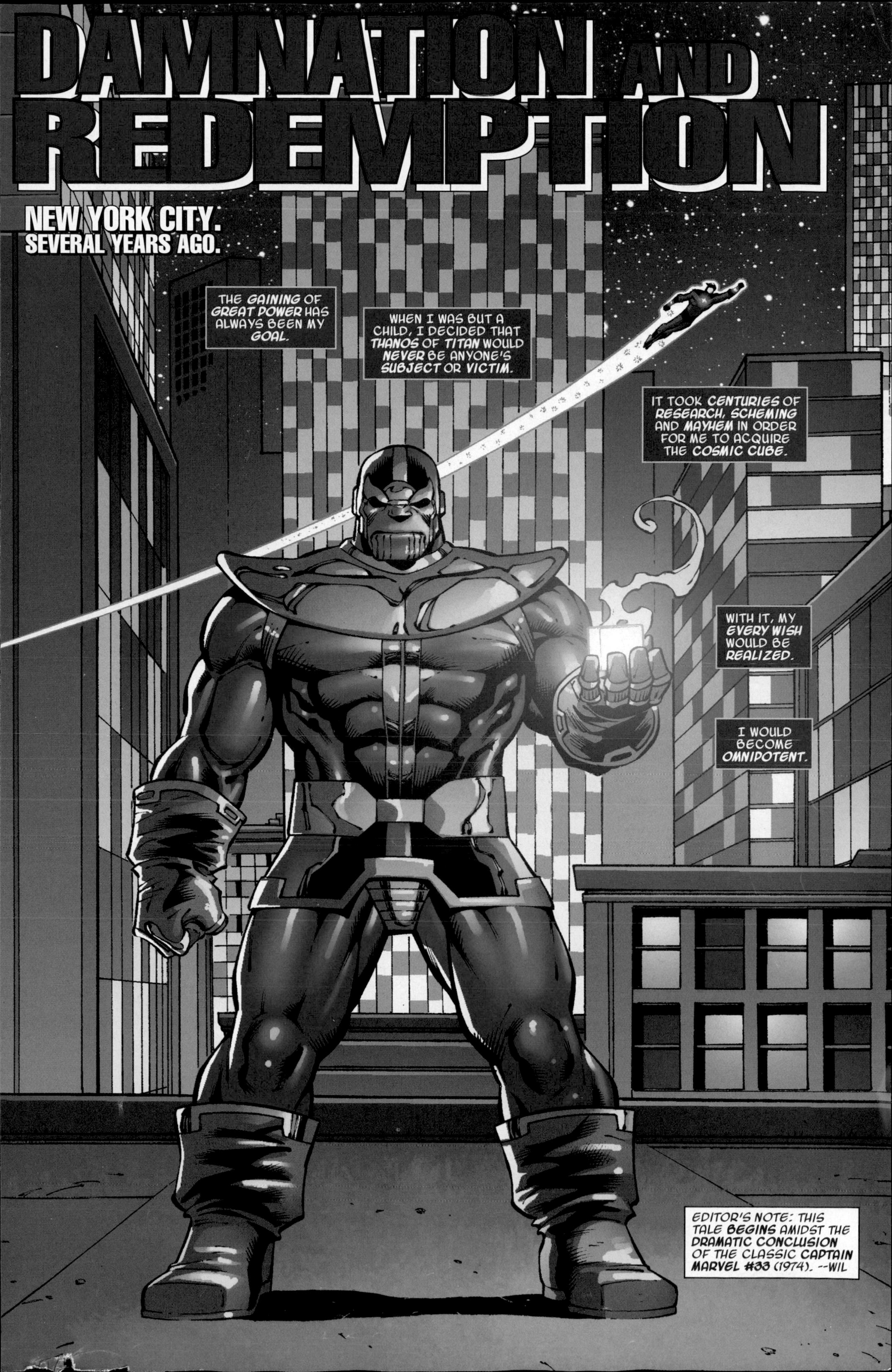
DAMNATION AND REDEMPTION
NEW YORK CITY. SEVERAL YEARS AGO.
THE GAINING OF GREAT POWER HAS ALWAYS BEEN MY GOAL.
WHEN I WAS BUT A CHILD, I DECIDED THAT THANOS OF TITAN WOULD NEVER BE ANYONE'S SUBJECT OR VICTIM.
IT TOOK CENTURIES OF RESEARCH, SCHEMING AND MAYHEM IN ORDER FOR ME TO ACQUIRE THE COSMIC CUBE.
WITH IT, MY EVERY WISH WOULD BE REALIZED.
I WOULD BECOME OMNIPOTENT.
EDITOR'S NOTE: THIS TALE BEGINS AMIDST THE DRAMATIC CONCLUSION OF THE CLASSIC CAPTAIN MARVEL #33 (1974). --WIL

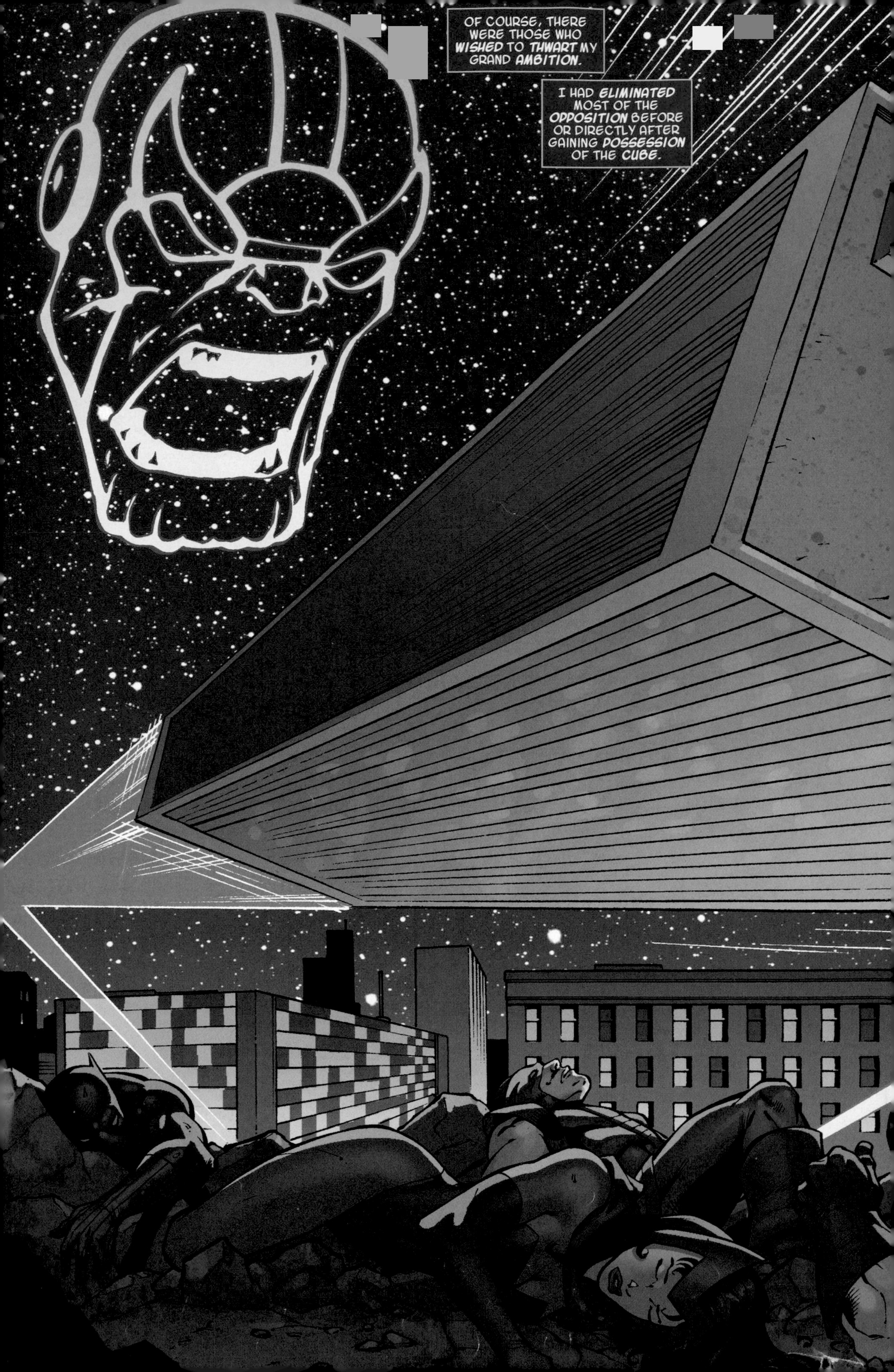
OF COURSE, THERE WERE THOSE WHO WISHED TO THWART MY GRAND AMBITION.
I HAD ELIMINATED MOST OF THE OPPOSITION BEFORE OR DIRECTLY AFTER GAINING POSSESSION OF THE CUBE.

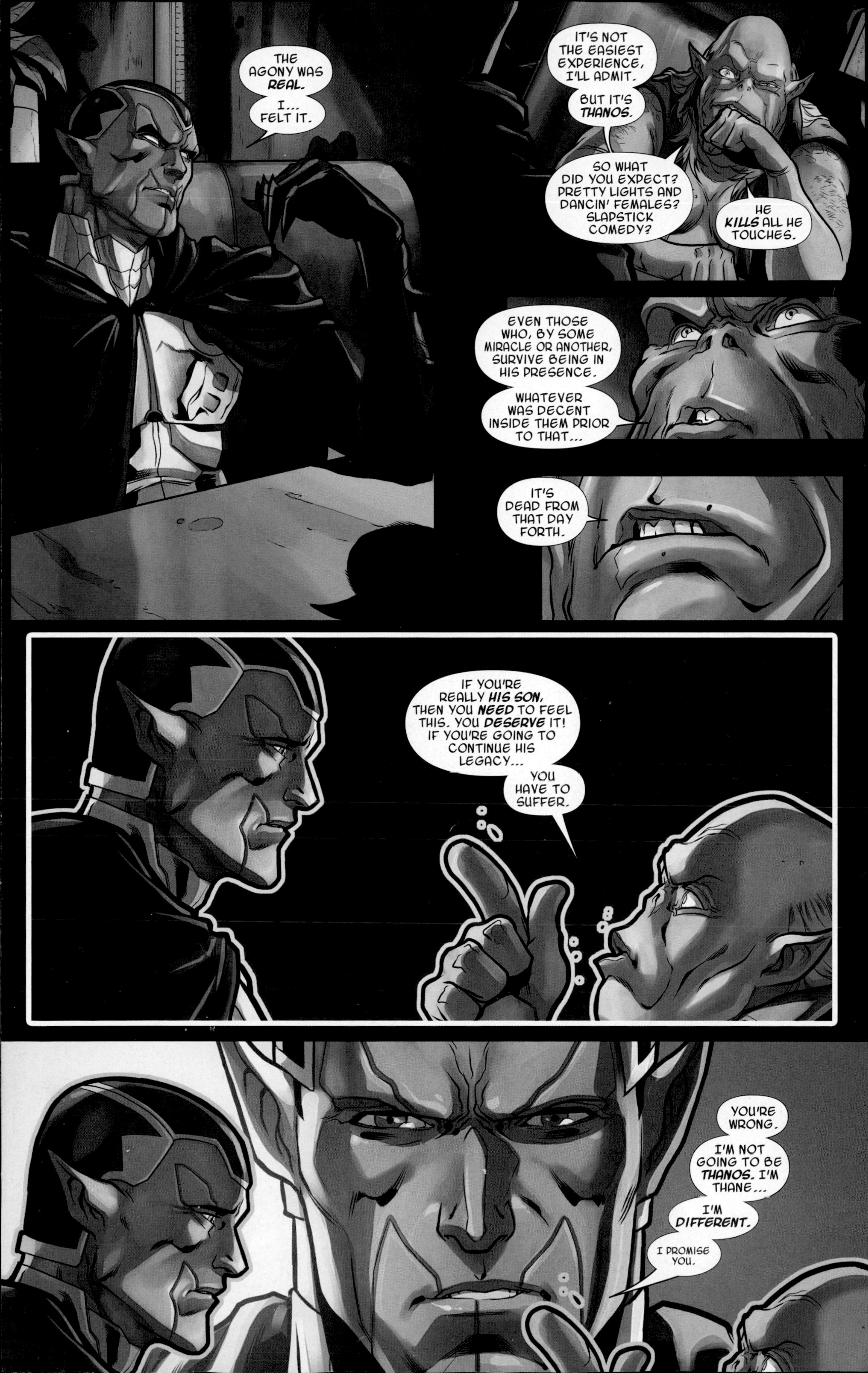
THE AGONY WAS REAL.
I... FELT IT.
IT'S NOT THE EASIEST EXPERIENCE, I'LL ADMIT.
BUT IT'S THANOS.
SO WHAT DID YOU EXPECT? PRETTY LIGHTS AND DANCIN' FEMALES? SLAPSTICK COMEDY?
HE KILLS ALL HE TOUCHES.
EVEN THOSE WHO, BY SOME MIRACLE OR ANOTHER, SURVIVE BEING IN HIS PRESENCE.
WHATEVER WAS DECENT INSIDE THEM PRIOR TO THAT...
IT'S DEAD FROM THAT DAY FORTH.
IF YOU'RE REALLY HIS SON, THEN YOU NEED TO FEEL THIS. YOU DESERVE IT! IF YOU'RE GOING TO CONTINUE HIS LEGACY...
YOU HAVE TO SUFFER.
YOU'RE WRONG.
I'M NOT GOING TO BE THANOS. I'M THANE...
I'M DIFFERENT.
I PROMISE YOU.

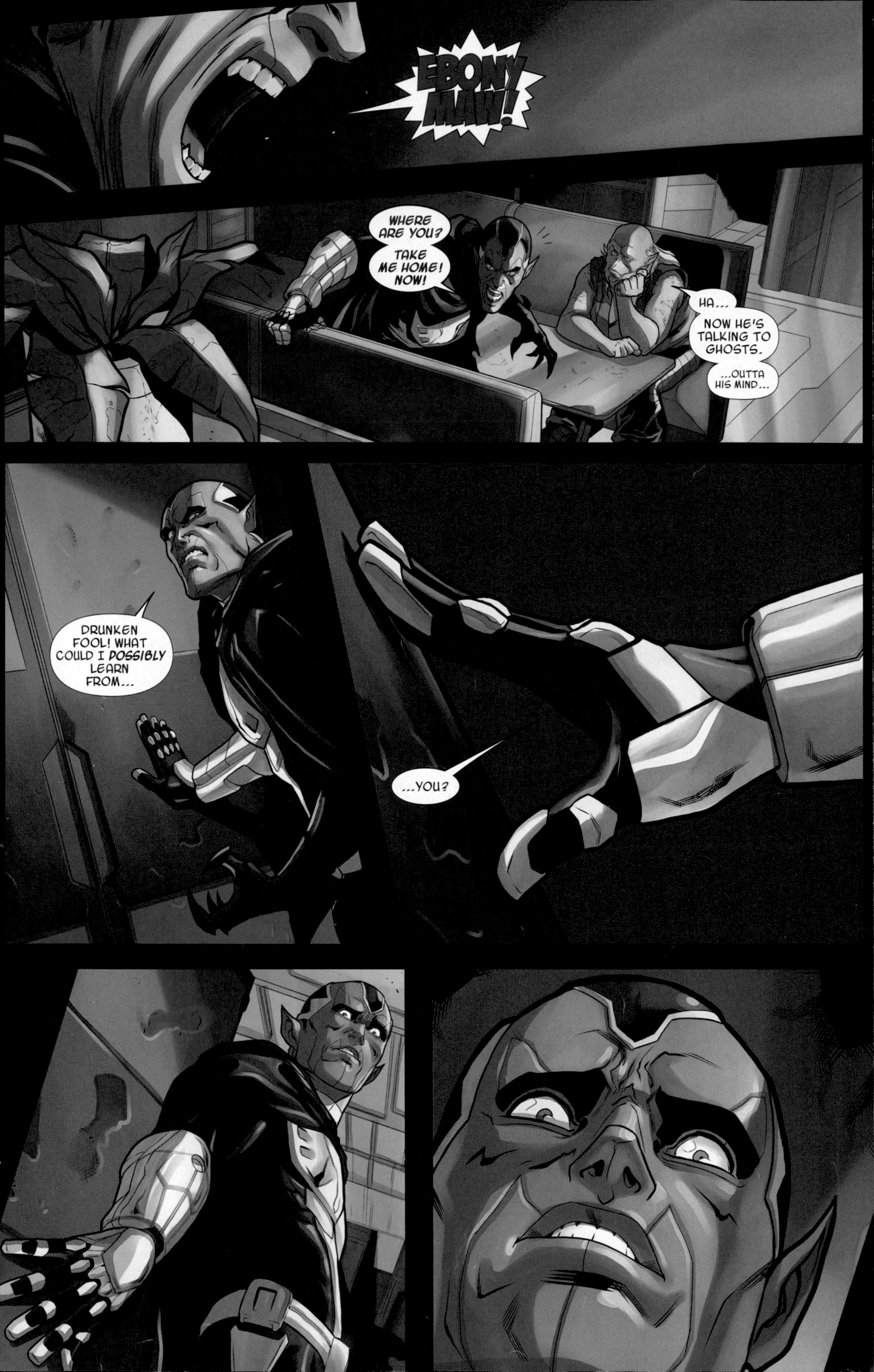
EBONY MAW!
WHERE ARE YOU?
TAKE ME HOME! NOW!
HA...
NOW HE'S TALKING TO GHOSTS.
...OUTTA HIS MIND...
DRUNKEN FOOL! WHAT COULD I POSSIBLY LEARN FROM...
...YOU?

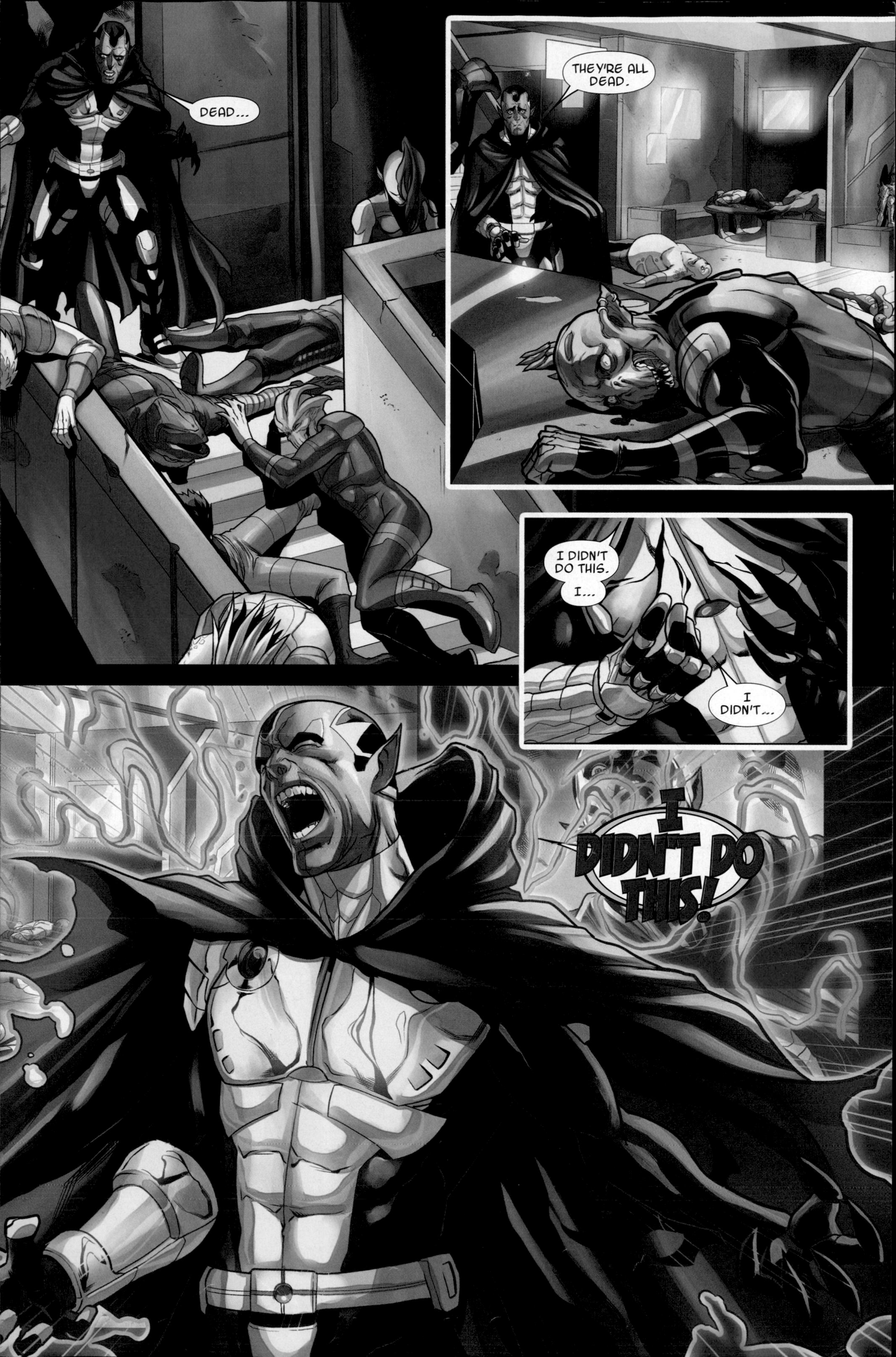
DEAD...
THEY'RE ALL DEAD.
I DIDN'T DO THIS.
I...
I DIDN'T...
I DIDN'T DO THIS!

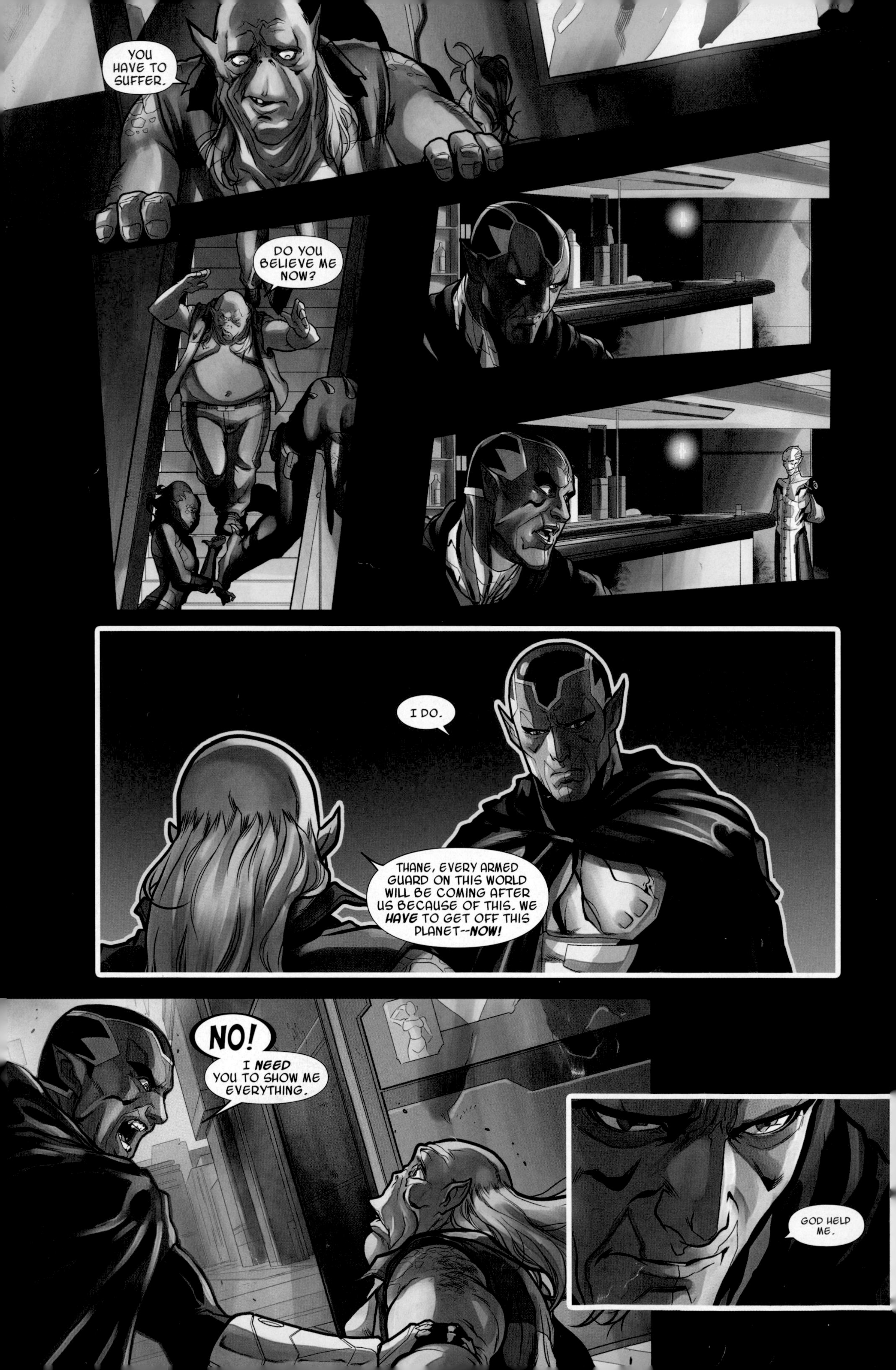
YOU HAVE TO SUFFER.
DO YOU BELIEVE ME NOW?
I DO.
THANE, EVERY ARMED GUARD ON THIS WORLD WILL BE COMING AFTER US BECAUSE OF THIS. WE *HAVE* TO GET OFF THIS PLANET--*NOW!*
NO!
I *NEED* YOU TO SHOW ME EVERYTHING.
GOD HELD ME.

"SHOW YOU EVERYTHING?"

"JUST OPEN YOUR EYES, THANE. YOU'RE *THERE*."

"*EGO THE LIVING PLANET* WAS TRIUMPHANT."

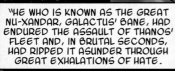
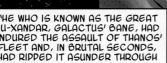

"HE WHO IS KNOWN AS THE GREAT NU-XANDAR, GALACTUS' BANE, HAD ENDURED THE ASSAULT OF THANOS' FLEET AND, IN BRUTAL SECONDS, HAD RIPPED IT ASUNDER THROUGH GREAT EXHALATIONS OF HATE."

"AND AS *THANOS* FELL DEEP INTO *EGO*, A PLANET'S WORTH OF MALICE RUMBLED WITH UNHOLY CONSIDERATIONS OF WHAT TO DO WITH THIS CANCEROUS *ABOMINATION*."

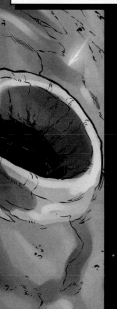
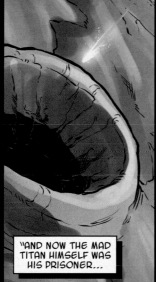

"AND NOW THE MAD TITAN HIMSELF WAS HIS PRISONER..."

"HOW MANY WAYS COULD HE MAKE THE KING OF SUFFERING *DIE*?"

COME THEN, EGO...

COME SHOW THANOS YOUR HEART SO THAT HE MIGHT EAT IT!

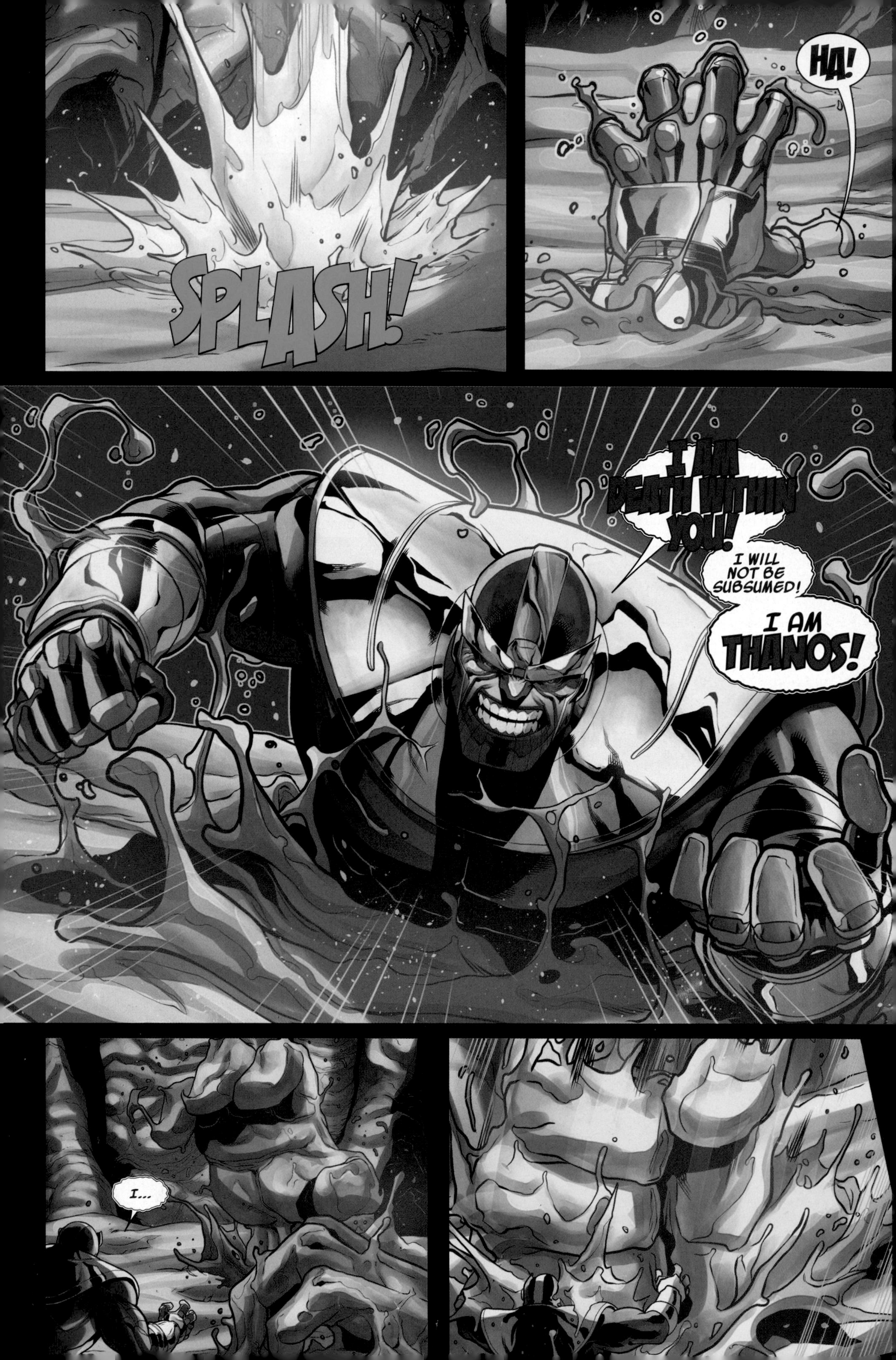
SPLASH!
HA!
I AM DEATH WITHIN YOU!
I WILL NOT BE SUBSUMED!
I AM THANOS!
I...

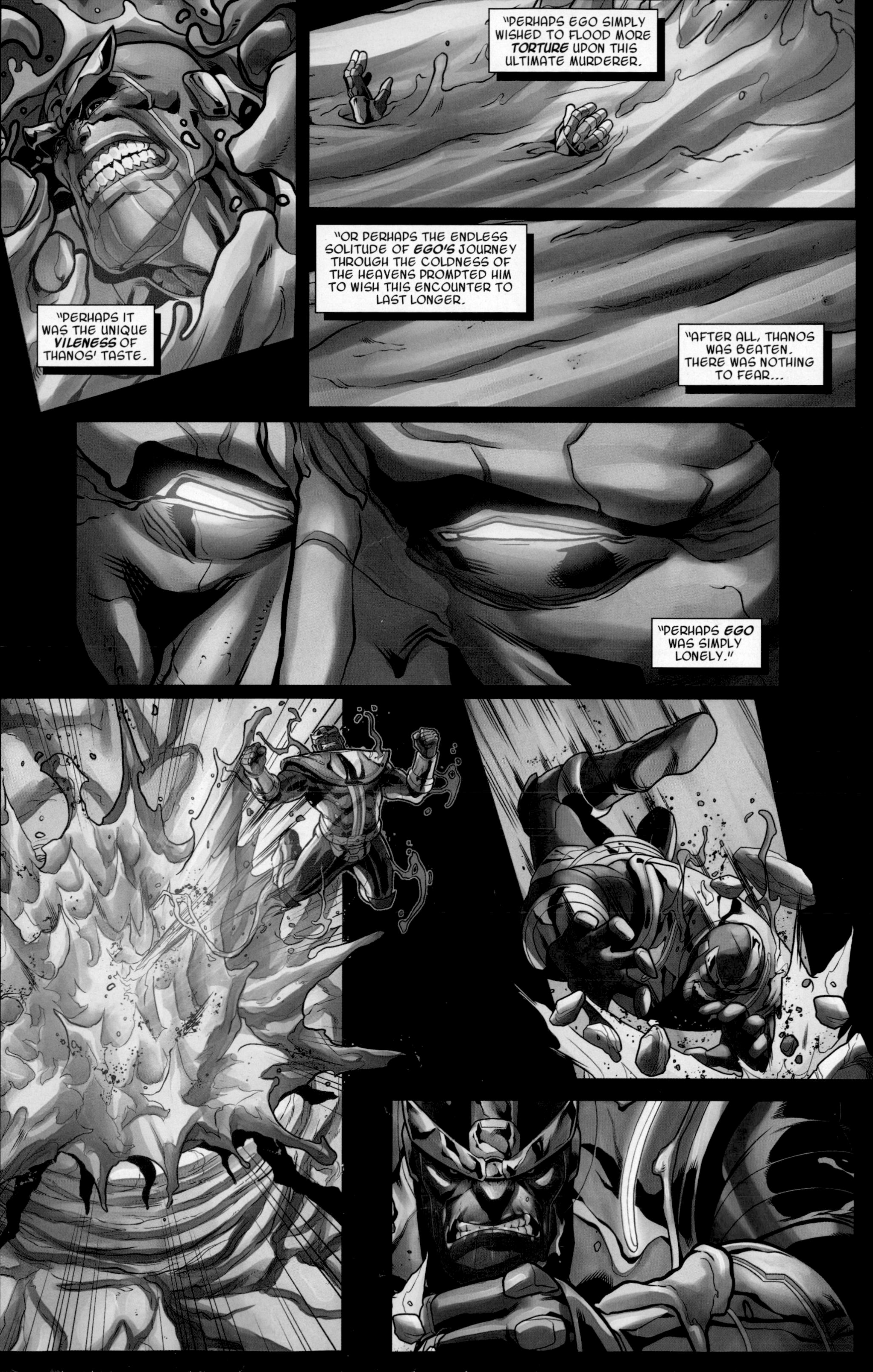
"PERHAPS IT WAS THE UNIQUE VILENESS OF THANOS' TASTE.
"PERHAPS EGO SIMPLY WISHED TO FLOOD MORE TORTURE UPON THIS ULTIMATE MURDERER.
"OR PERHAPS THE ENDLESS SOLITUDE OF EGO'S JOURNEY THROUGH THE COLDNESS OF THE HEAVENS PROMPTED HIM TO WISH THIS ENCOUNTER TO LAST LONGER.
"AFTER ALL, THANOS WAS BEATEN. THERE WAS NOTHING TO FEAR...
"PERHAPS EGO WAS SIMPLY LONELY."

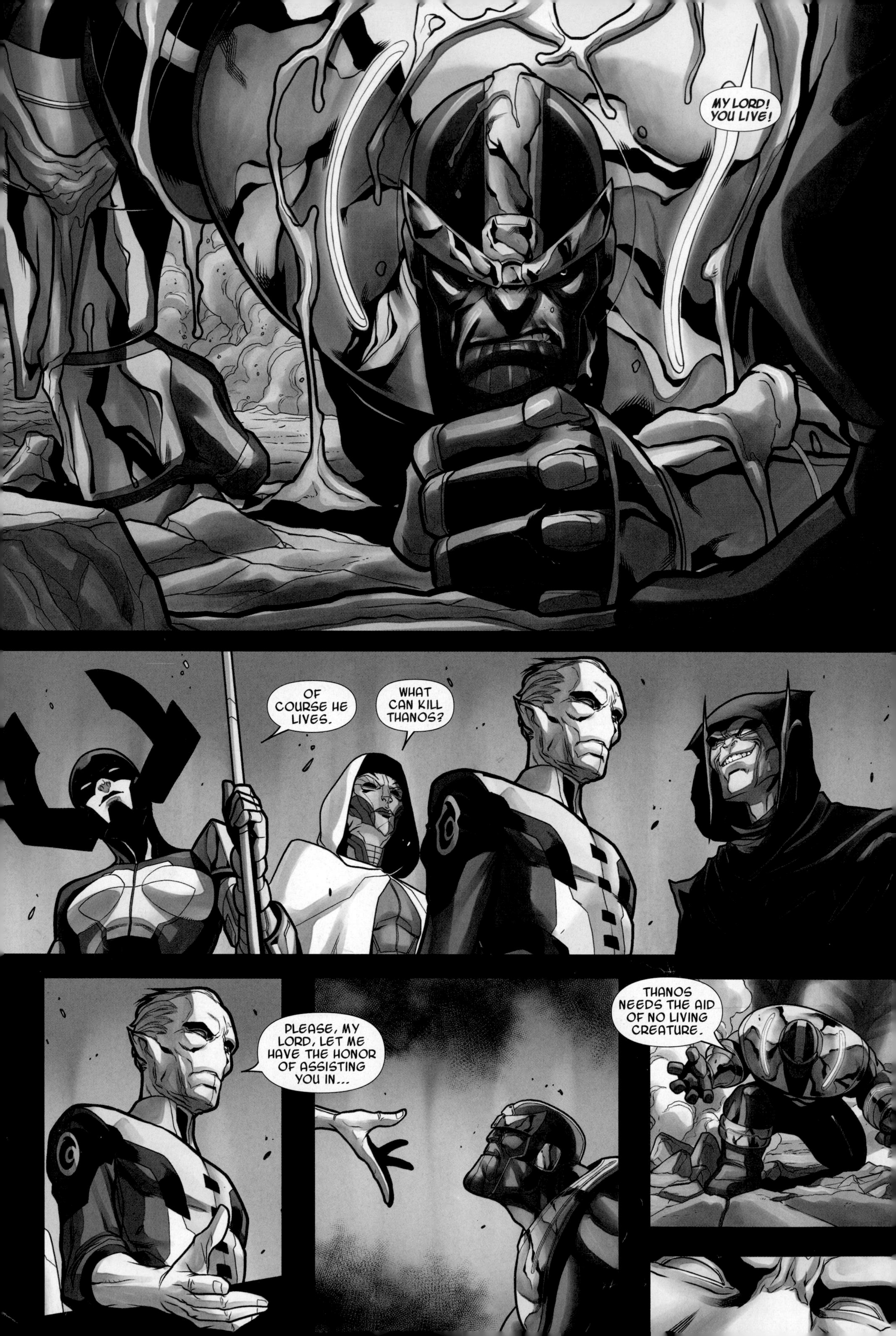
MY LORD! YOU LIVE!
OF COURSE HE LIVES.
WHAT CAN KILL THANOS?
PLEASE, MY LORD, LET ME HAVE THE HONOR OF ASSISTING YOU IN...
THANOS NEEDS THE AID OF NO LIVING CREATURE.

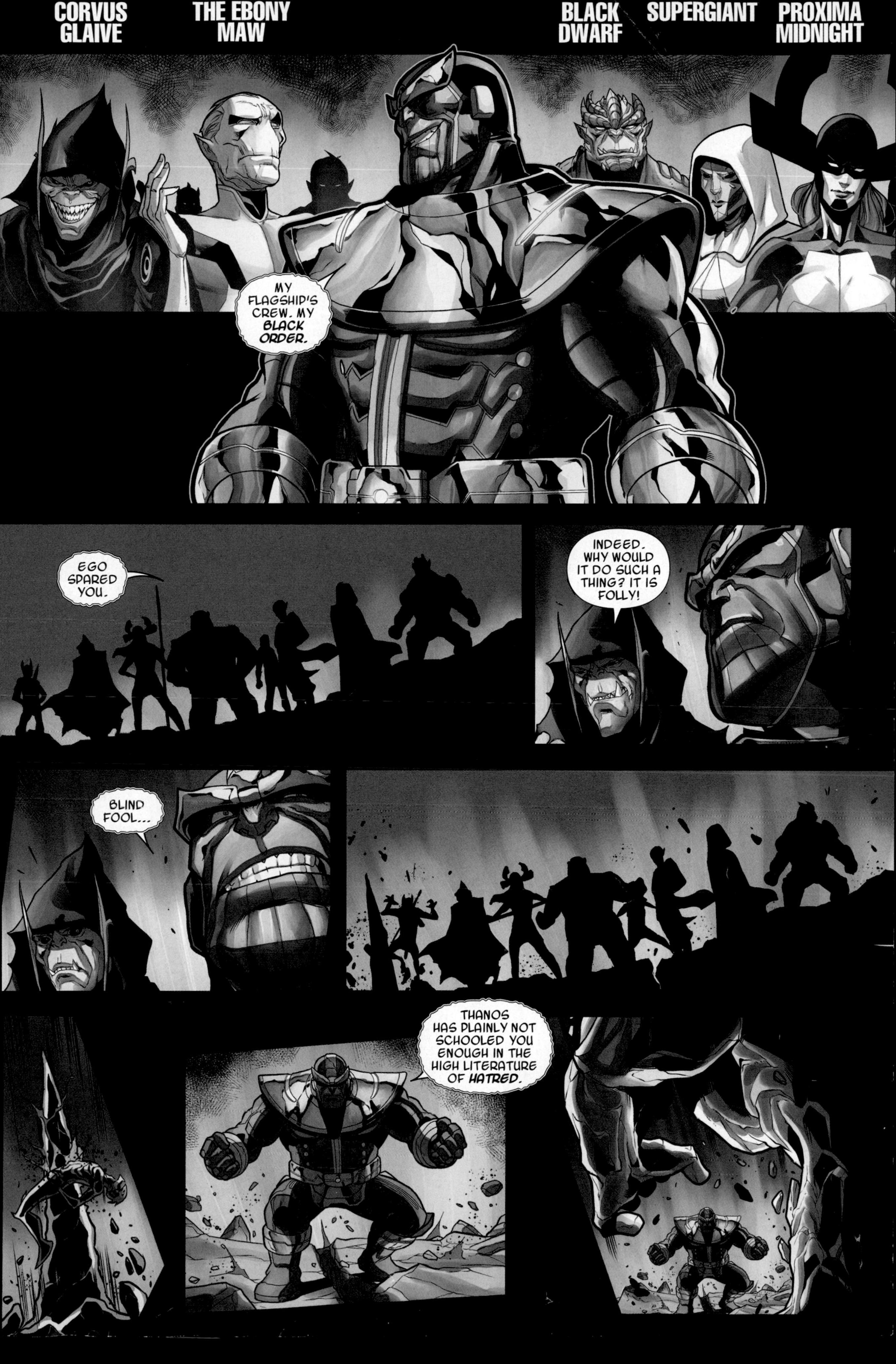
CORVUS GLAIVE
THE EBONY MAW
BLACK DWARF
SUPERGIANT
PROXIMA MIDNIGHT
MY FLAGSHIP'S CREW. MY BLACK ORDER.
EGO SPARED YOU.
INDEED. WHY WOULD IT DO SUCH A THING? IT IS FOLLY!
BLIND FOOL...
THANOS HAS PLAINLY NOT SCHOOLED YOU ENOUGH IN THE HIGH LITERATURE OF HATRED.

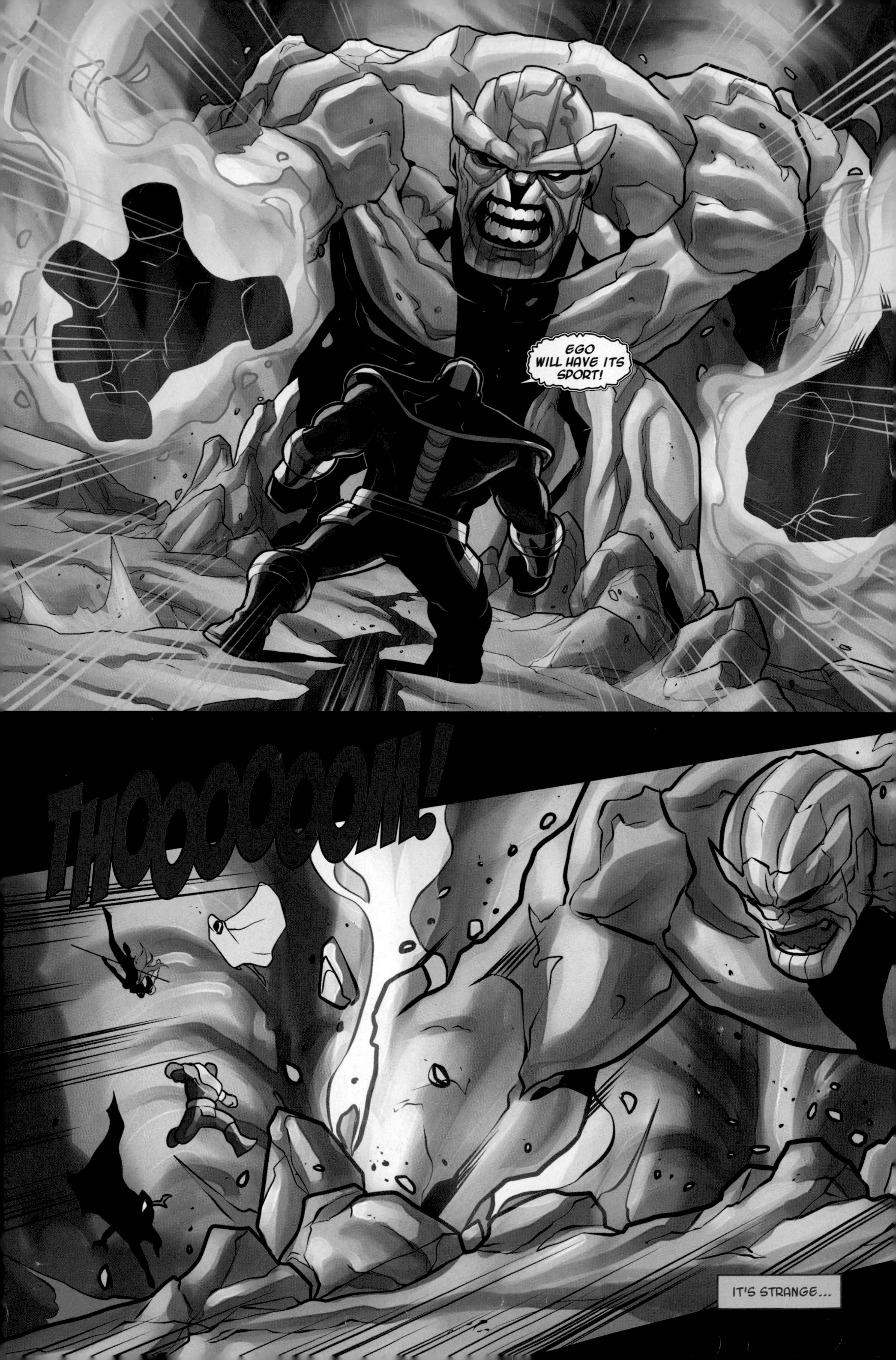
EGO WILL HAVE ITS SPORT!
THOOOOOOM!
IT'S STRANGE...

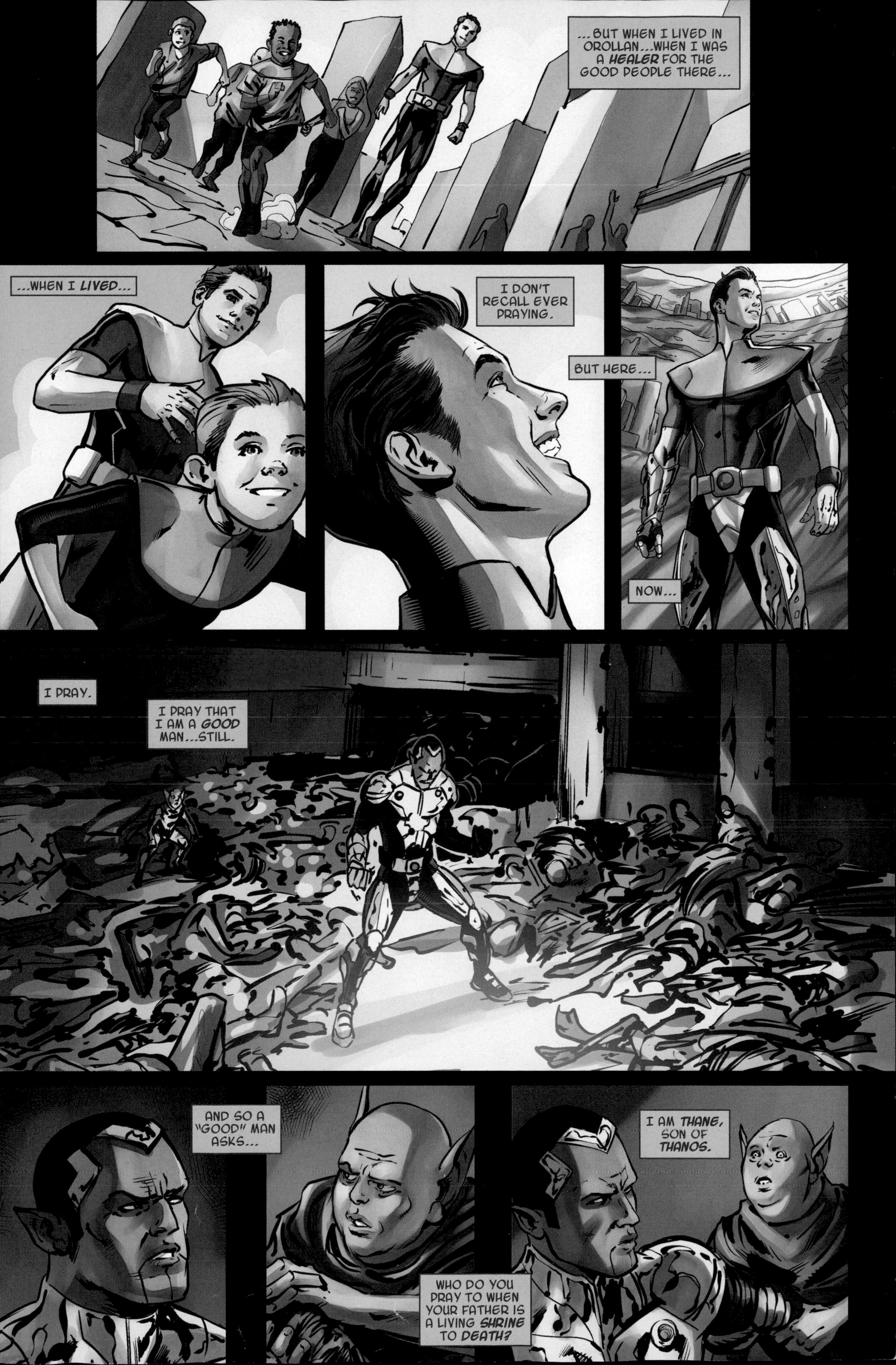
...BUT WHEN I LIVED IN OROLLAN...WHEN I WAS A HEALER FOR THE GOOD PEOPLE THERE...
...WHEN I LIVED...
I DON'T RECALL EVER PRAYING.
BUT HERE...
NOW...
I PRAY.
I PRAY THAT I AM A GOOD MAN...STILL.
AND SO A "GOOD" MAN ASKS...
WHO DO YOU PRAY TO WHEN YOUR FATHER IS A LIVING SHRINE TO DEATH?
I AM THANE, SON OF THANOS.

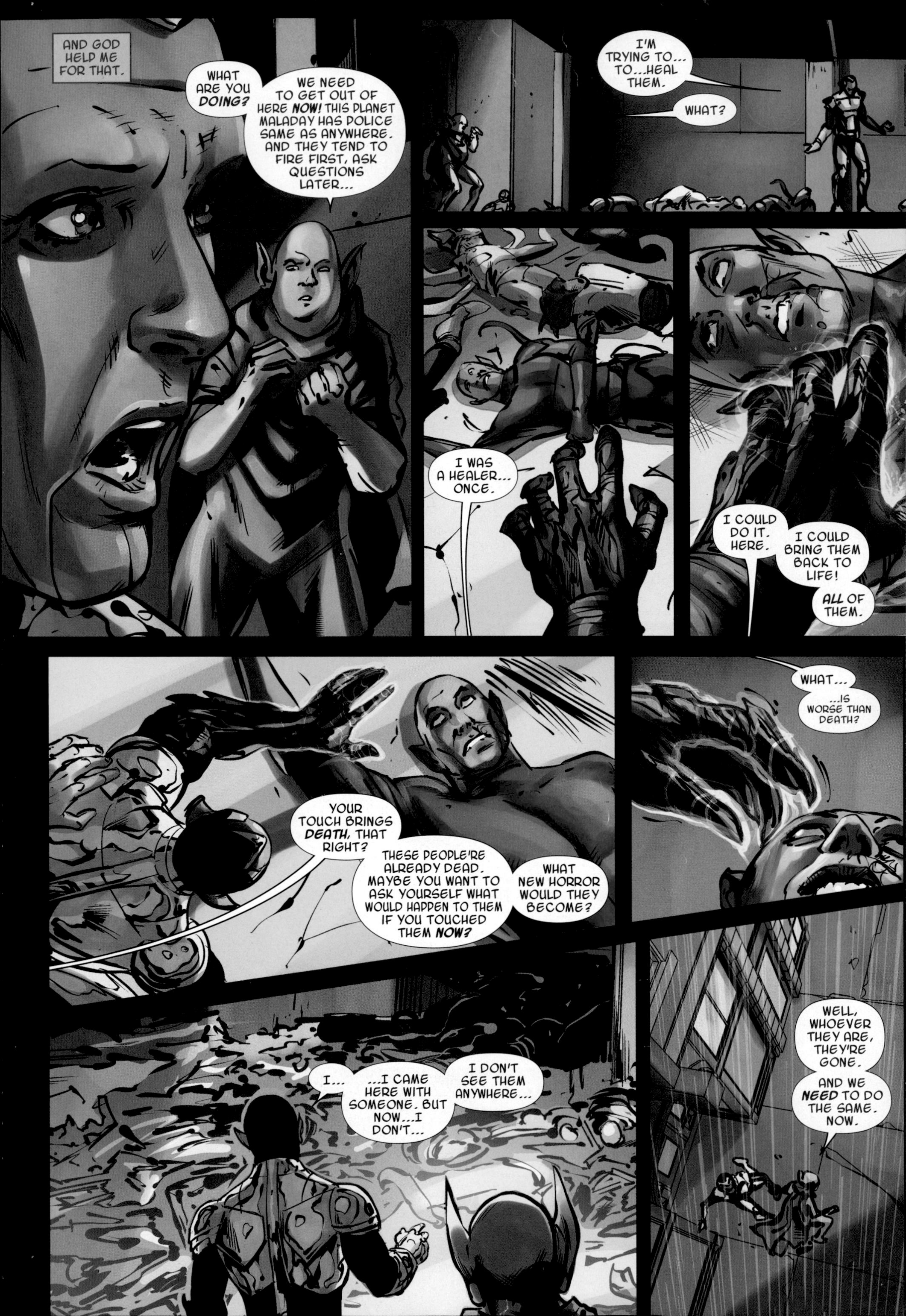
AND GOD HELP ME FOR THAT.
WHAT ARE YOU DOING?
WE NEED TO GET OUT OF HERE NOW! THIS PLANET MALADAY HAS POLICE SAME AS ANYWHERE. AND THEY TEND TO FIRE FIRST, ASK QUESTIONS LATER...
I'M TRYING TO... TO...HEAL THEM.
WHAT?
I WAS A HEALER... ONCE.
I COULD DO IT. HERE.
I COULD BRING THEM BACK TO LIFE!
ALL OF THEM.
YOUR TOUCH BRINGS DEATH, THAT RIGHT?
THESE PEOPLE'RE ALREADY DEAD. MAYBE YOU WANT TO ASK YOURSELF WHAT WOULD HAPPEN TO THEM IF YOU TOUCHED THEM NOW?
WHAT NEW HORROR WOULD THEY BECOME?
WHAT...
...IS WORSE THAN DEATH?
I...
...I CAME HERE WITH SOMEONE. BUT NOW...I DON'T...
I DON'T SEE THEM ANYWHERE...
WELL, WHOEVER THEY ARE, THEY'RE GONE.
AND WE NEED TO DO THE SAME. NOW.

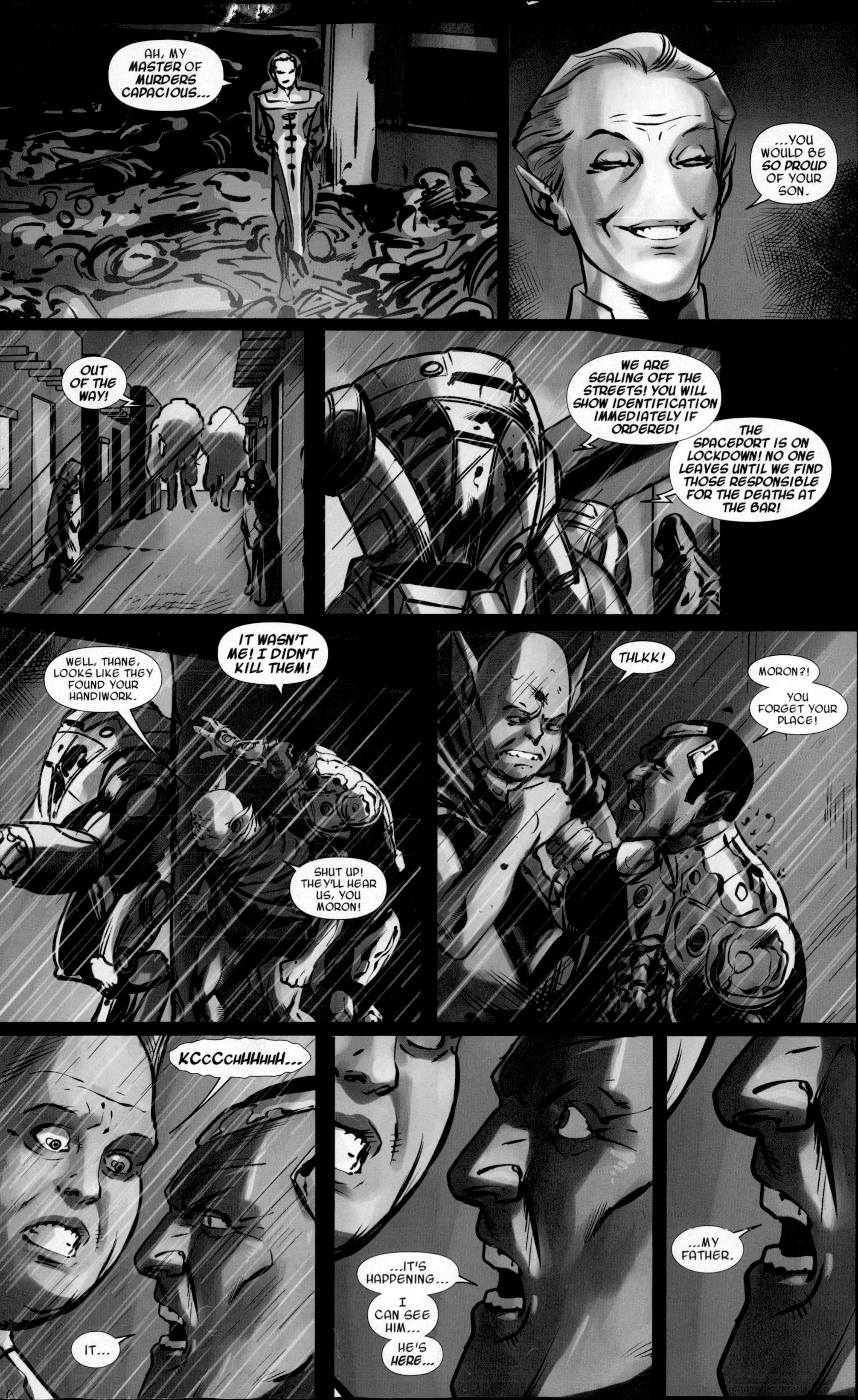
AH, MY MASTER OF MURDERS CAPACIOUS...
...YOU WOULD BE SO PROUD OF YOUR SON.
OUT OF THE WAY!
WE ARE SEALING OFF THE STREETS! YOU WILL SHOW IDENTIFICATION IMMEDIATELY IF ORDERED!
THE SPACEPORT IS ON LOCKDOWN! NO ONE LEAVES UNTIL WE FIND THOSE RESPONSIBLE FOR THE DEATHS AT THE BAR!
WELL, THANE, LOOKS LIKE THEY FOUND YOUR HANDIWORK.
IT WASN'T ME! I DIDN'T KILL THEM!
SHUT UP! THEY'LL HEAR US, YOU MORON!
THLKK!
MORON?!
YOU FORGET YOUR PLACE!
KCCCCHHHHH...
IT...
...IT'S HAPPENING...
I CAN SEE HIM...
HE'S HERE...
...MY FATHER.

YOU WOULD DEFILE MY IMAGE, EGO...?

YOU WOULD DEFILE THE IMAGE OF THANOS, THE MAD TITAN?!

YESSS!

KRRRASSSSHHH!

THE GIANT...IT IS EGO ITSELF.

EGO WHO WOULD ENJOY ITS KILLING OF US, IT SEEMS, MY DEAR PROXIMA.

IT... MOCKS YOU, SIRE.

THE LIVING PLANET SHALL PAY FOR THIS INSULT.

THOSSSSE WHO WOULDDDD LOUDLY ATTACKKKK EGO...!

SHALL HAVVVVE INFINITTTE SSSSSILENNCCEE TO TASTTTTE REMORSSSSEE!

THOOOOOOOM!

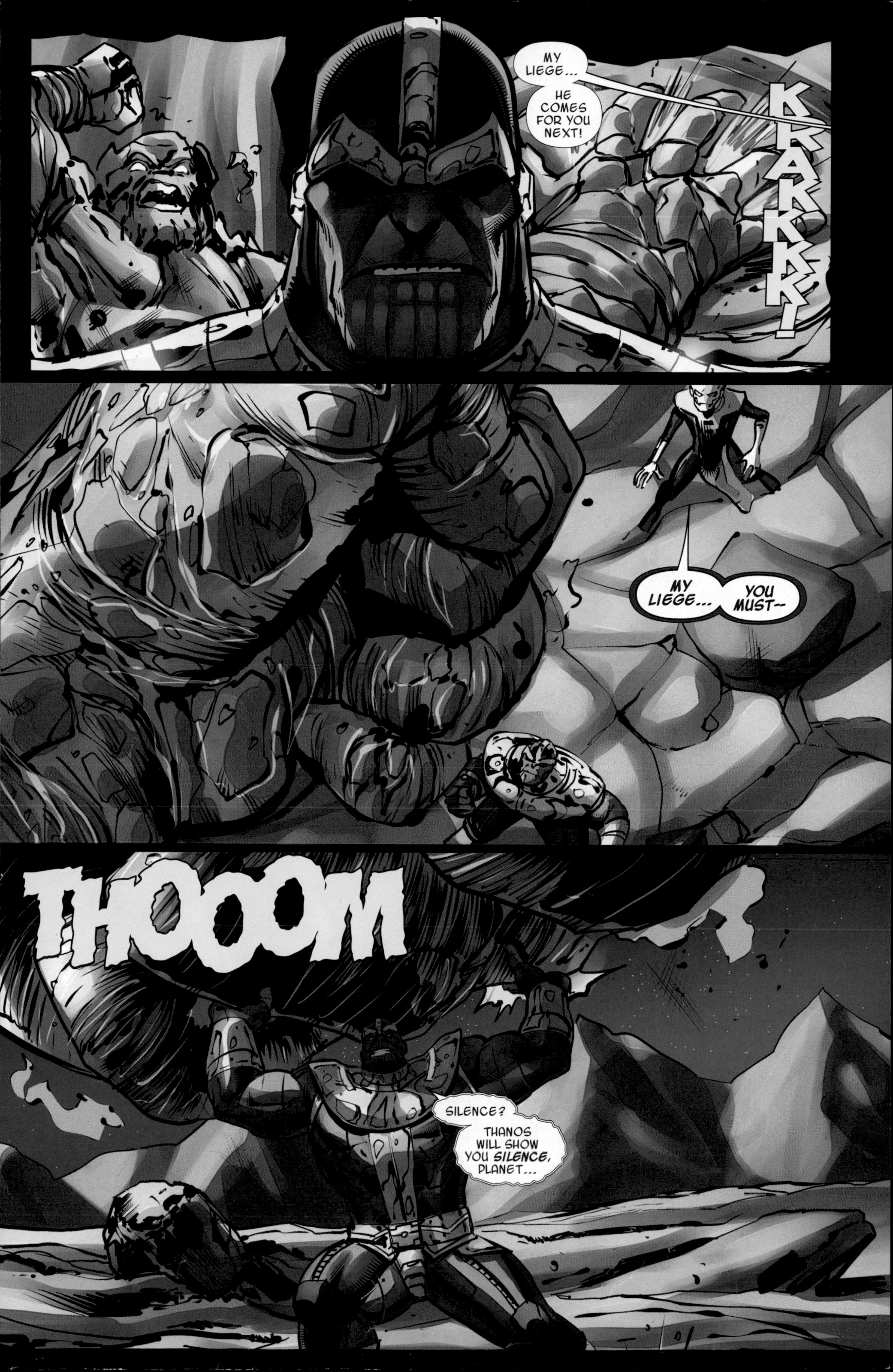
MY LIEGE...
HE COMES FOR YOU NEXT!
KRAKKKK!
MY LIEGE...
YOU MUST--
THOOOM
SILENCE?
THANOS WILL SHOW YOU SILENCE, PLANET...

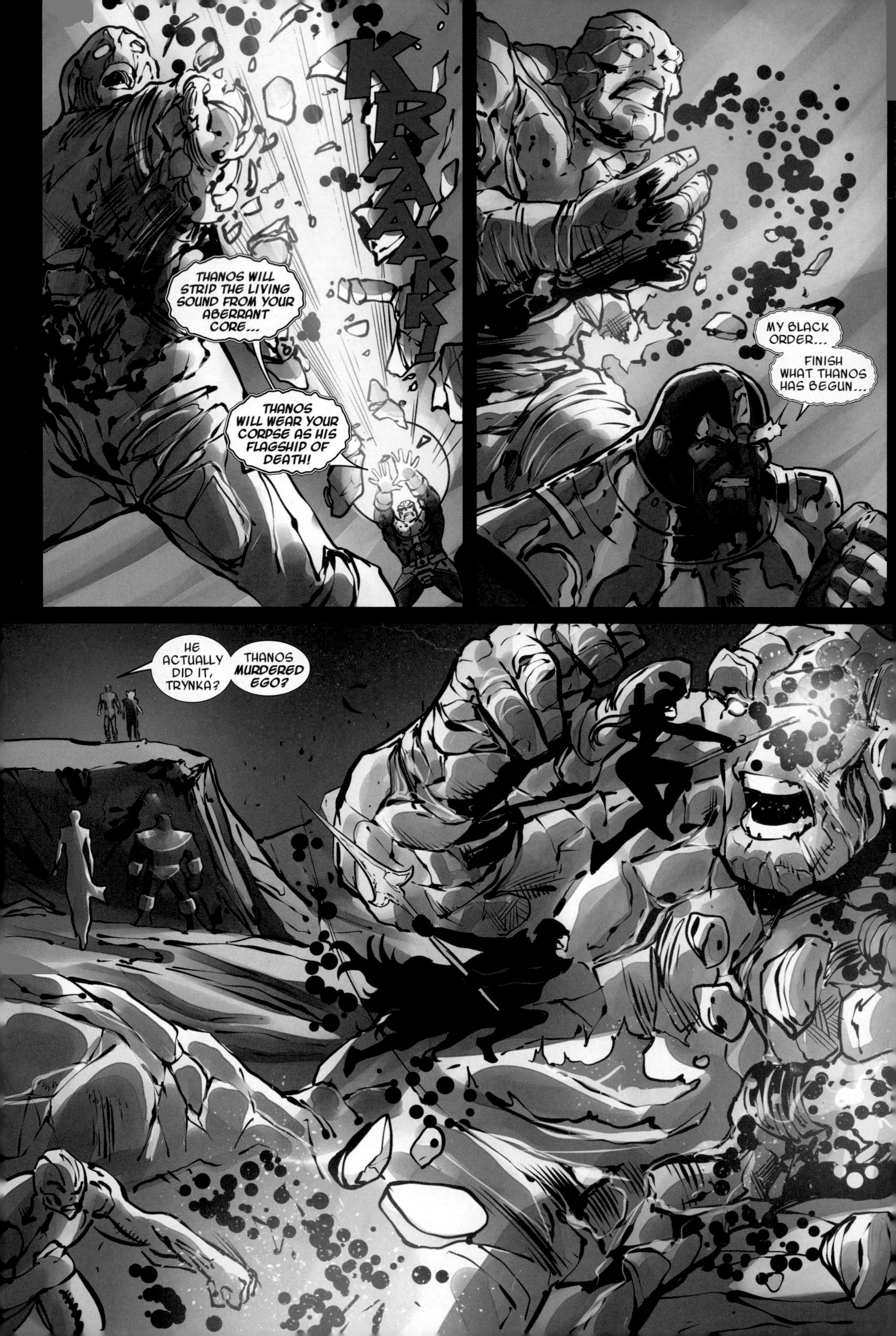
KRAAAAAKK!
THANOS WILL STRIP THE LIVING SOUND FROM YOUR ABERRANT CORE...
THANOS WILL WEAR YOUR CORPSE AS HIS FLAGSHIP OF DEATH!
MY BLACK ORDER...
FINISH WHAT THANOS HAS BEGUN...
HE ACTUALLY DID IT, TRYNKA?
THANOS MURDERED EGO?

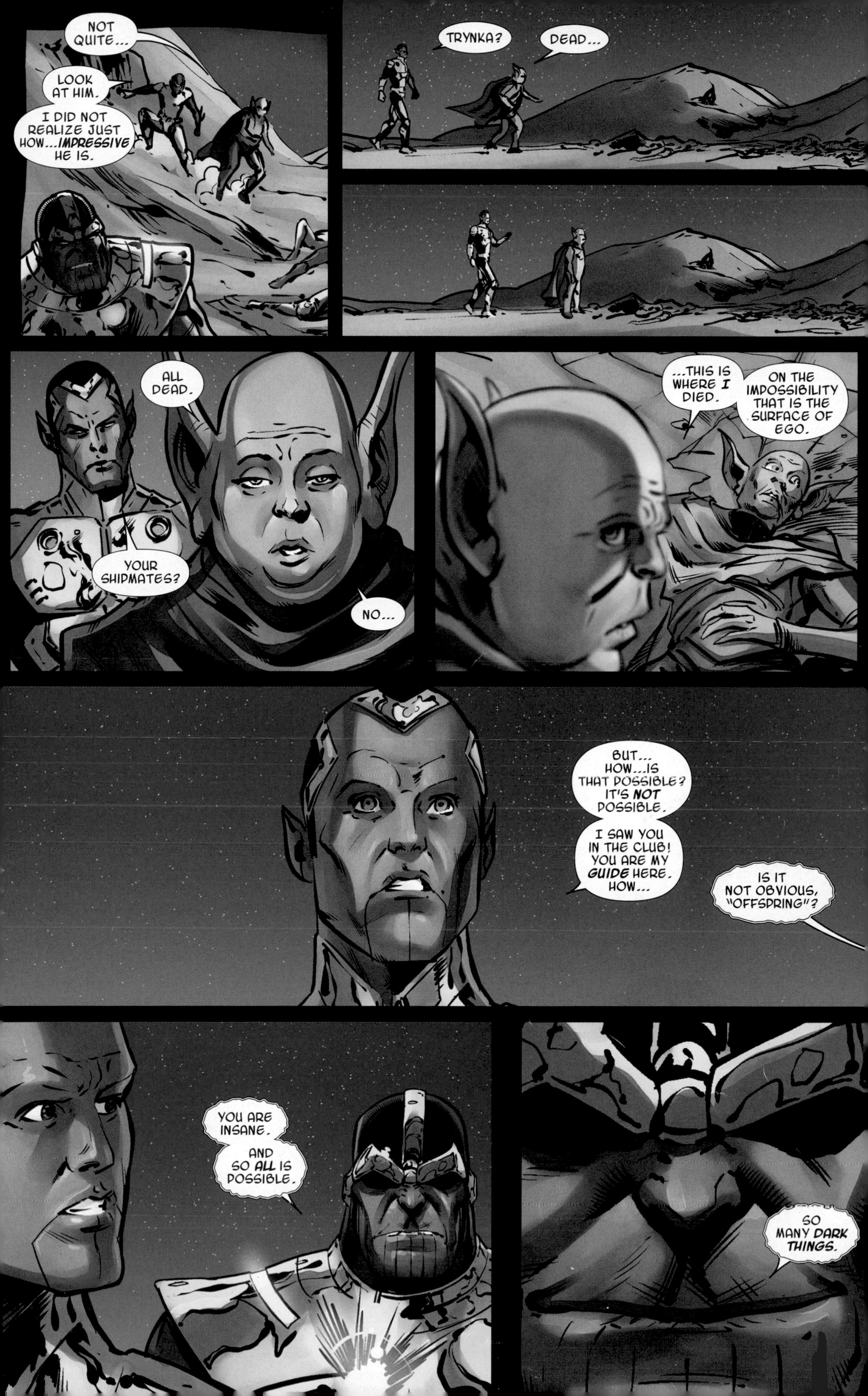

NOT QUITE...
LOOK AT HIM.
I DID NOT REALIZE JUST HOW...IMPRESSIVE HE IS.
TRYNKA?
DEAD...
ALL DEAD.
YOUR SHIPMATES?
NO...
...THIS IS WHERE I DIED.
ON THE IMPOSSIBILITY THAT IS THE SURFACE OF EGO.
BUT... HOW...IS THAT POSSIBLE? IT'S NOT POSSIBLE.
I SAW YOU IN THE CLUB! YOU ARE MY GUIDE HERE. HOW...
IS IT NOT OBVIOUS, "OFFSPRING"?
YOU ARE INSANE.
AND SO ALL IS POSSIBLE.
SO MANY DARK THINGS.

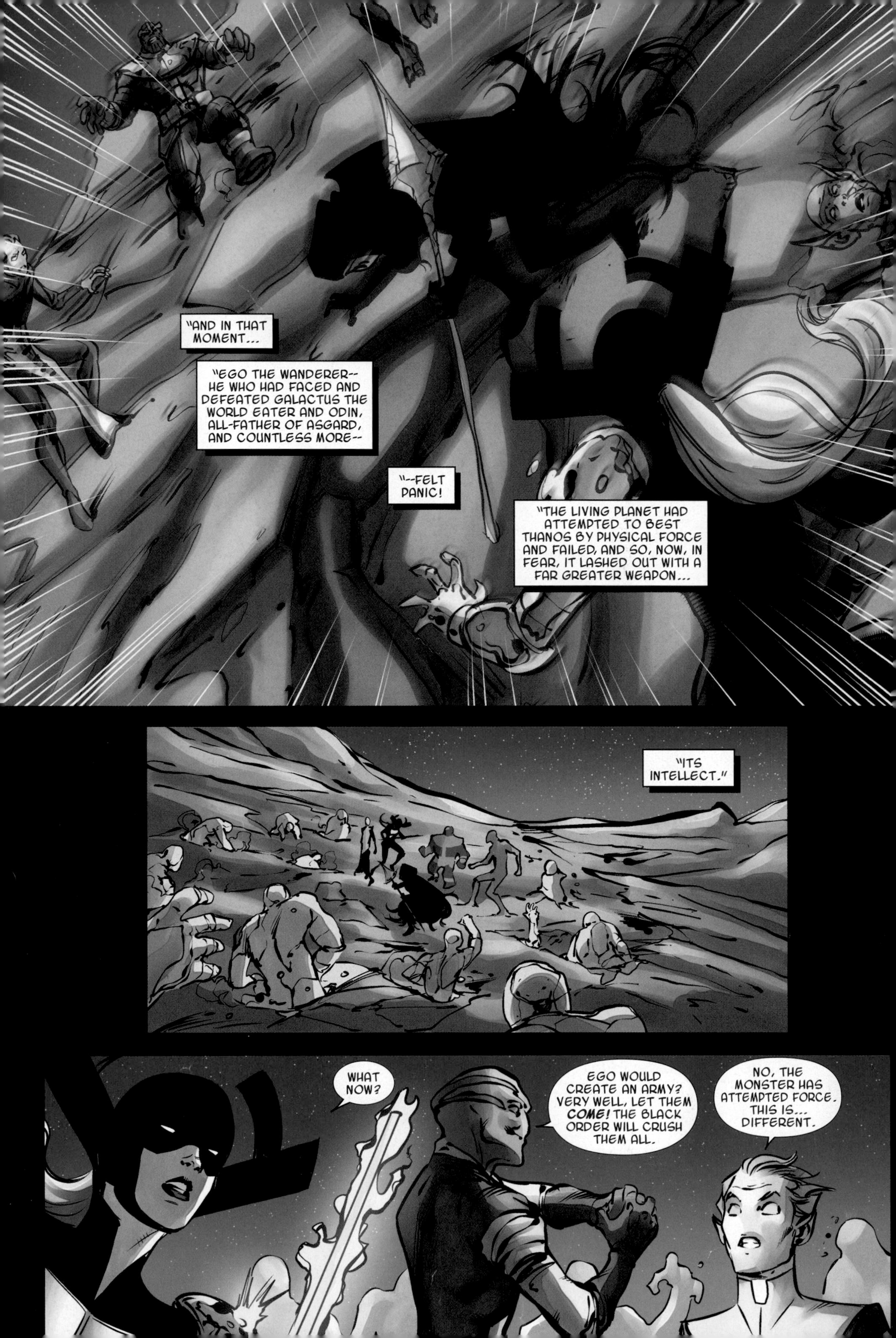
"AND IN THAT MOMENT...
"EGO THE WANDERER--HE WHO HAD FACED AND DEFEATED GALACTUS THE WORLD EATER AND ODIN, ALL-FATHER OF ASGARD, AND COUNTLESS MORE--
"--FELT PANIC!
"THE LIVING PLANET HAD ATTEMPTED TO BEST THANOS BY PHYSICAL FORCE AND FAILED, AND SO, NOW, IN FEAR, IT LASHED OUT WITH A FAR GREATER WEAPON...
"ITS INTELLECT."
WHAT NOW?
EGO WOULD CREATE AN ARMY? VERY WELL, LET THEM COME! THE BLACK ORDER WILL CRUSH THEM ALL.
NO, THE MONSTER HAS ATTEMPTED FORCE. THIS IS... DIFFERENT.

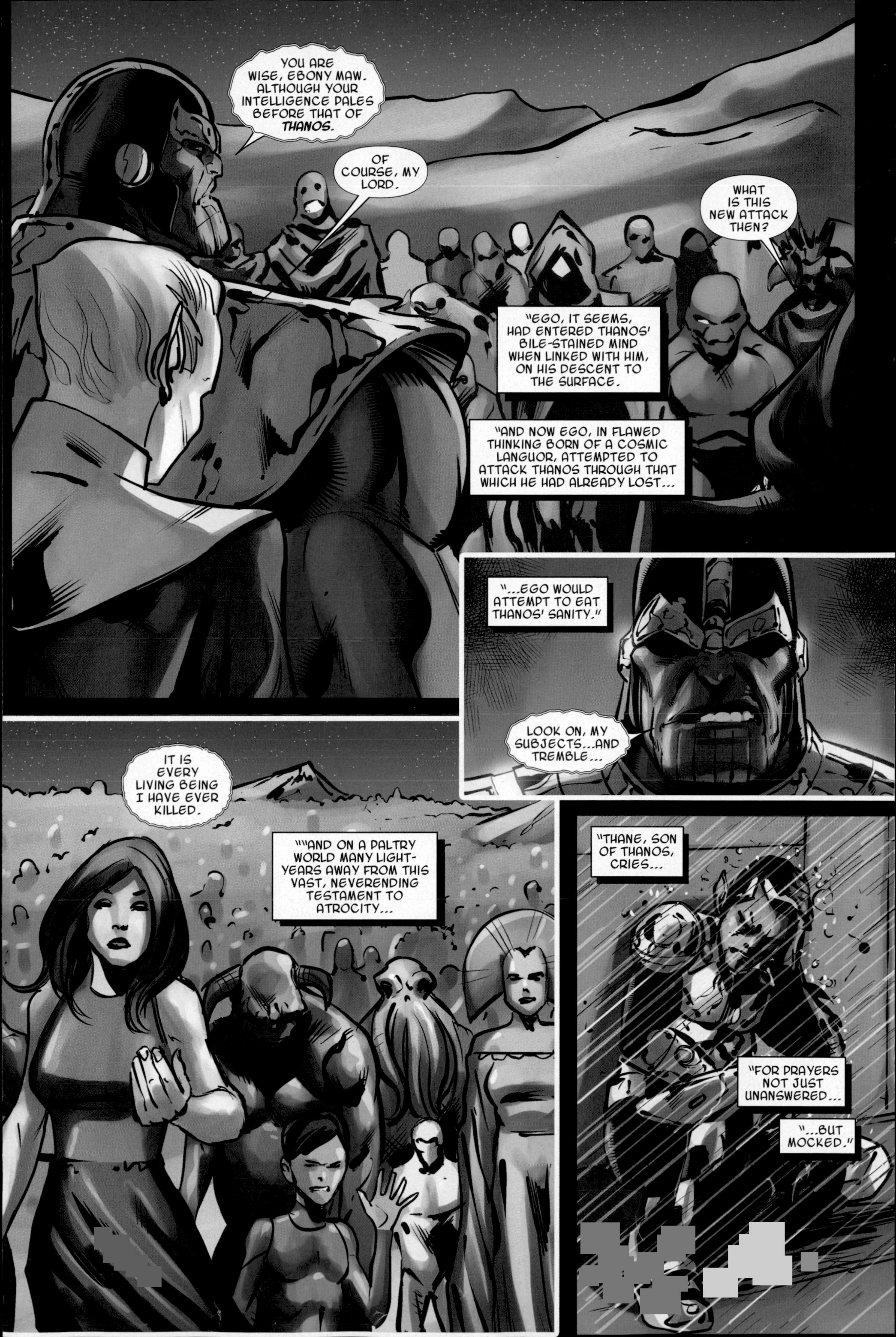

YOU ARE WISE, EBONY MAW. ALTHOUGH YOUR INTELLIGENCE PALES BEFORE THAT OF *THANOS*.
OF COURSE, MY LORD.
WHAT IS THIS NEW ATTACK THEN?
"EGO, IT SEEMS, HAD ENTERED THANOS' BILE-STAINED MIND WHEN LINKED WITH HIM, ON HIS DESCENT TO THE SURFACE.
"AND NOW EGO, IN FLAWED THINKING BORN OF A COSMIC LANGUOR, ATTEMPTED TO ATTACK THANOS THROUGH THAT WHICH HE HAD ALREADY LOST...
"...EGO WOULD ATTEMPT TO EAT THANOS' SANITY."
LOOK ON, MY SUBJECTS...AND TREMBLE...
IT IS EVERY LIVING BEING I HAVE EVER KILLED.
"'"AND ON A PALTRY WORLD MANY LIGHT-YEARS AWAY FROM THIS VAST, NEVERENDING TESTAMENT TO ATROCITY...
"THANE, SON OF THANOS, CRIES...
"FOR PRAYERS NOT JUST UNANSWERED...
"...BUT MOCKED."

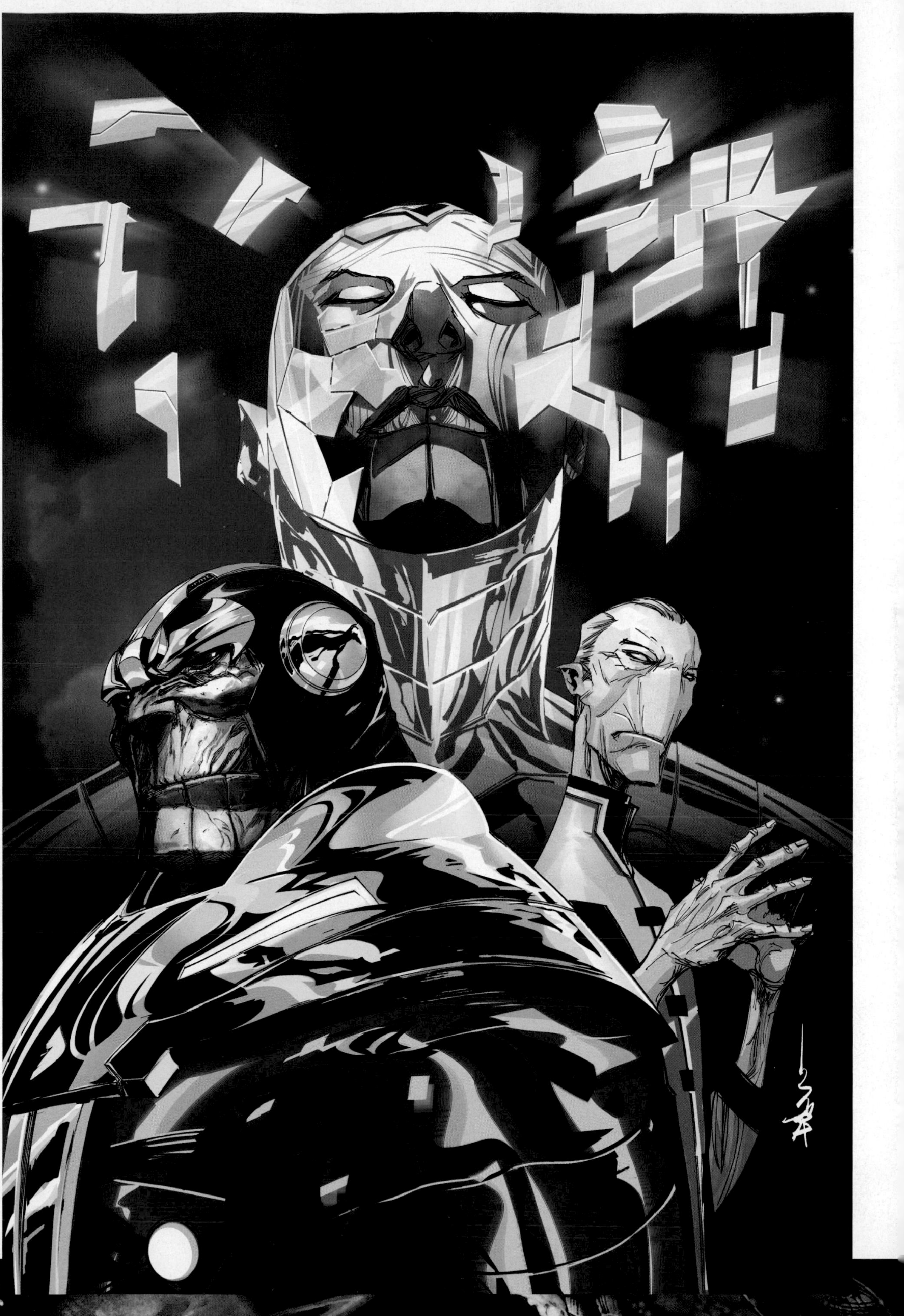

FOUR

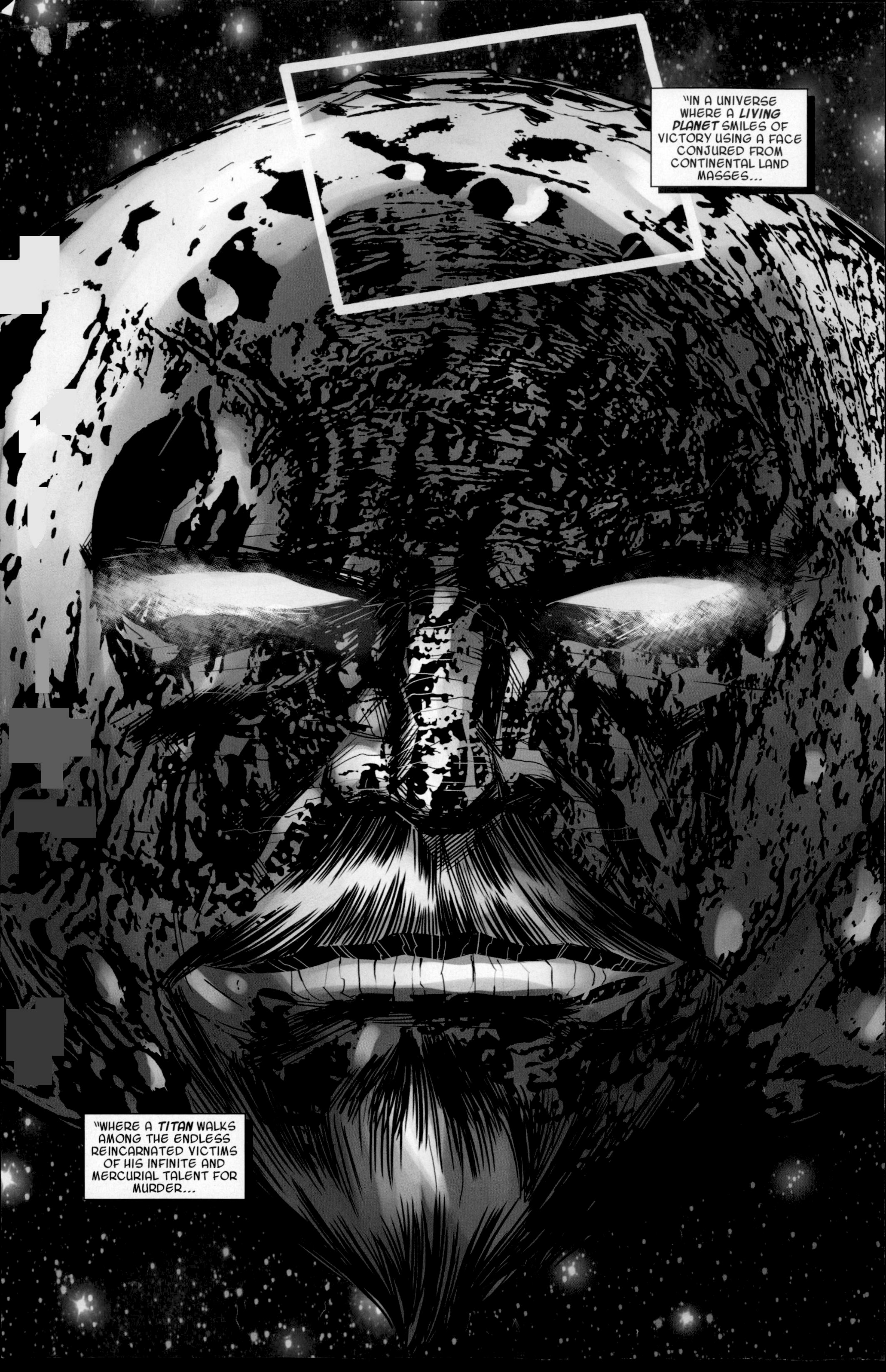
"IN A UNIVERSE WHERE A LIVING PLANET SMILES OF VICTORY USING A FACE CONJURED FROM CONTINENTAL LAND MASSES...
"WHERE A TITAN WALKS AMONG THE ENDLESS REINCARNATED VICTIMS OF HIS INFINITE AND MERCURIAL TALENT FOR MURDER...

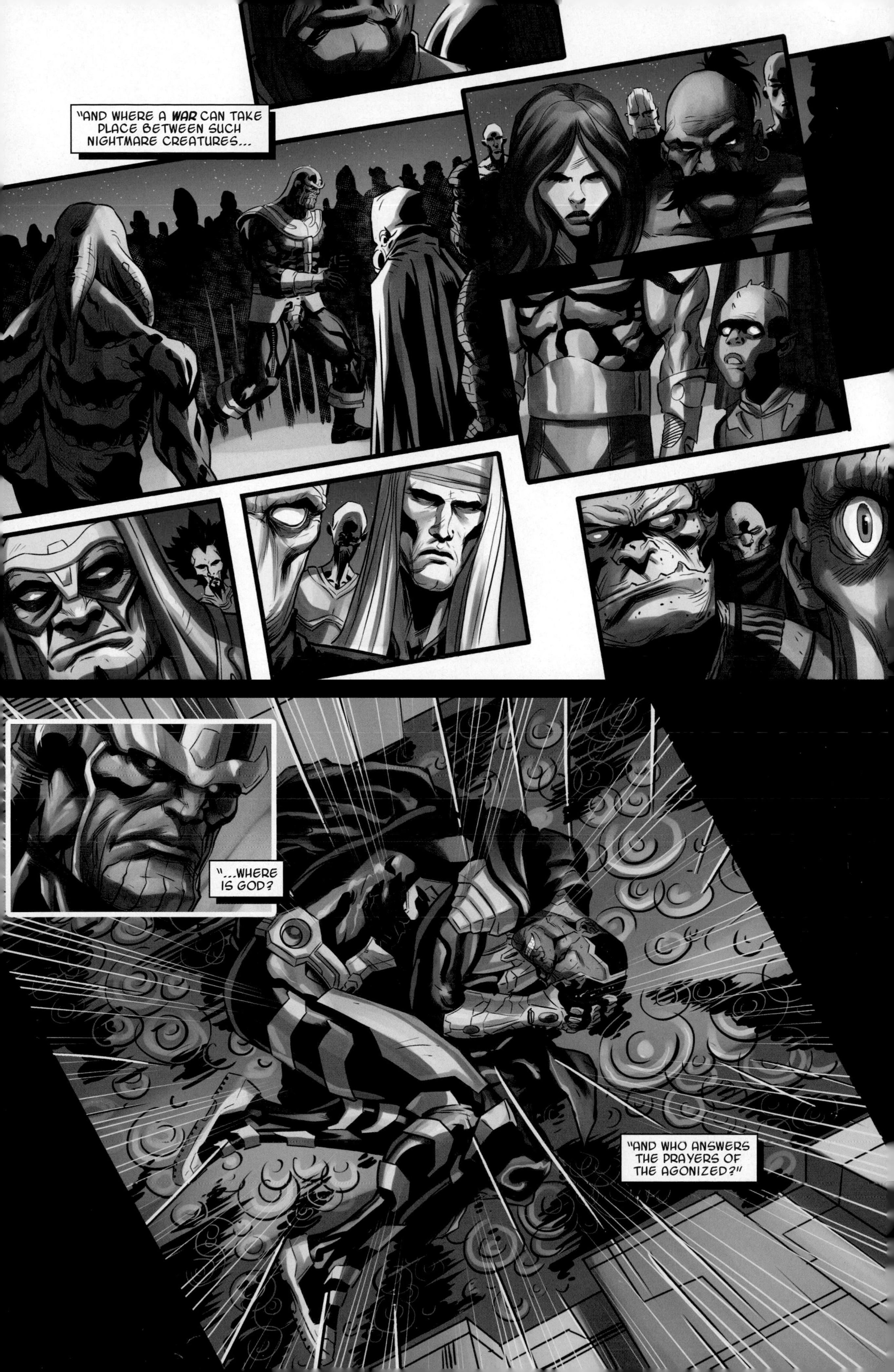
"AND WHERE A WAR CAN TAKE PLACE BETWEEN SUCH NIGHTMARE CREATURES...
"...WHERE IS GOD?
"AND WHO ANSWERS THE PRAYERS OF THE AGONIZED?"

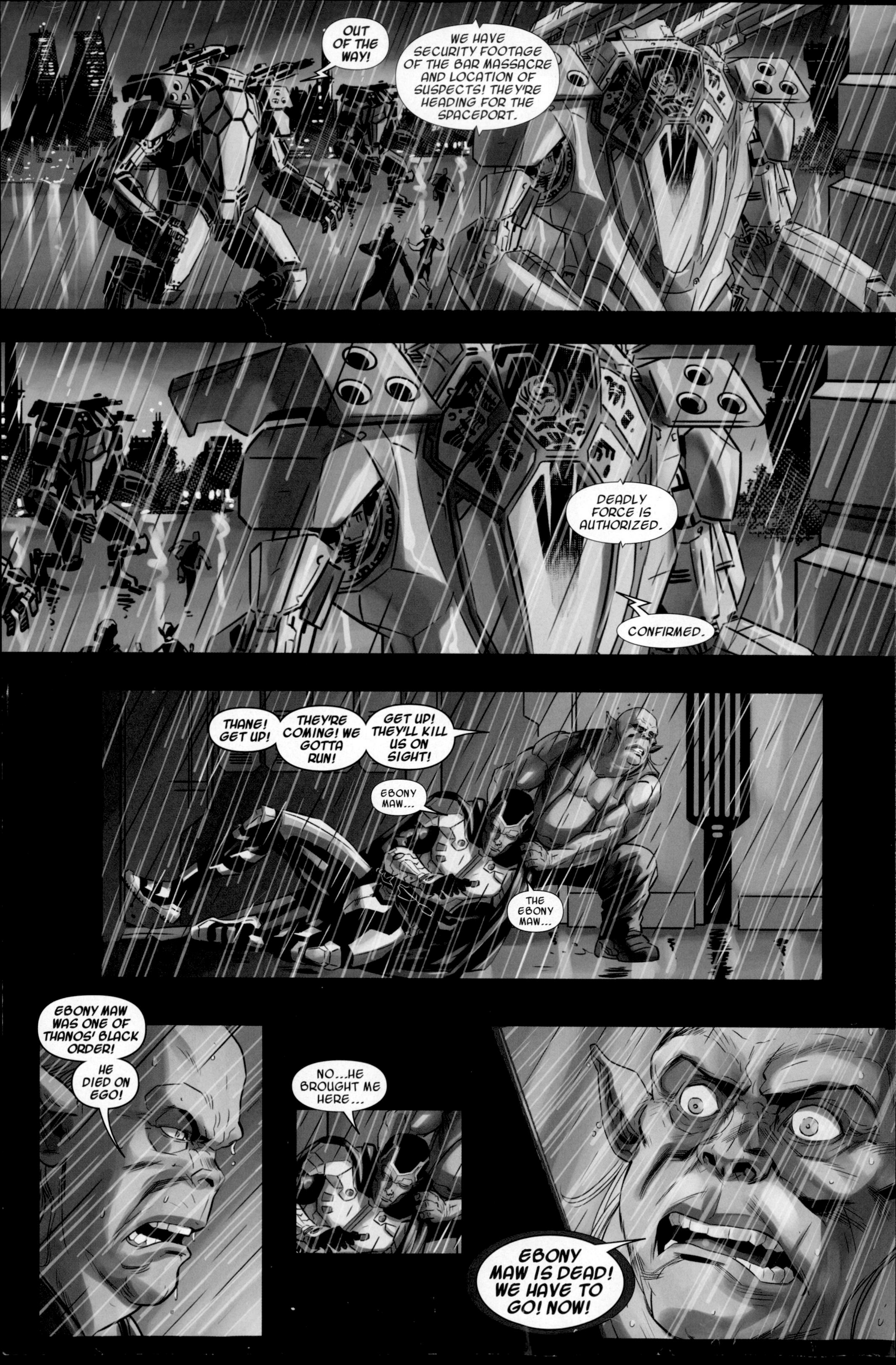
OUT OF THE WAY!
WE HAVE SECURITY FOOTAGE OF THE BAR MASSACRE AND LOCATION OF SUSPECTS! THEY'RE HEADING FOR THE SPACEPORT.
DEADLY FORCE IS AUTHORIZED.
CONFIRMED.
THANE! GET UP!
THEY'RE COMING! WE GOTTA RUN!
GET UP! THEY'LL KILL US ON SIGHT!
EBONY MAW...
THE EBONY MAW...
EBONY MAW WAS ONE OF THANOS' BLACK ORDER!
HE DIED ON EGO!
NO...HE BROUGHT ME HERE...
EBONY MAW IS DEAD! WE HAVE TO GO! NOW!

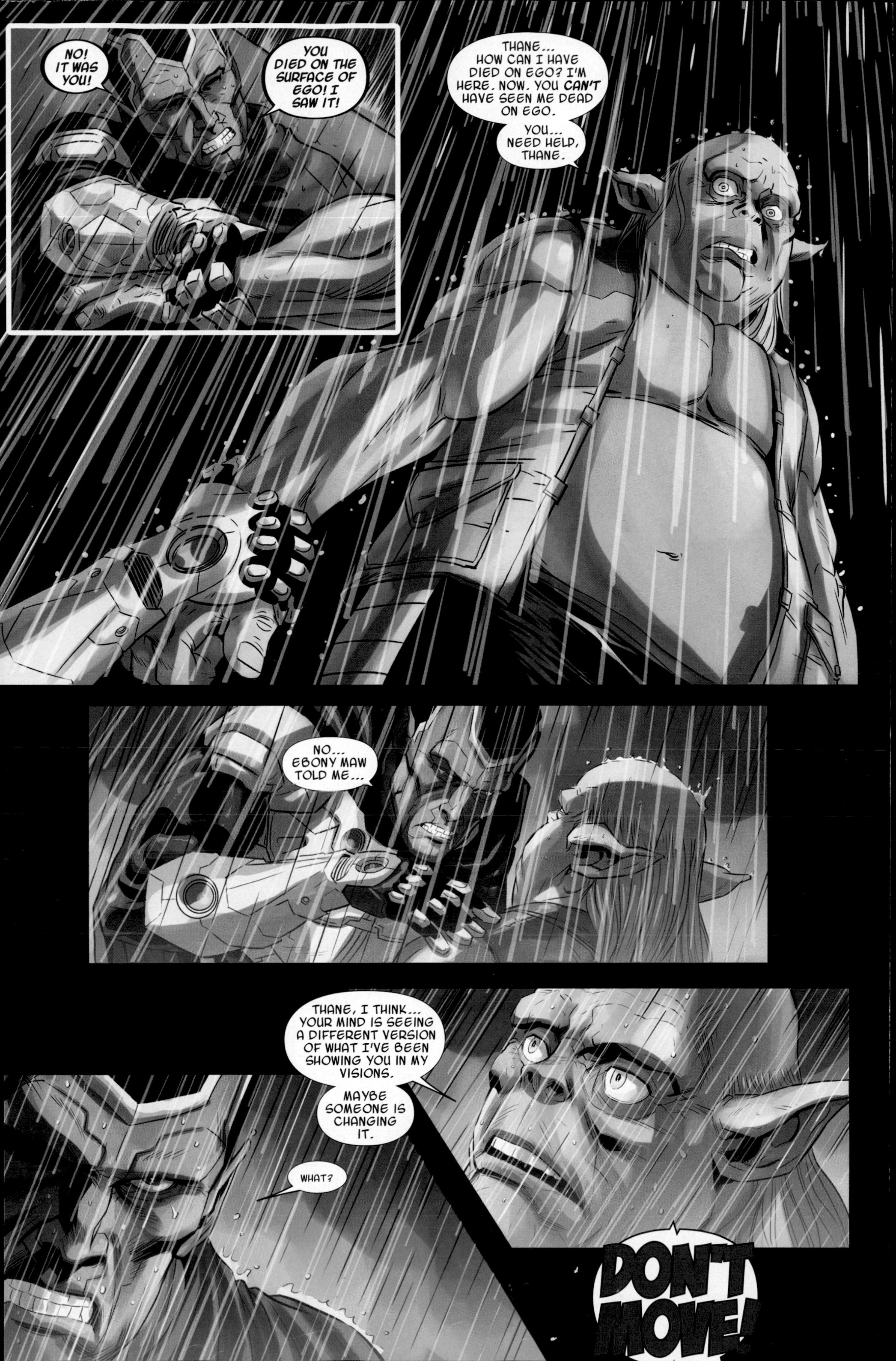
NO! IT WAS YOU!
YOU DIED ON THE SURFACE OF EGO! I SAW IT!
THANE... HOW CAN I HAVE DIED ON EGO? I'M HERE. NOW. YOU CAN'T HAVE SEEN ME DEAD ON EGO.
YOU... NEED HELP, THANE.
NO... EBONY MAW TOLD ME...
THANE, I THINK... YOUR MIND IS SEEING A DIFFERENT VERSION OF WHAT I'VE BEEN SHOWING YOU IN MY VISIONS.
MAYBE SOMEONE IS CHANGING IT.
WHAT?
DON'T MOVE!

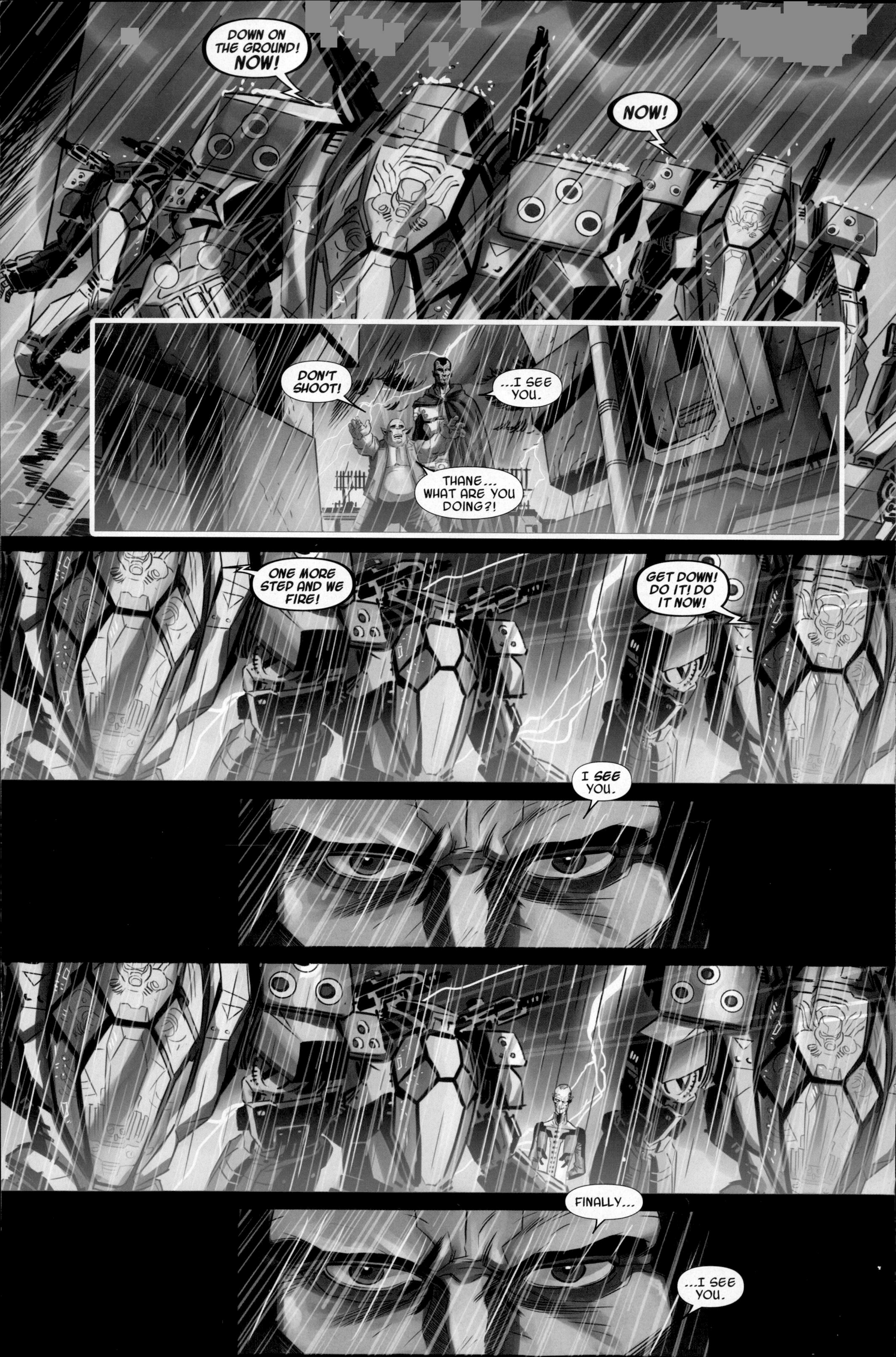

DOWN ON THE GROUND! NOW!
NOW!
DON'T SHOOT!
...I SEE YOU.
THANE... WHAT ARE YOU DOING?!
ONE MORE STEP AND WE FIRE!
GET DOWN! DO IT! DO IT NOW!
I SEE YOU.
FINALLY...
...I SEE YOU.

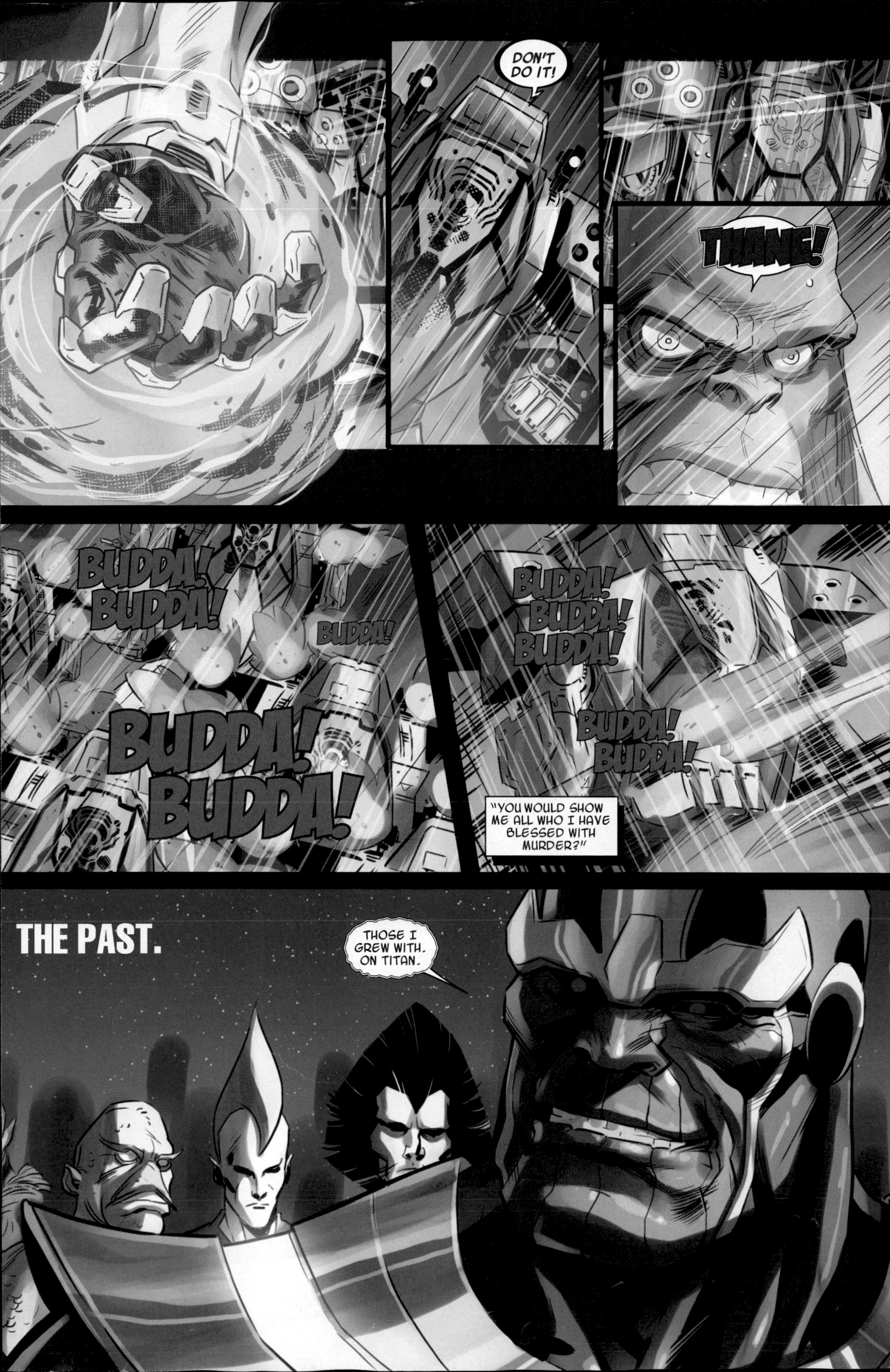

DON'T DO IT!
THANE!
BUDDA! BUDDA!
BUDDA!
BUDDA! BUDDA!
BUDDA! BUDDA! BUDDA!
BUDDA! BUDDA!
"YOU WOULD SHOW ME ALL WHO I HAVE BLESSED WITH MURDER?"
THE PAST.
THOSE I GREW WITH. ON TITAN.

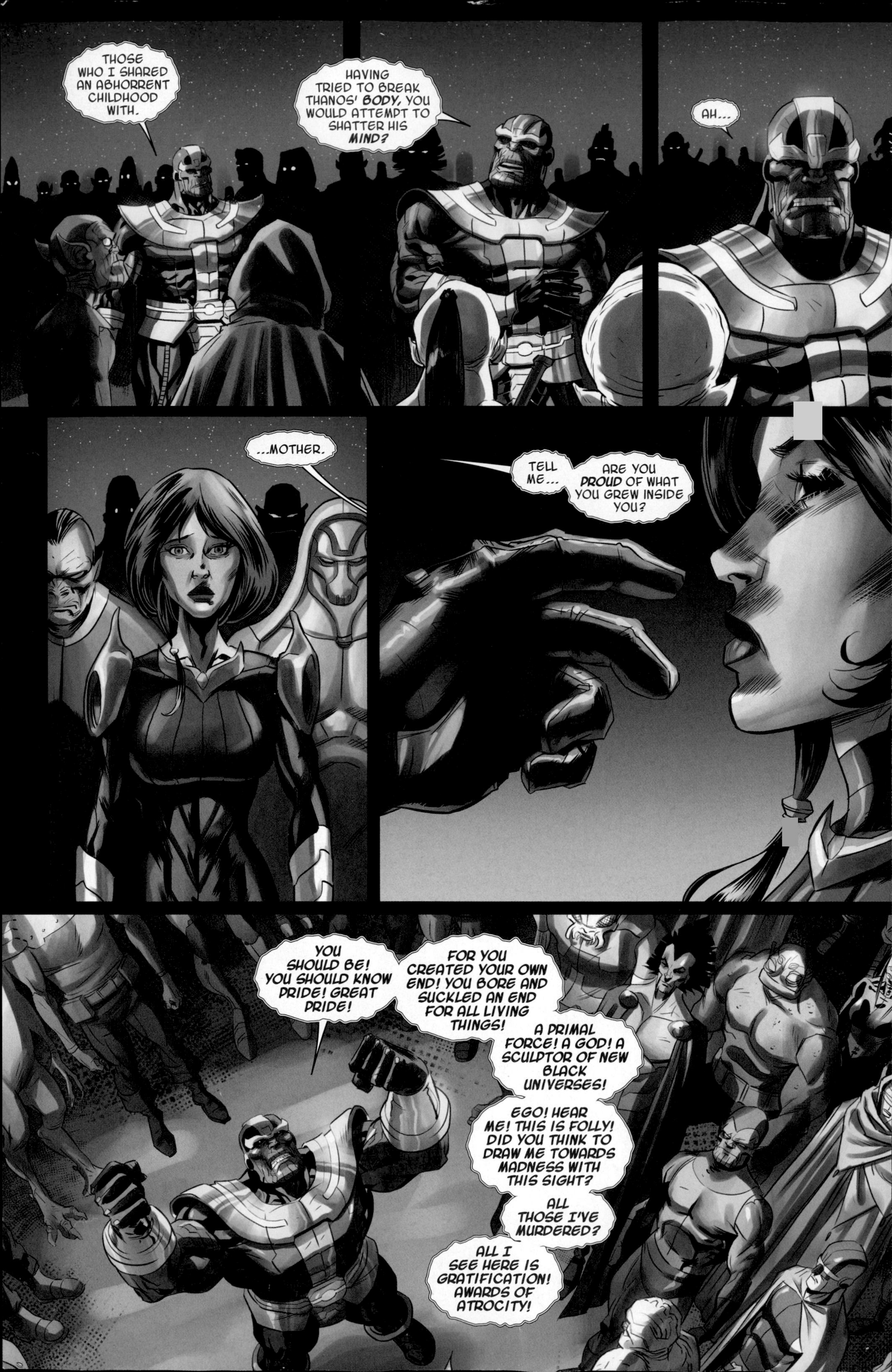
THOSE WHO I SHARED AN ABHORRENT CHILDHOOD WITH.
HAVING TRIED TO BREAK THANOS' BODY, YOU WOULD ATTEMPT TO SHATTER HIS MIND?
AH...
...MOTHER.
TELL ME...
ARE YOU PROUD OF WHAT YOU GREW INSIDE YOU?
YOU SHOULD BE! YOU SHOULD KNOW PRIDE! GREAT PRIDE!
FOR YOU CREATED YOUR OWN END! YOU BORE AND SUCKLED AN END FOR ALL LIVING THINGS!
A PRIMAL FORCE! A GOD! A SCULPTOR OF NEW BLACK UNIVERSES!
EGO! HEAR ME! THIS IS FOLLY! DID YOU THINK TO DRAW ME TOWARDS MADNESS WITH THIS SIGHT?
ALL THOSE I'VE MURDERED?
ALL I SEE HERE IS GRATIFICATION! AWARDS OF ATROCITY!

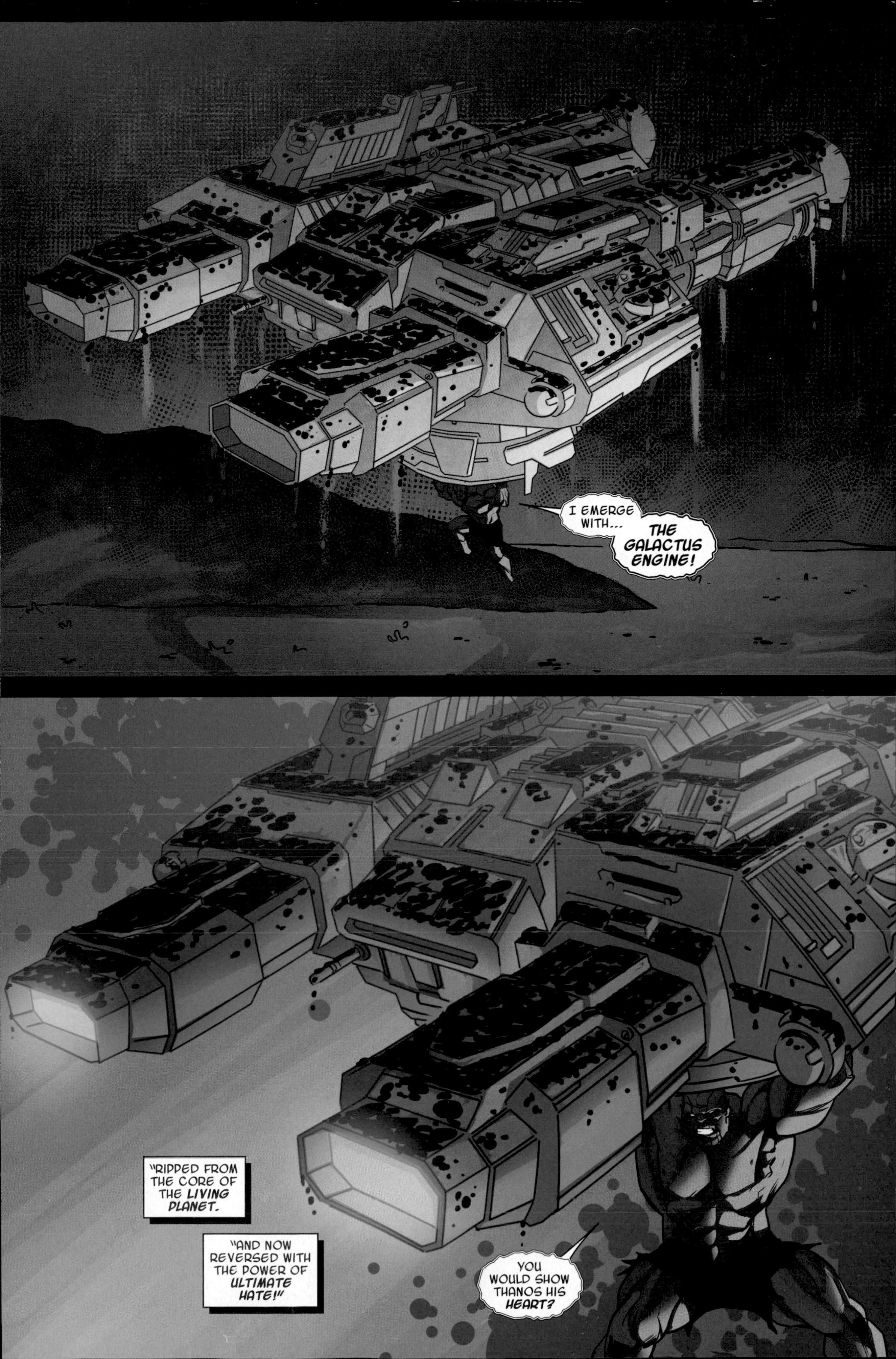
I EMERGE WITH... THE GALACTUS ENGINE!
"RIPPED FROM THE CORE OF THE LIVING PLANET.
"AND NOW REVERSED WITH THE POWER OF ULTIMATE HATE!"
YOU WOULD SHOW THANOS HIS HEART?

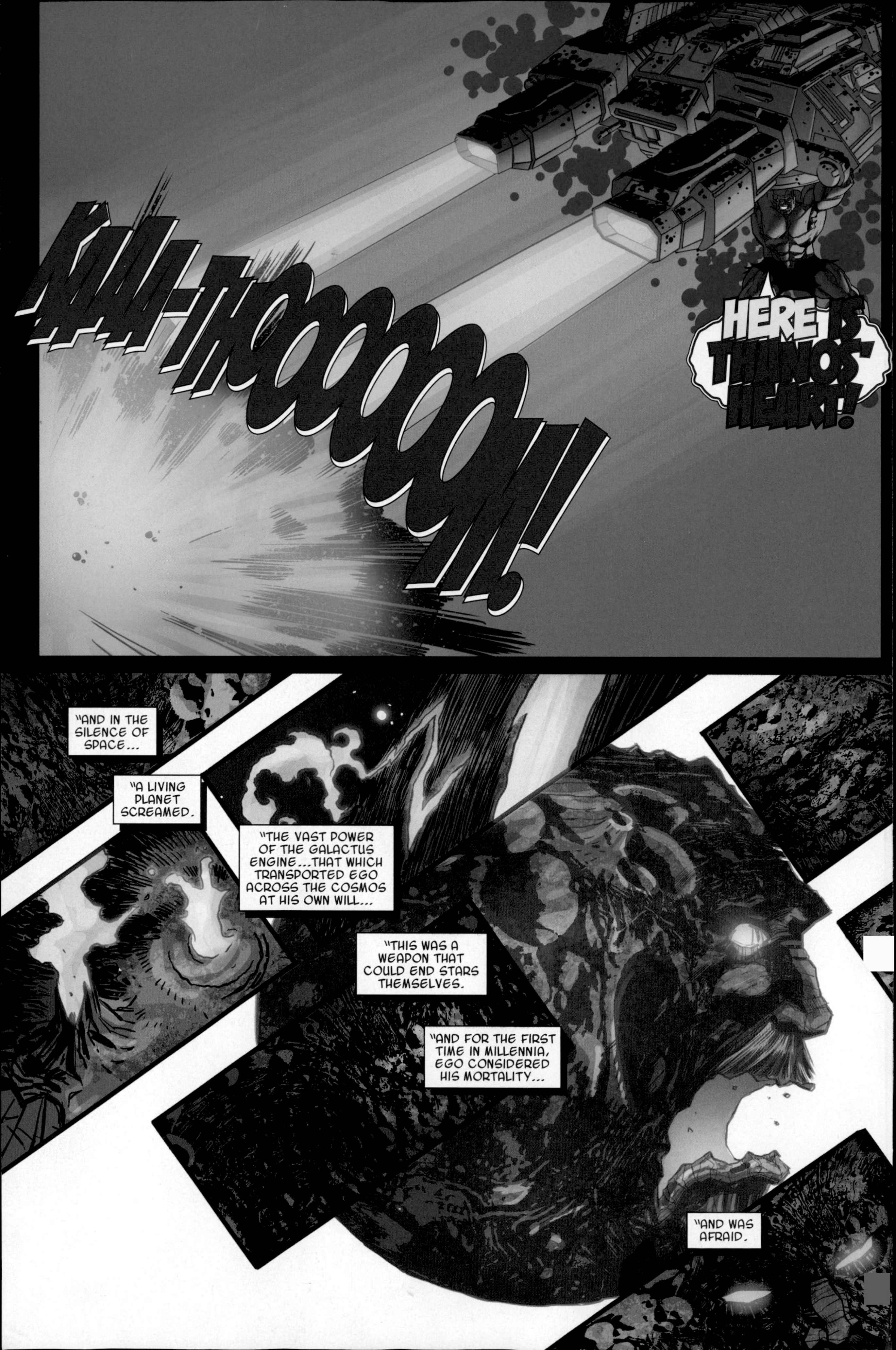
KRAAA-THOOOOOOM!!
HERE IS THANOS' HEART!!
"AND IN THE SILENCE OF SPACE...
"A LIVING PLANET SCREAMED.
"THE VAST POWER OF THE GALACTUS ENGINE...THAT WHICH TRANSPORTED EGO ACROSS THE COSMOS AT HIS OWN WILL...
"THIS WAS A WEAPON THAT COULD END STARS THEMSELVES.
"AND FOR THE FIRST TIME IN MILLENNIA, EGO CONSIDERED HIS MORTALITY...
"AND WAS AFRAID.

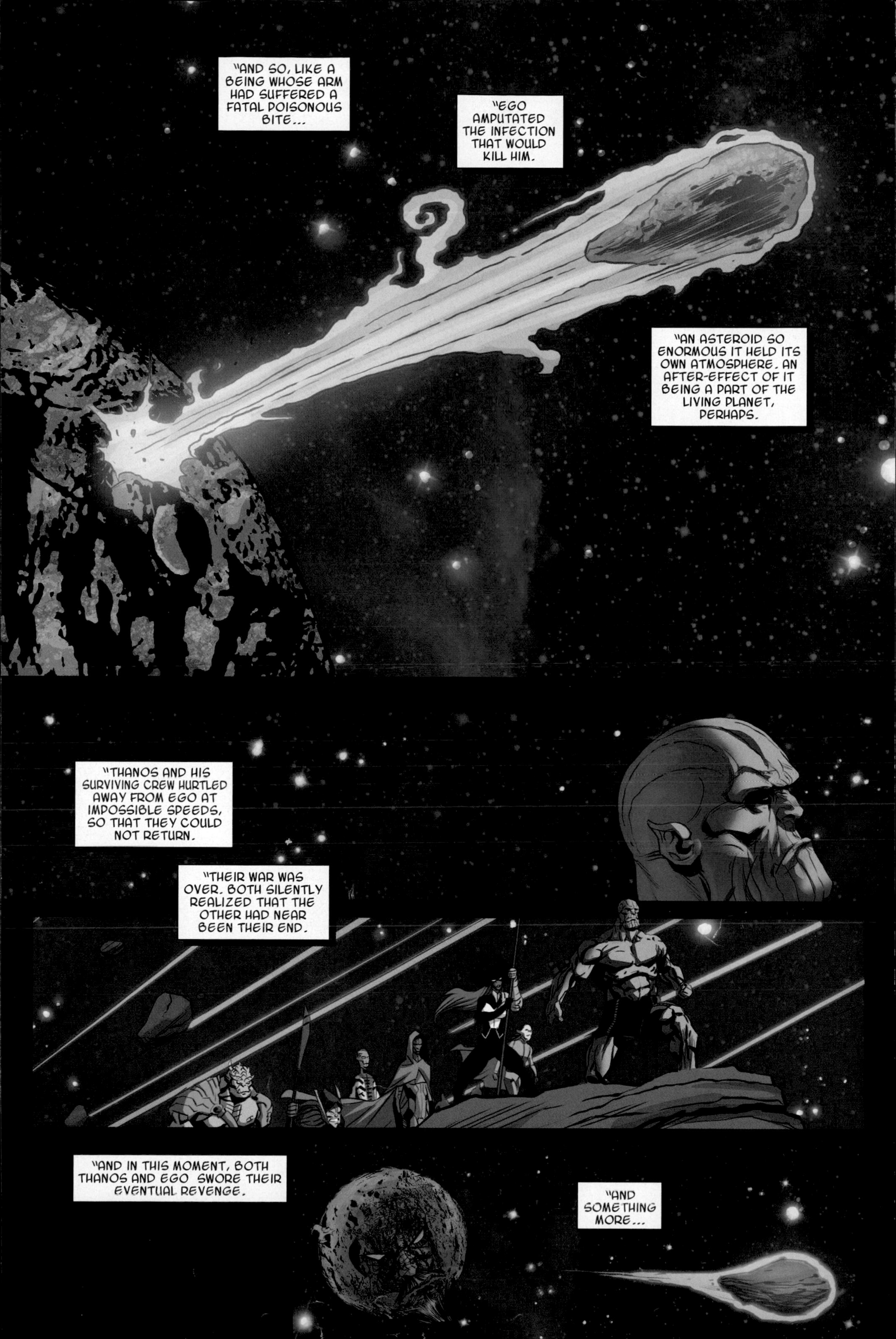
"AND SO, LIKE A BEING WHOSE ARM HAD SUFFERED A FATAL POISONOUS BITE...
"EGO AMPUTATED THE INFECTION THAT WOULD KILL HIM.
"AN ASTEROID SO ENORMOUS IT HELD ITS OWN ATMOSPHERE. AN AFTER-EFFECT OF IT BEING A PART OF THE LIVING PLANET, PERHAPS.
"THANOS AND HIS SURVIVING CREW HURTLED AWAY FROM EGO AT IMPOSSIBLE SPEEDS, SO THAT THEY COULD NOT RETURN.
"THEIR WAR WAS OVER. BOTH SILENTLY REALIZED THAT THE OTHER HAD NEAR BEEN THEIR END.
"AND IN THIS MOMENT, BOTH THANOS AND EGO SWORE THEIR EVENTUAL REVENGE.
"AND SOMETHING MORE...

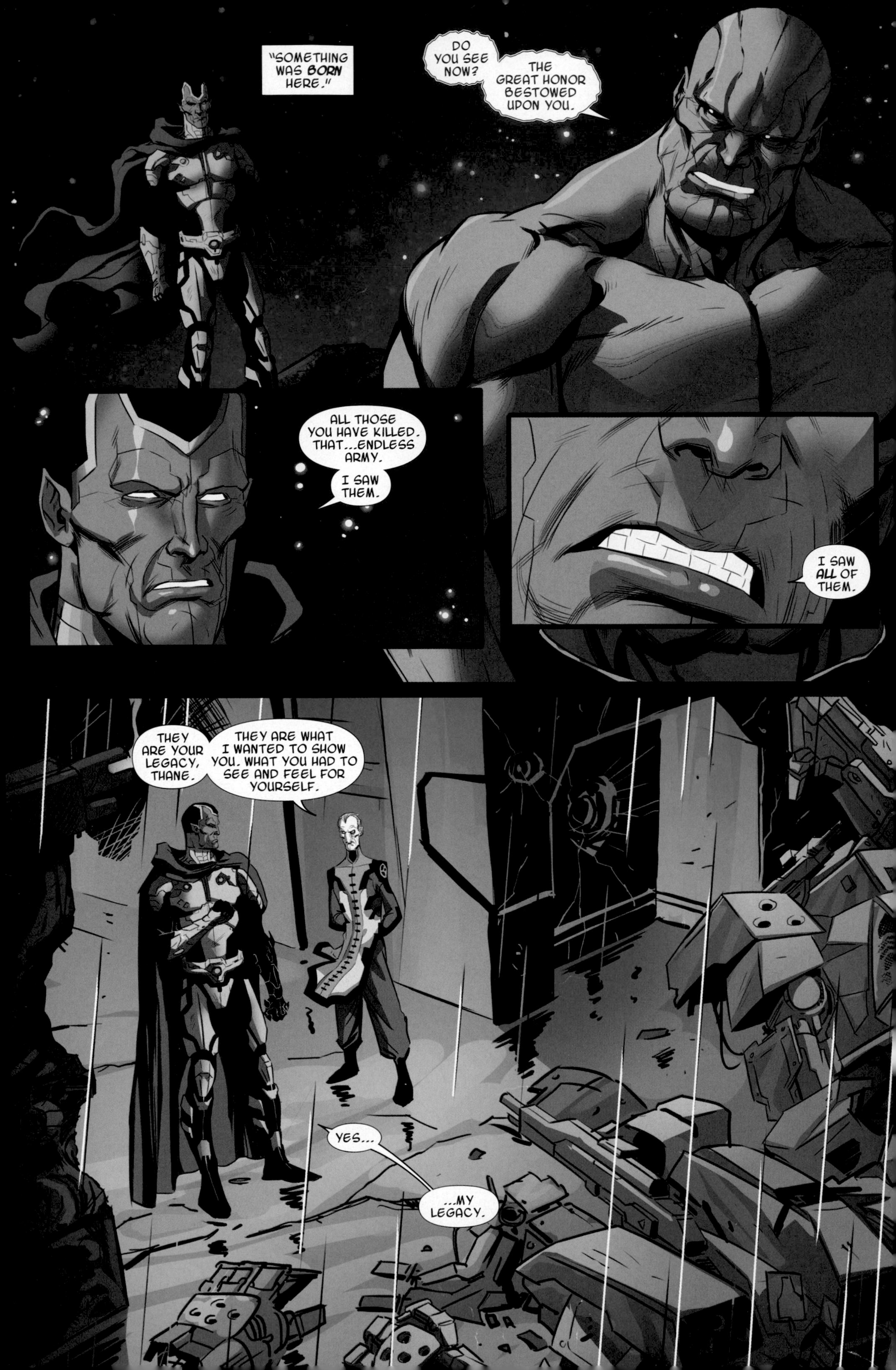
"SOMETHING WAS BORN HERE."
DO YOU SEE NOW?
THE GREAT HONOR BESTOWED UPON YOU.
ALL THOSE YOU HAVE KILLED. THAT...ENDLESS ARMY.
I SAW THEM.
I SAW ALL OF THEM.
THEY ARE YOUR LEGACY, THANE.
THEY ARE WHAT I WANTED TO SHOW YOU. WHAT YOU HAD TO SEE AND FEEL FOR YOURSELF.
YES...
...MY LEGACY.

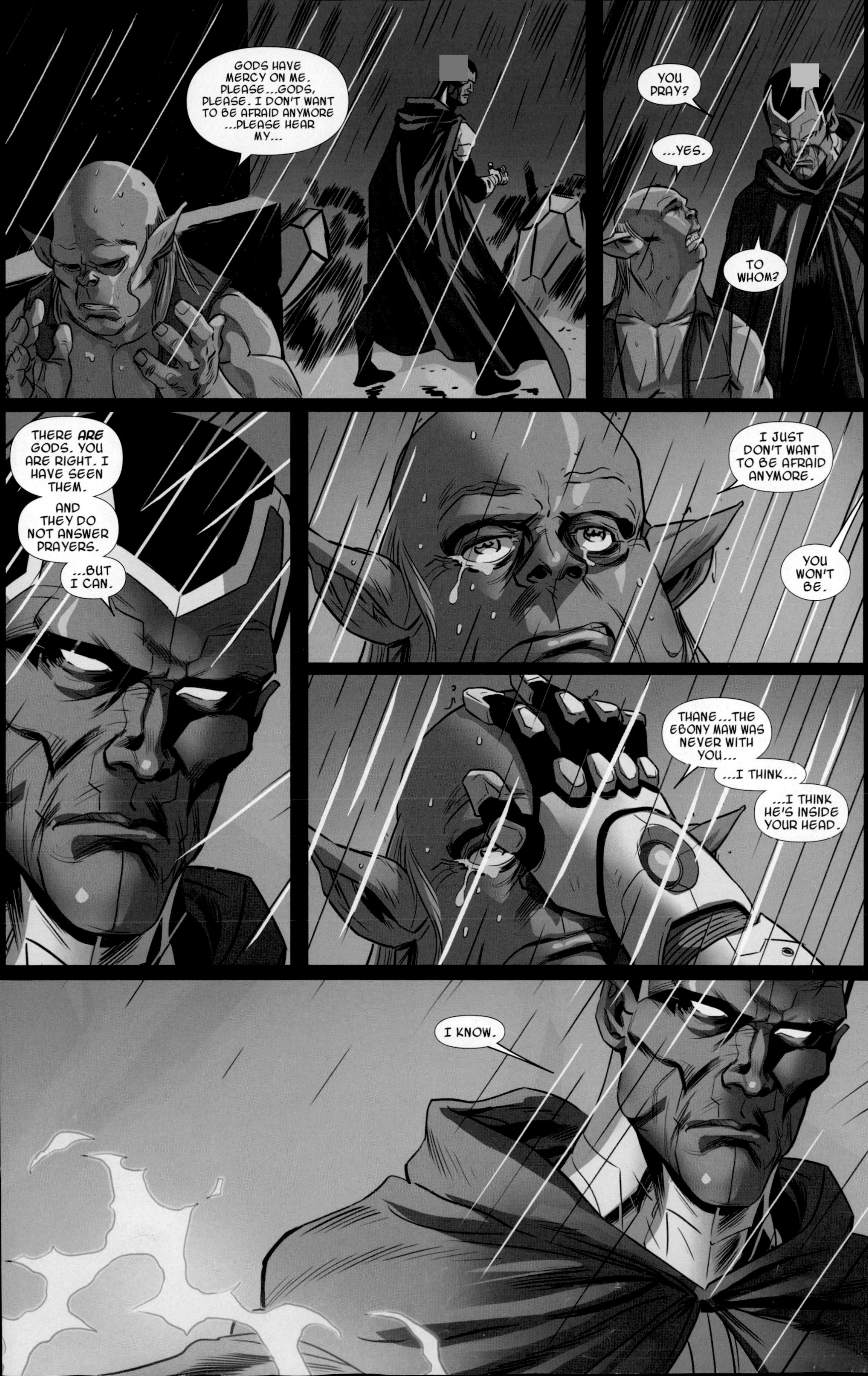
GODS HAVE MERCY ON ME. PLEASE...GODS, PLEASE. I DON'T WANT TO BE AFRAID ANYMORE ...PLEASE HEAR MY...
YOU PRAY?
...YES.
TO WHOM?
THERE *ARE* GODS. YOU ARE RIGHT. I HAVE SEEN THEM.
AND THEY DO NOT ANSWER PRAYERS.
...BUT I CAN.
I JUST DON'T WANT TO BE AFRAID ANYMORE.
YOU WON'T BE.
THANE...THE EBONY MAW WAS NEVER WITH YOU...
...I THINK...
...I THINK HE'S INSIDE YOUR HEAD.
I KNOW.

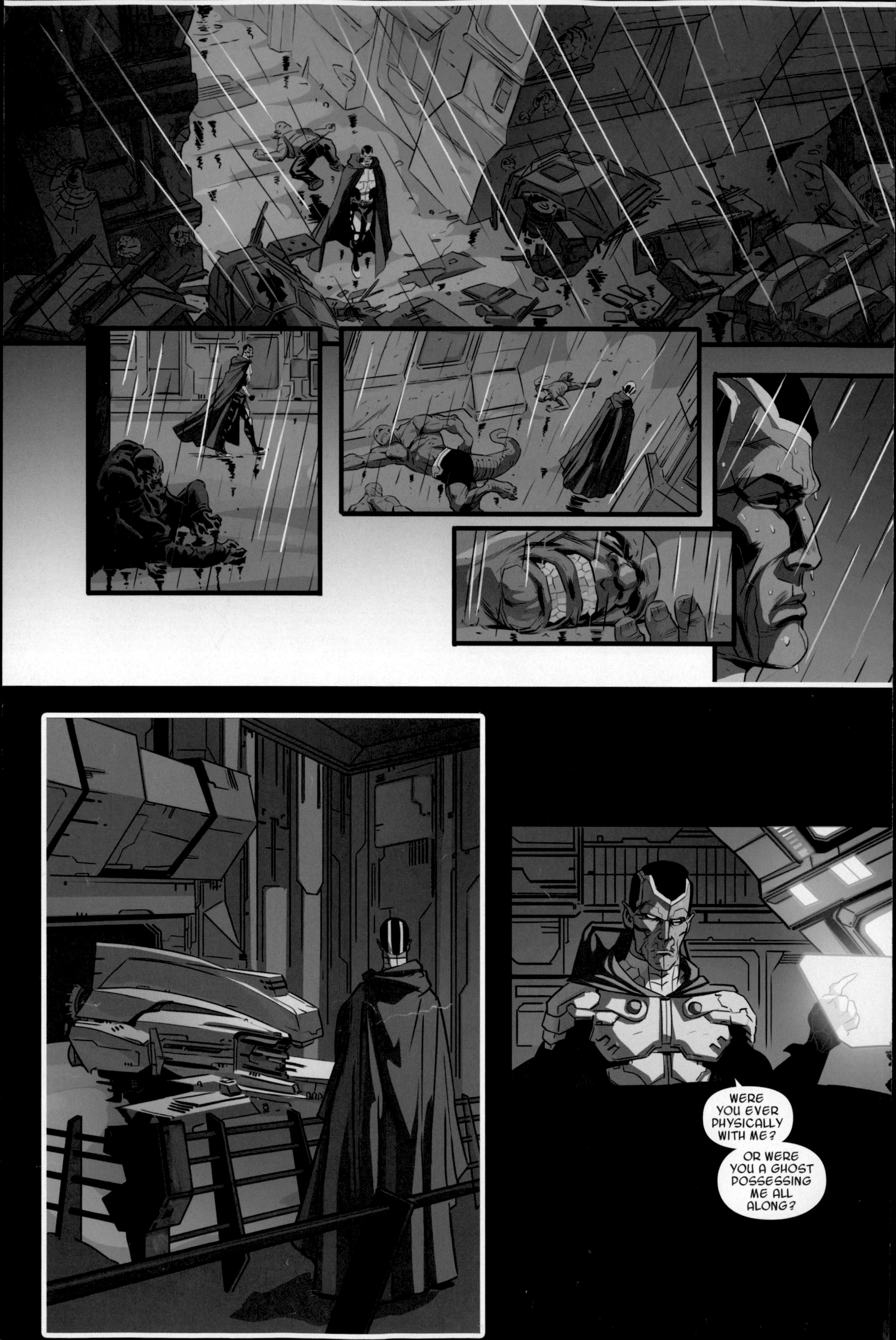
WERE YOU EVER PHYSICALLY WITH ME?
OR WERE YOU A GHOST POSSESSING ME ALL ALONG?

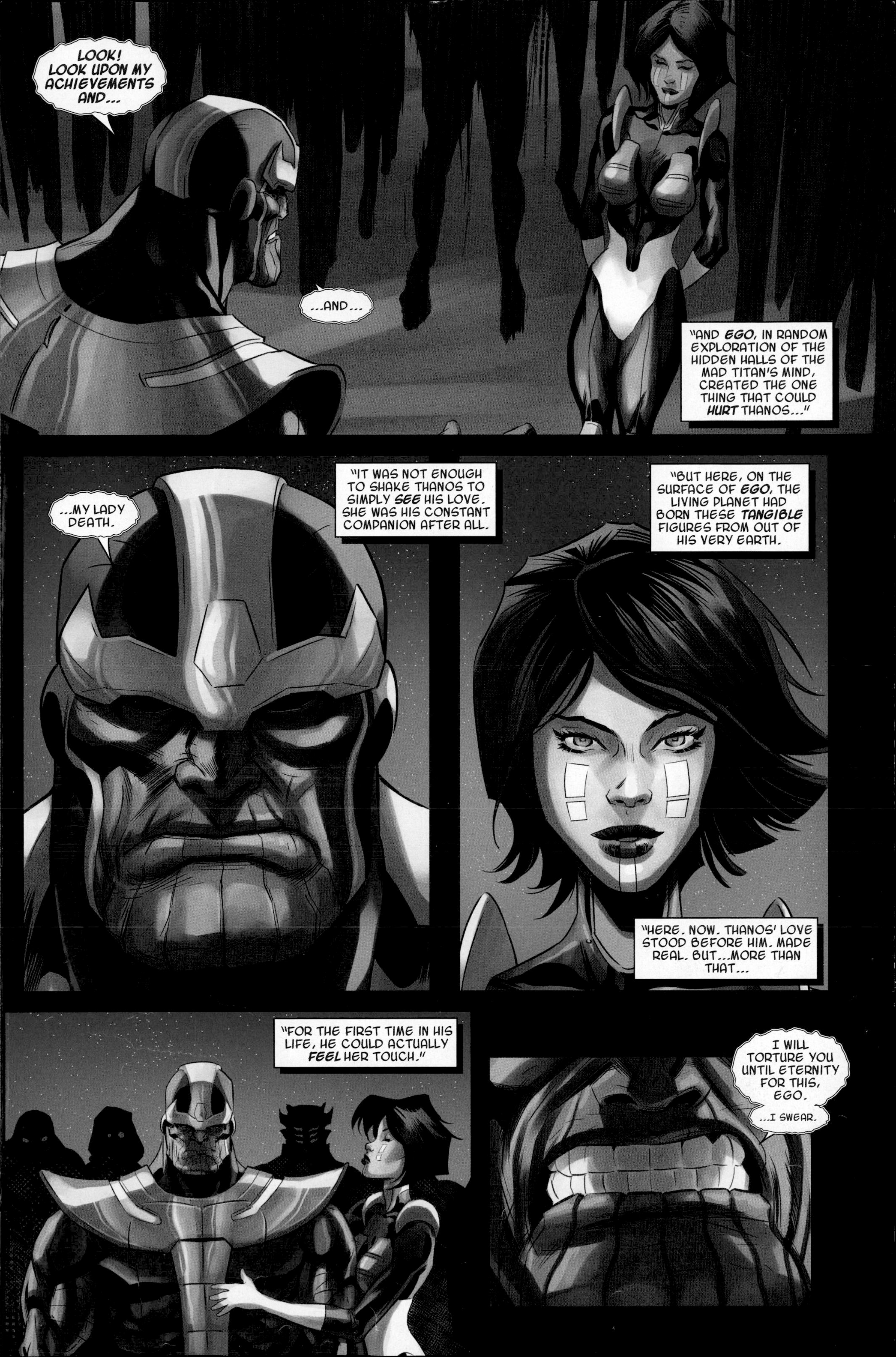
LOOK! LOOK UPON MY ACHIEVEMENTS AND...
...AND...
"AND EGO, IN RANDOM EXPLORATION OF THE HIDDEN HALLS OF THE MAD TITAN'S MIND, CREATED THE ONE THING THAT COULD HURT THANOS..."
...MY LADY DEATH.
"IT WAS NOT ENOUGH TO SHAKE THANOS TO SIMPLY SEE HIS LOVE. SHE WAS HIS CONSTANT COMPANION AFTER ALL.
"BUT HERE, ON THE SURFACE OF EGO, THE LIVING PLANET HAD BORN THESE TANGIBLE FIGURES FROM OUT OF HIS VERY EARTH.
"HERE. NOW. THANOS' LOVE STOOD BEFORE HIM. MADE REAL. BUT...MORE THAN THAT...
"FOR THE FIRST TIME IN HIS LIFE, HE COULD ACTUALLY FEEL HER TOUCH."
I WILL TORTURE YOU UNTIL ETERNITY FOR THIS, EGO.
...I SWEAR.

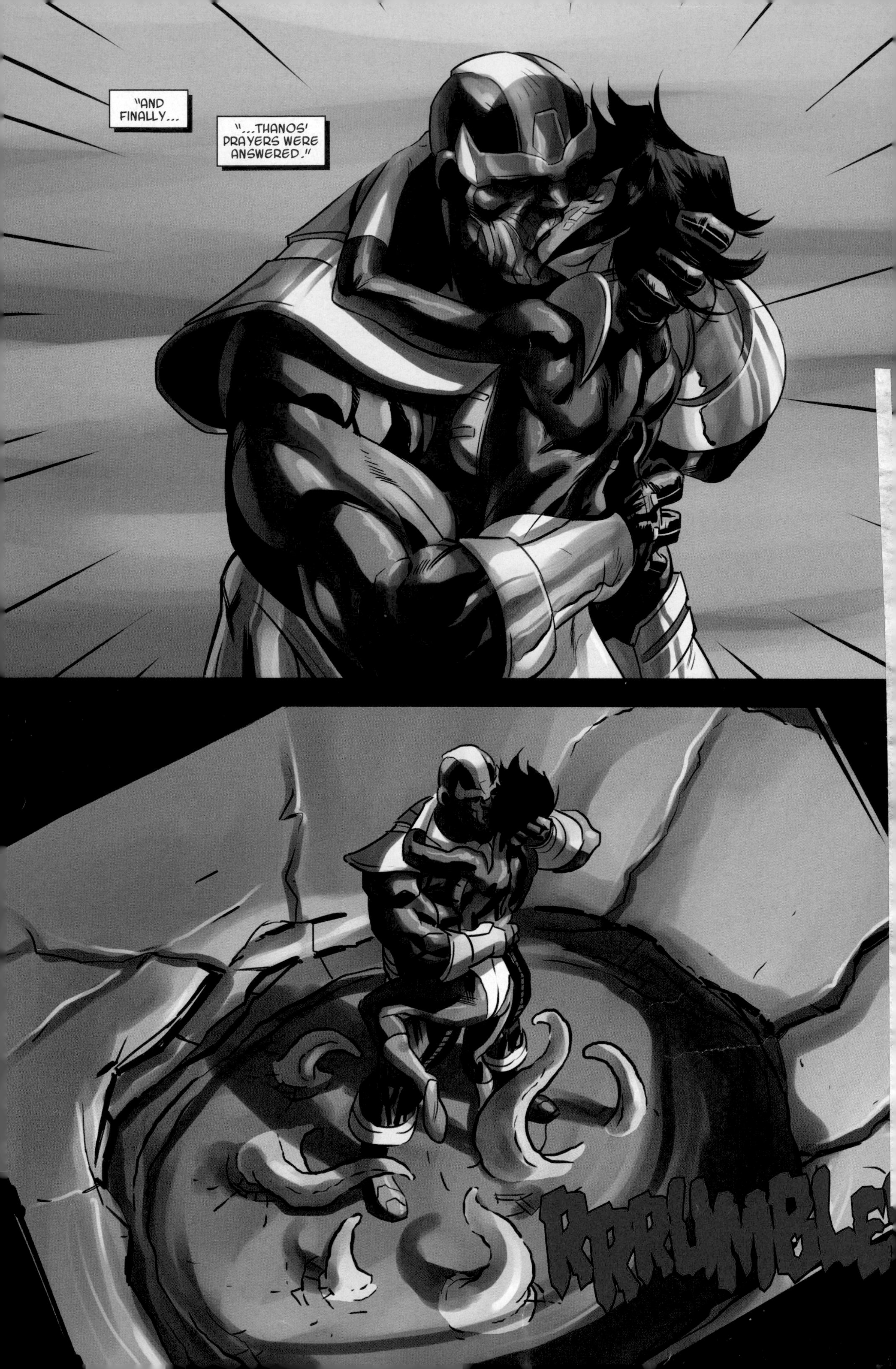
"AND FINALLY...
"...THANOS' PRAYERS WERE ANSWERED."
RRRUMBLE

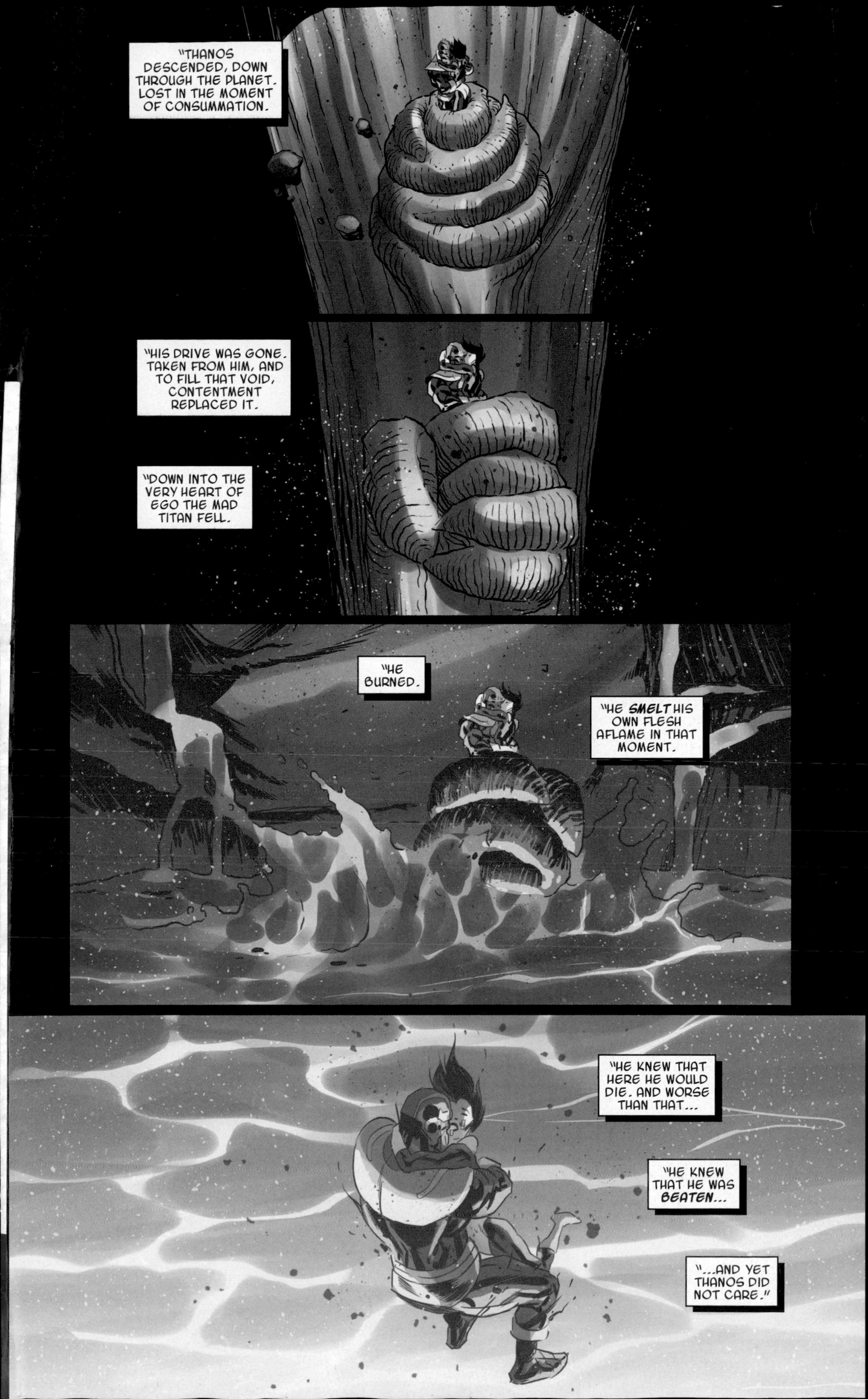
"THANOS DESCENDED, DOWN THROUGH THE PLANET. LOST IN THE MOMENT OF CONSUMMATION.
"HIS DRIVE WAS GONE. TAKEN FROM HIM, AND TO FILL THAT VOID, CONTENTMENT REPLACED IT.
"DOWN INTO THE VERY HEART OF EGO THE MAD TITAN FELL.
"HE BURNED.
"HE SMELT HIS OWN FLESH AFLAME IN THAT MOMENT.
"HE KNEW THAT HERE HE WOULD DIE. AND WORSE THAN THAT...
"HE KNEW THAT HE WAS BEATEN...
"...AND YET THANOS DID NOT CARE."

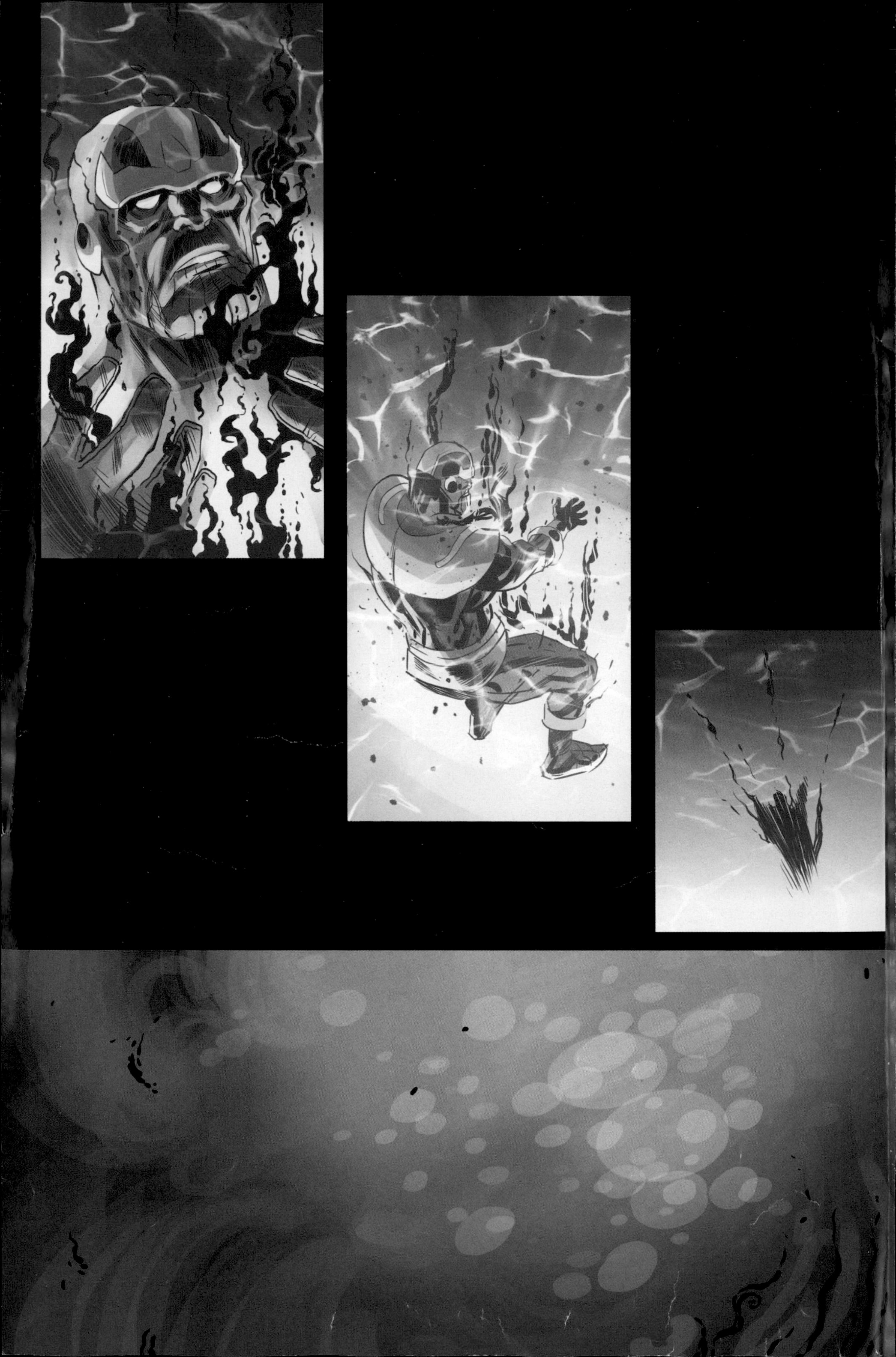

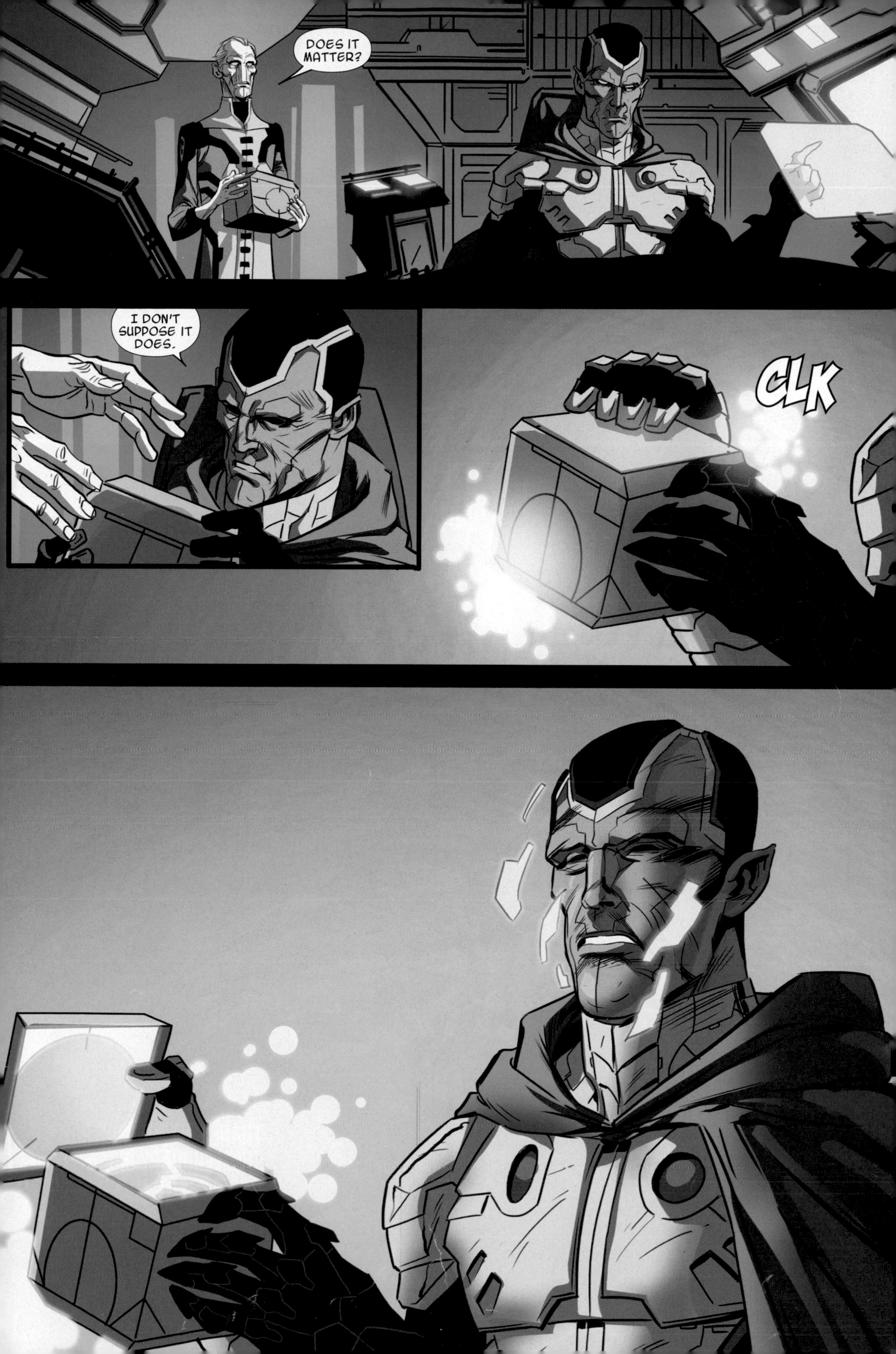
DOES IT MATTER?
I DON'T SUPPOSE IT DOES.
CLK

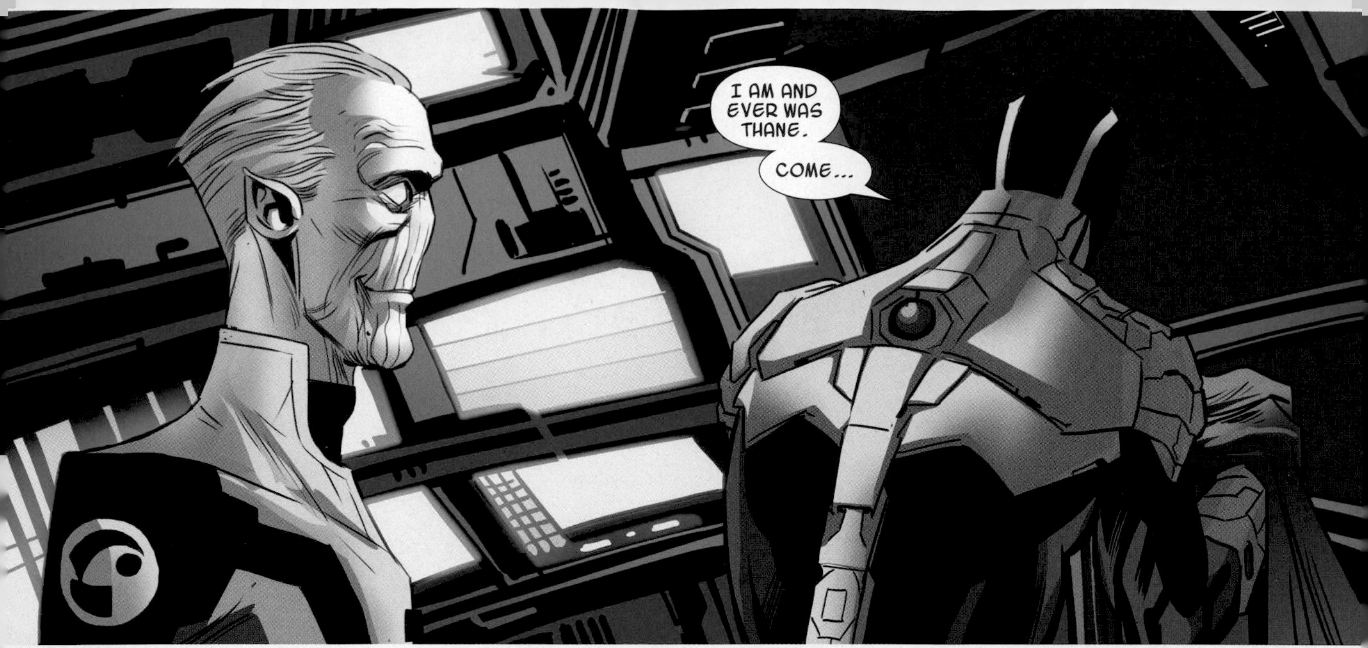
I AM AND EVER WAS THANE.
COME...

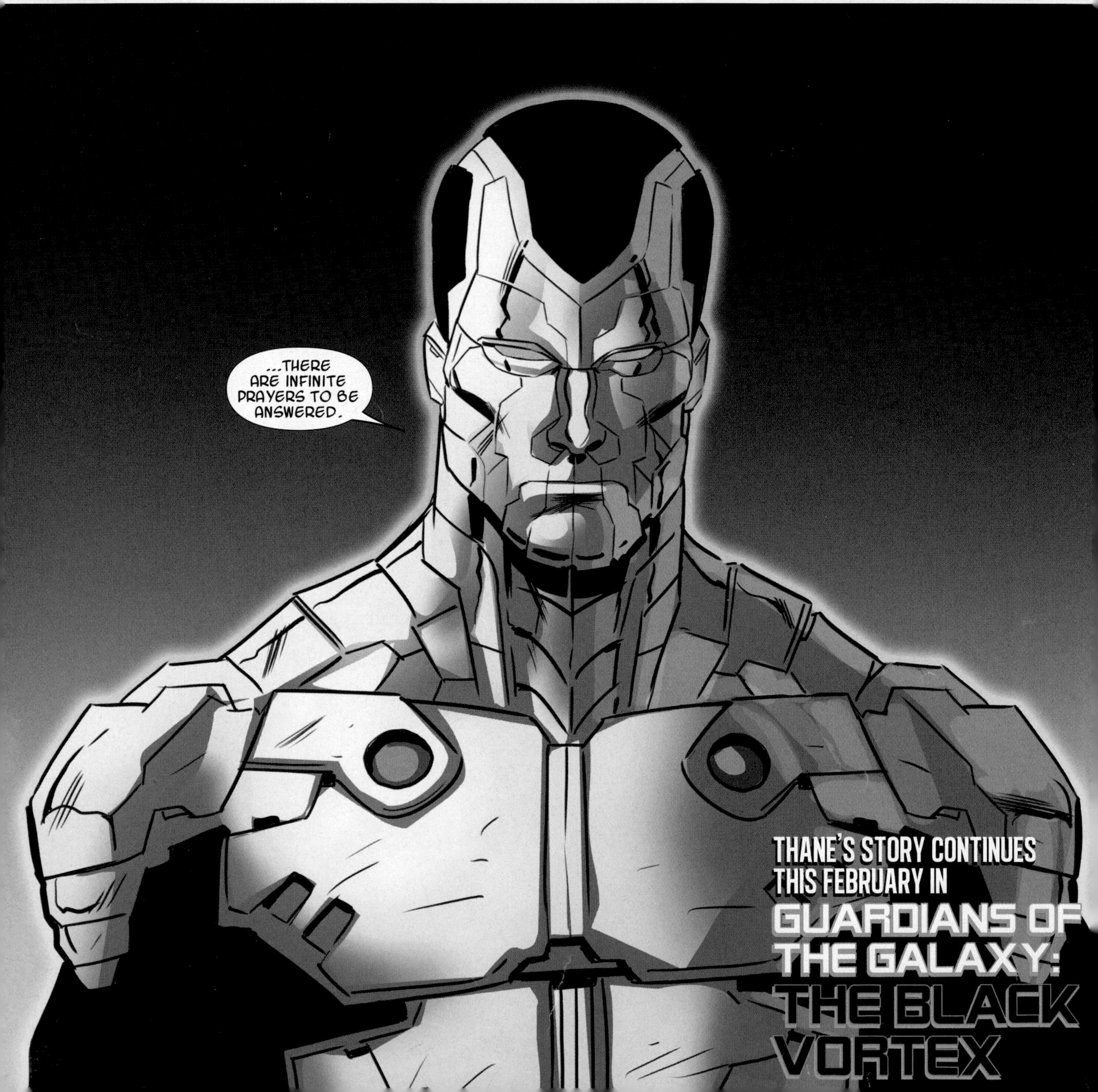
...THERE ARE INFINITE PRAYERS TO BE ANSWERED.
THANE'S STORY CONTINUES THIS FEBRUARY IN
GUARDIANS OF THE GALAXY: THE BLACK VORTEX

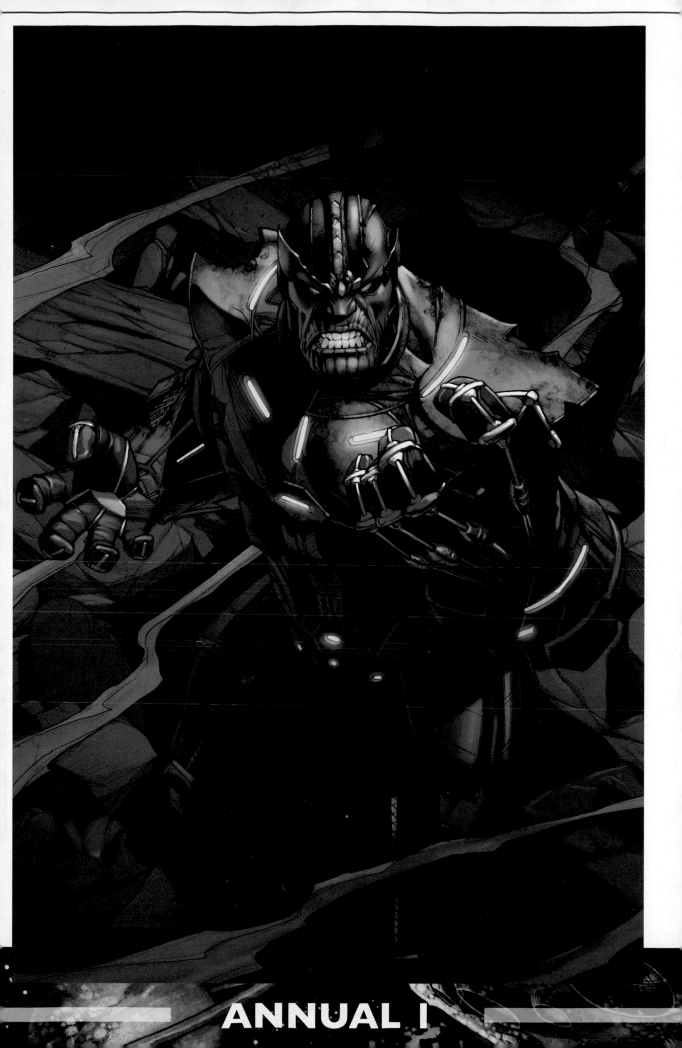

ANNUAL 1

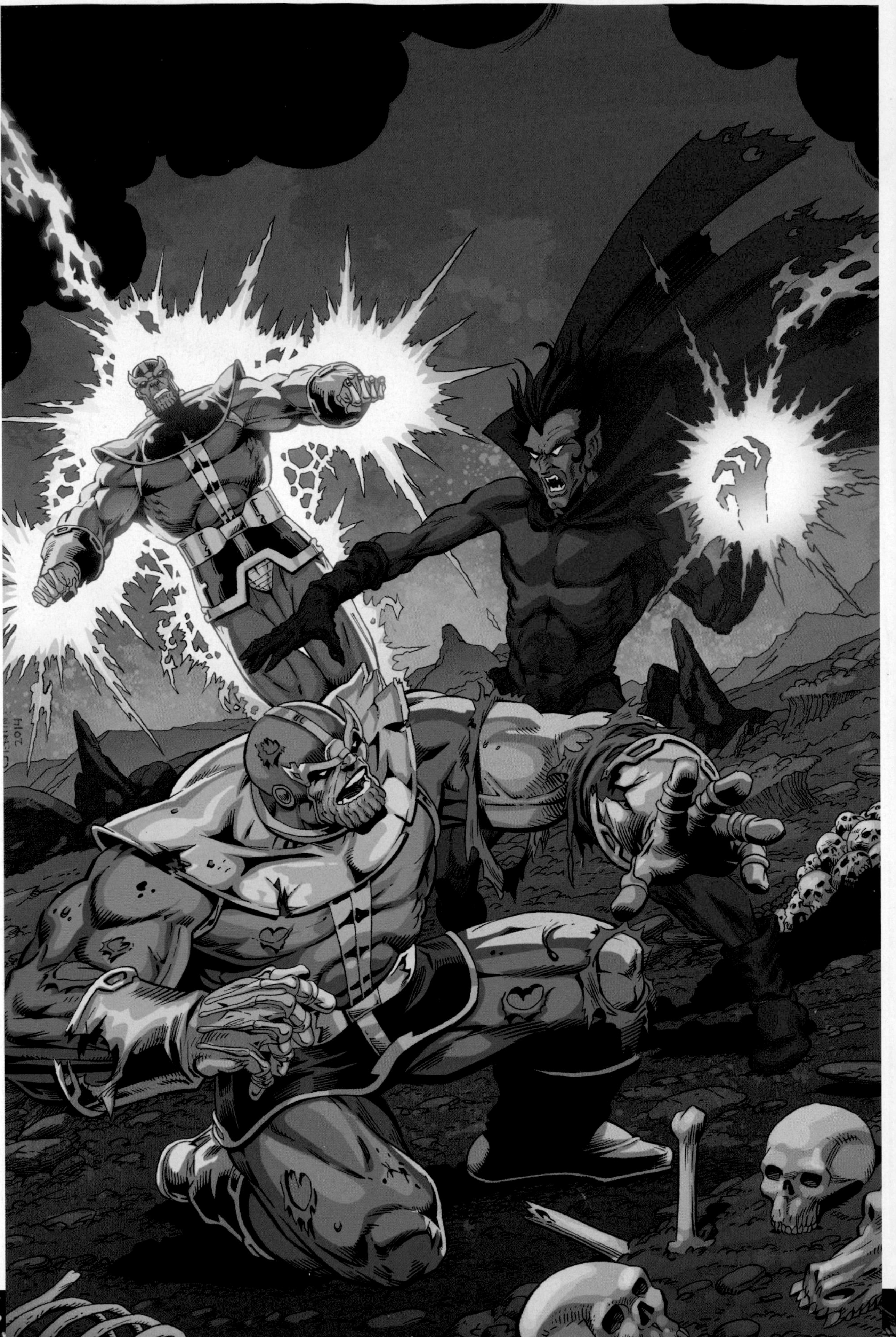
STARLIN 2014

ANNUAL #1 VARIANT
BY JIM STARLIN, AL MILGROM, & BRAD ANDERSON

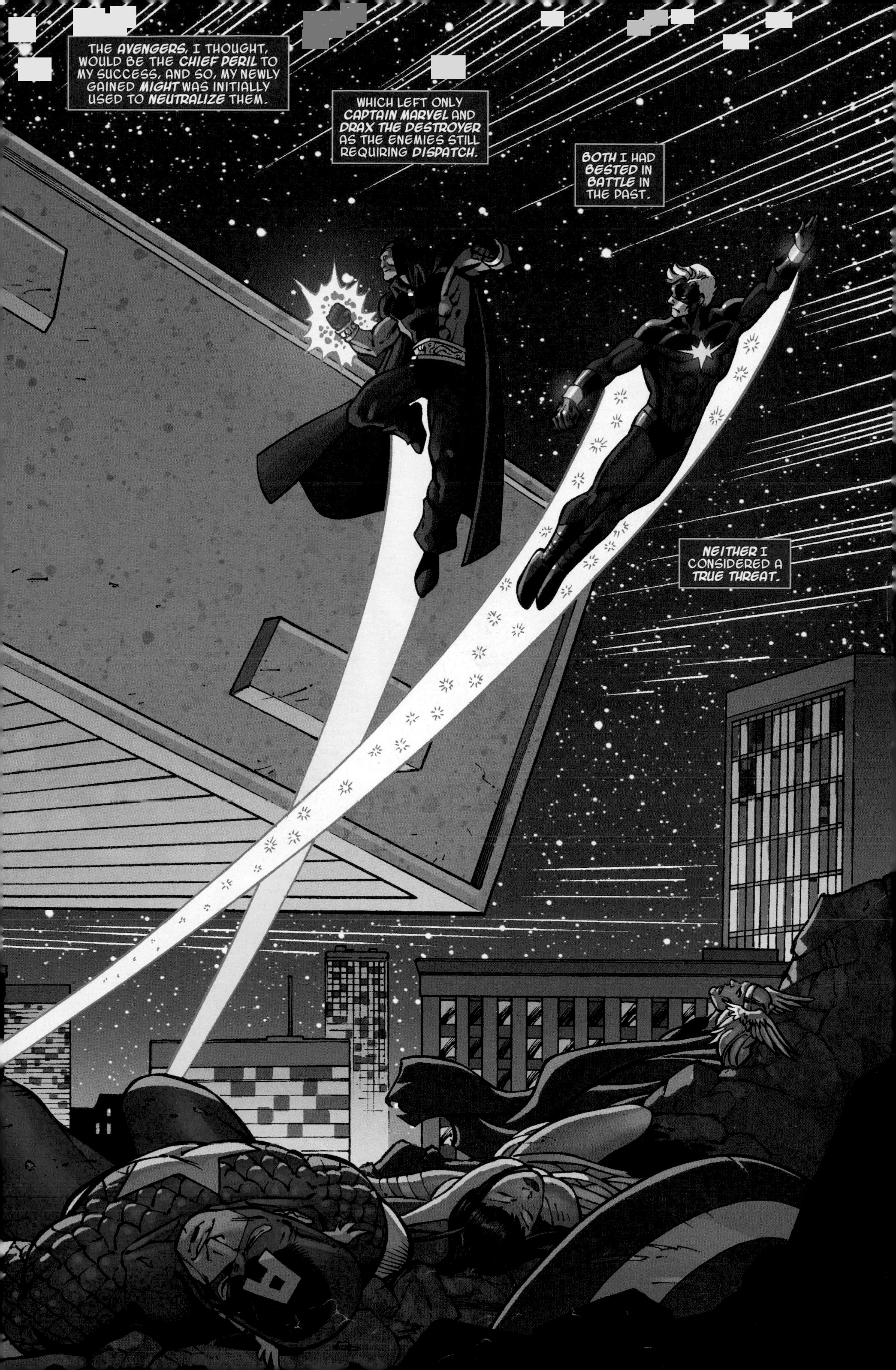
THE AVENGERS, I THOUGHT, WOULD BE THE CHIEF PERIL TO MY SUCCESS, AND SO, MY NEWLY GAINED MIGHT WAS INITIALLY USED TO NEUTRALIZE THEM.
WHICH LEFT ONLY CAPTAIN MARVEL AND DRAX THE DESTROYER AS THE ENEMIES STILL REQUIRING DISPATCH.
BOTH I HAD BESTED IN BATTLE IN THE PAST.
NEITHER I CONSIDERED A TRUE THREAT.

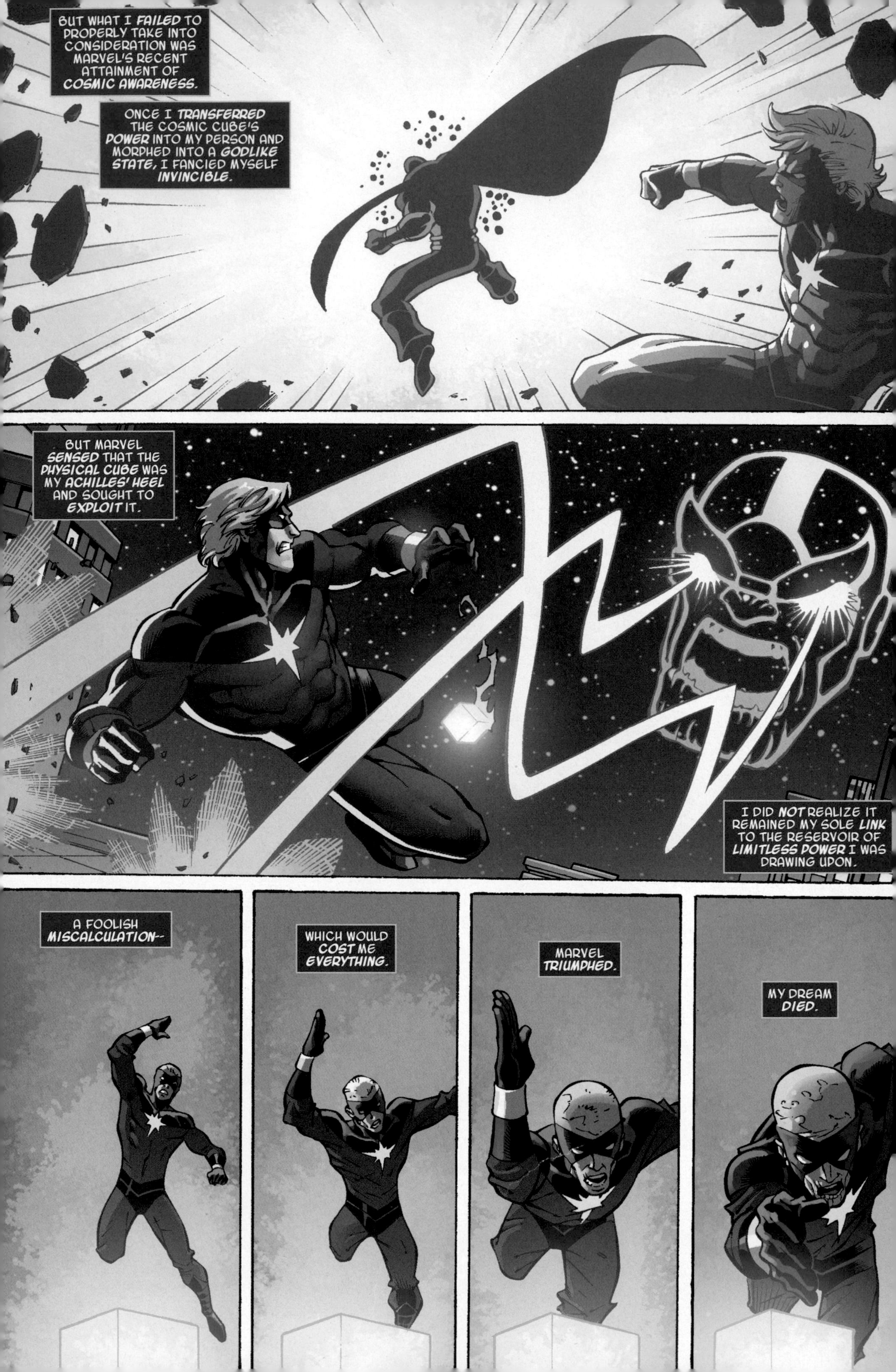
BUT WHAT I FAILED TO PROPERLY TAKE INTO CONSIDERATION WAS MARVEL'S RECENT ATTAINMENT OF COSMIC AWARENESS.
ONCE I TRANSFERRED THE COSMIC CUBE'S POWER INTO MY PERSON AND MORPHED INTO A GODLIKE STATE, I FANCIED MYSELF INVINCIBLE.
BUT MARVEL SENSED THAT THE PHYSICAL CUBE WAS MY ACHILLES' HEEL AND SOUGHT TO EXPLOIT IT.
I DID NOT REALIZE IT REMAINED MY SOLE LINK TO THE RESERVOIR OF LIMITLESS POWER I WAS DRAWING UPON.
A FOOLISH MISCALCULATION--
WHICH WOULD COST ME EVERYTHING.
MARVEL TRIUMPHED.
MY DREAM DIED.

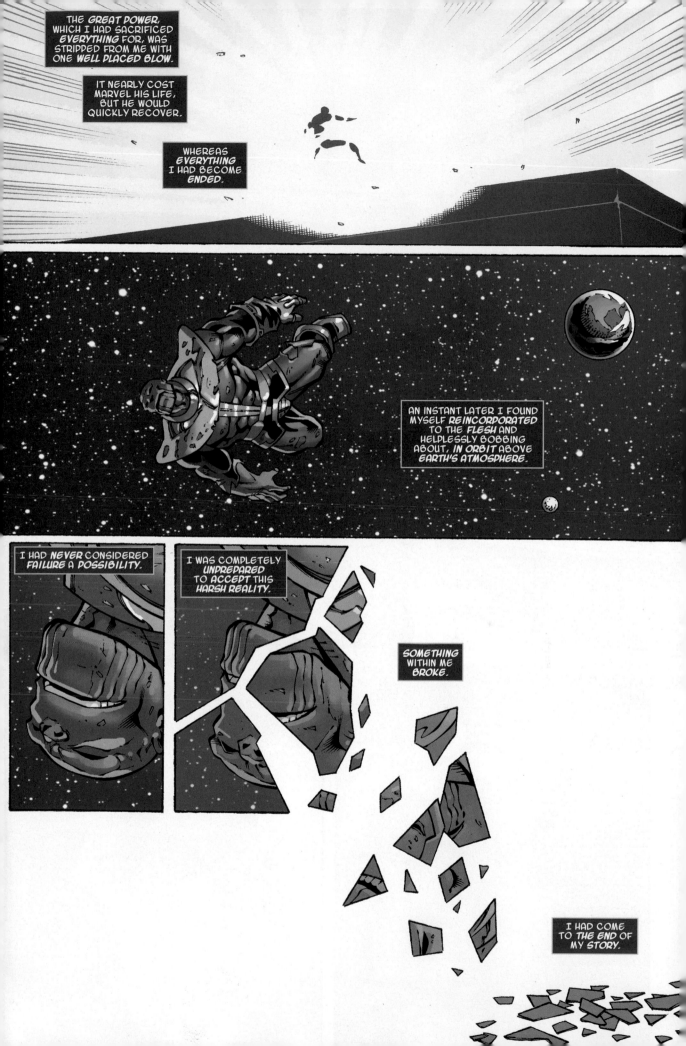

THE *GREAT POWER*, WHICH I HAD SACRIFICED *EVERYTHING* FOR, WAS STRIPPED FROM ME WITH ONE *WELL PLACED BLOW*.

IT NEARLY COST MARVEL HIS LIFE, BUT HE WOULD QUICKLY RECOVER.

WHEREAS *EVERYTHING* I HAD BECOME ENDED.

AN INSTANT LATER I FOUND MYSELF *REINCORPORATED* TO THE *FLESH* AND *HELPLESSLY BOBBING* ABOUT, *IN ORBIT* ABOVE EARTH'S ATMOSPHERE.

I HAD *NEVER* CONSIDERED FAILURE A *POSSIBILITY*.

I WAS COMPLETELY *UNPREPARED* TO ACCEPT THIS *HARSH REALITY*.

SOMETHING WITHIN ME BROKE.

I HAD COME TO *THE END* OF MY *STORY*.

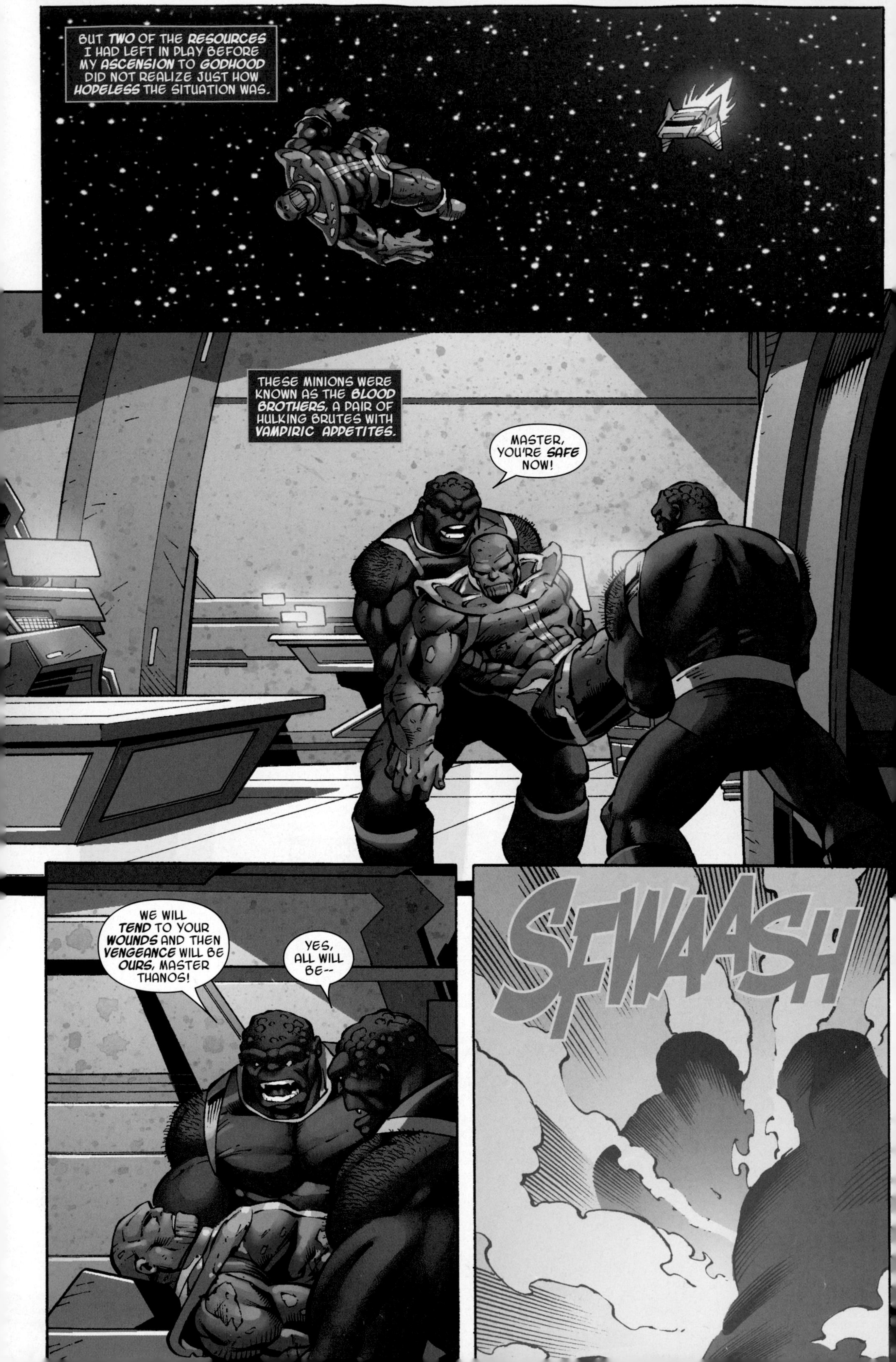
BUT TWO OF THE RESOURCES I HAD LEFT IN PLAY BEFORE MY ASCENSION TO GODHOOD DID NOT REALIZE JUST HOW HOPELESS THE SITUATION WAS.
THESE MINIONS WERE KNOWN AS THE BLOOD BROTHERS, A PAIR OF HULKING BRUTES WITH VAMPIRIC APPETITES.
MASTER, YOU'RE SAFE NOW!
WE WILL TEND TO YOUR WOUNDS AND THEN VENGEANCE WILL BE OURS, MASTER THANOS!
YES, ALL WILL BE--
SFWAASH

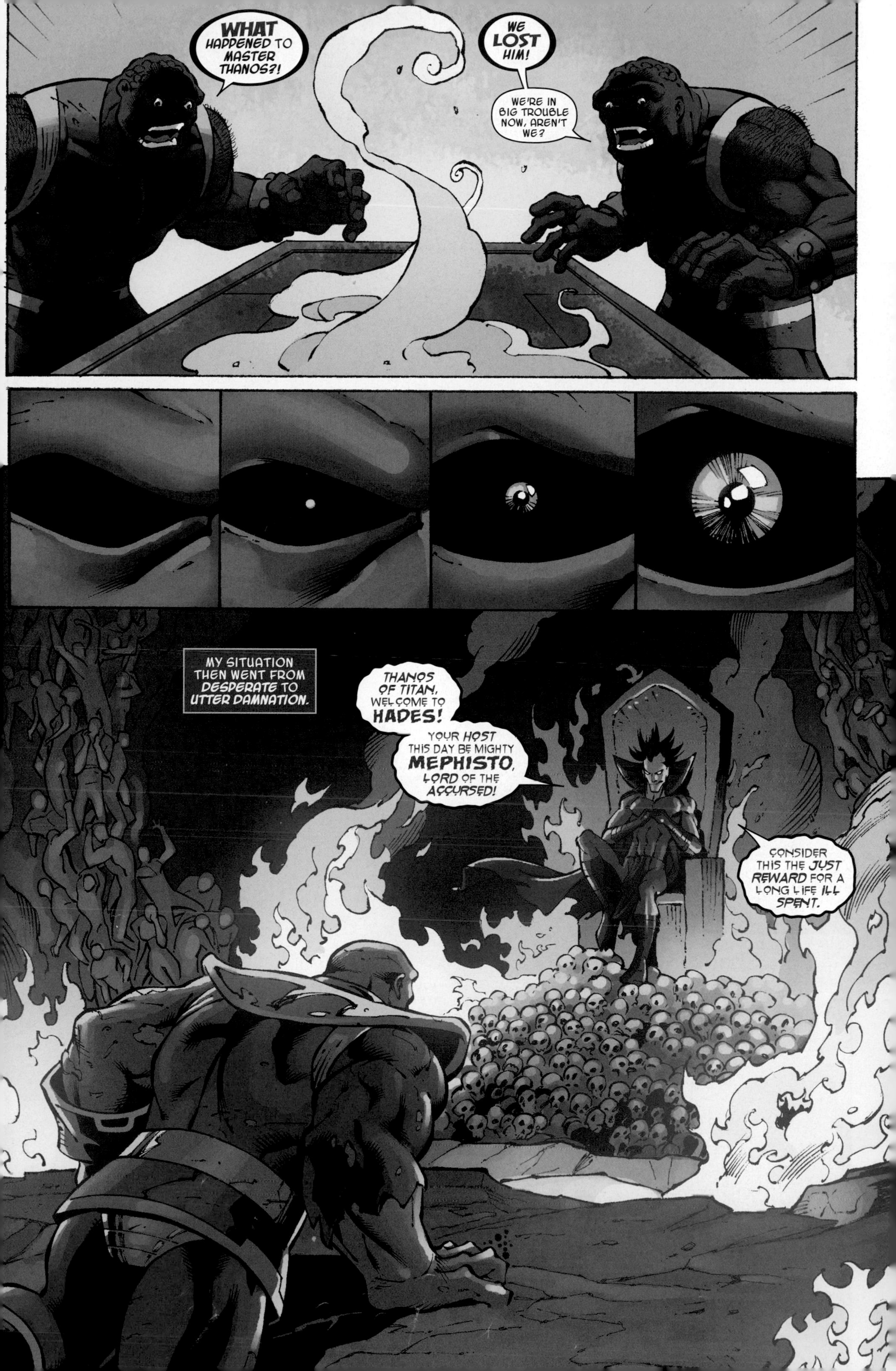
WHAT HAPPENED TO MASTER THANOS?!
WE LOST HIM!
WE'RE IN BIG TROUBLE NOW, AREN'T WE?
MY SITUATION THEN WENT FROM DESPERATE TO UTTER DAMNATION.
THANOS OF TITAN, WELCOME TO HADES!
YOUR HOST THIS DAY BE MIGHTY MEPHISTO, LORD OF THE ACCURSED!
CONSIDER THIS THE JUST REWARD FOR A LONG LIFE ILL SPENT.

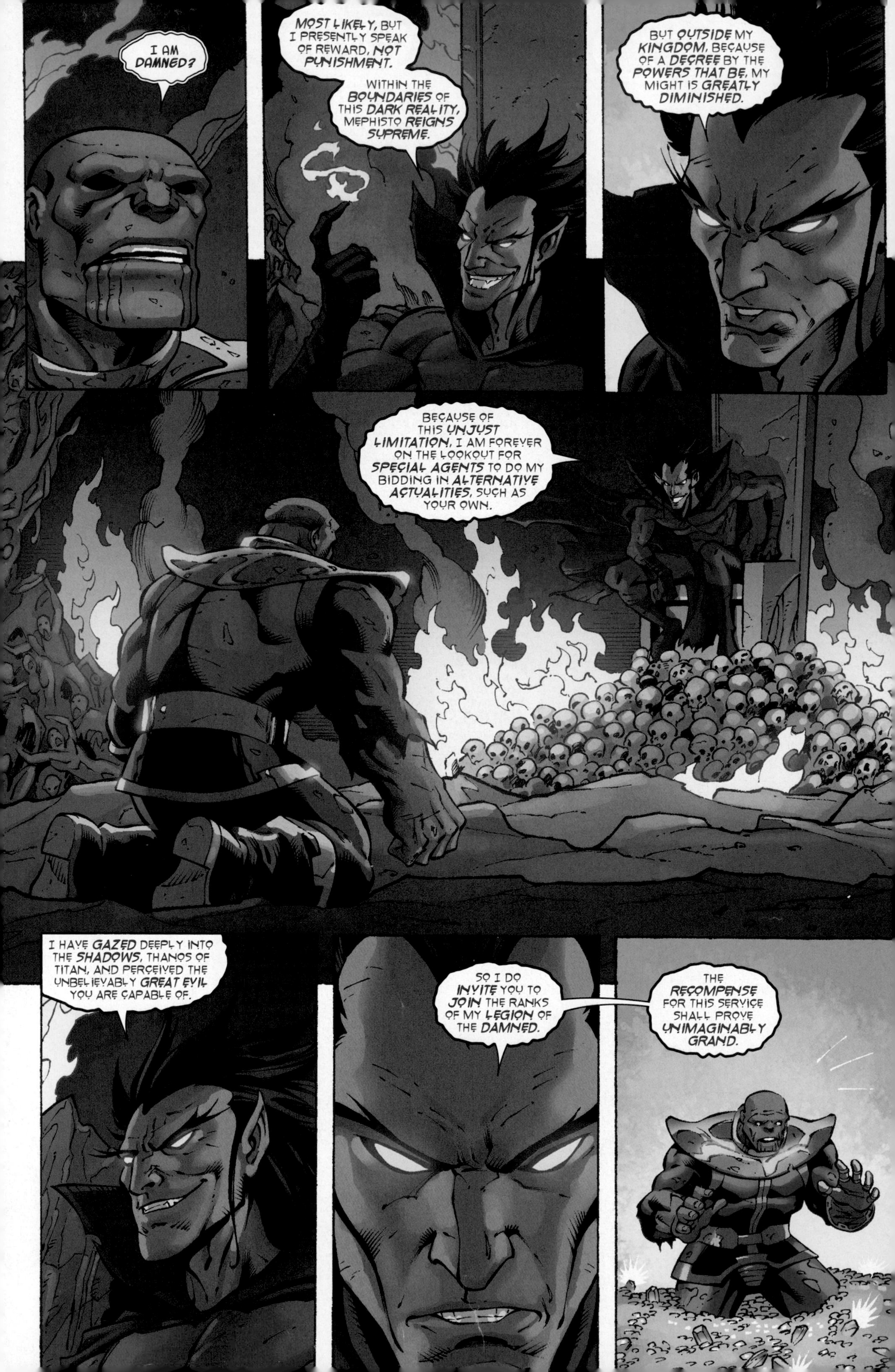
I AM DAMNED?
MOST LIKELY, BUT I PRESENTLY SPEAK OF REWARD, NOT PUNISHMENT.
WITHIN THE BOUNDARIES OF THIS DARK REALITY, MEPHISTO REIGNS SUPREME.
BUT OUTSIDE MY KINGDOM, BECAUSE OF A DECREE BY THE POWERS THAT BE, MY MIGHT IS GREATLY DIMINISHED.
BECAUSE OF THIS UNJUST LIMITATION, I AM FOREVER ON THE LOOKOUT FOR SPECIAL AGENTS TO DO MY BIDDING IN ALTERNATIVE ACTUALITIES, SUCH AS YOUR OWN.
I HAVE GAZED DEEPLY INTO THE SHADOWS, THANOS OF TITAN, AND PERCEIVED THE UNBELIEVABLY GREAT EVIL YOU ARE CAPABLE OF.
SO I DO INVITE YOU TO JOIN THE RANKS OF MY LEGION OF THE DAMNED.
THE RECOMPENSE FOR THIS SERVICE SHALL PROVE UNIMAGINABLY GRAND.

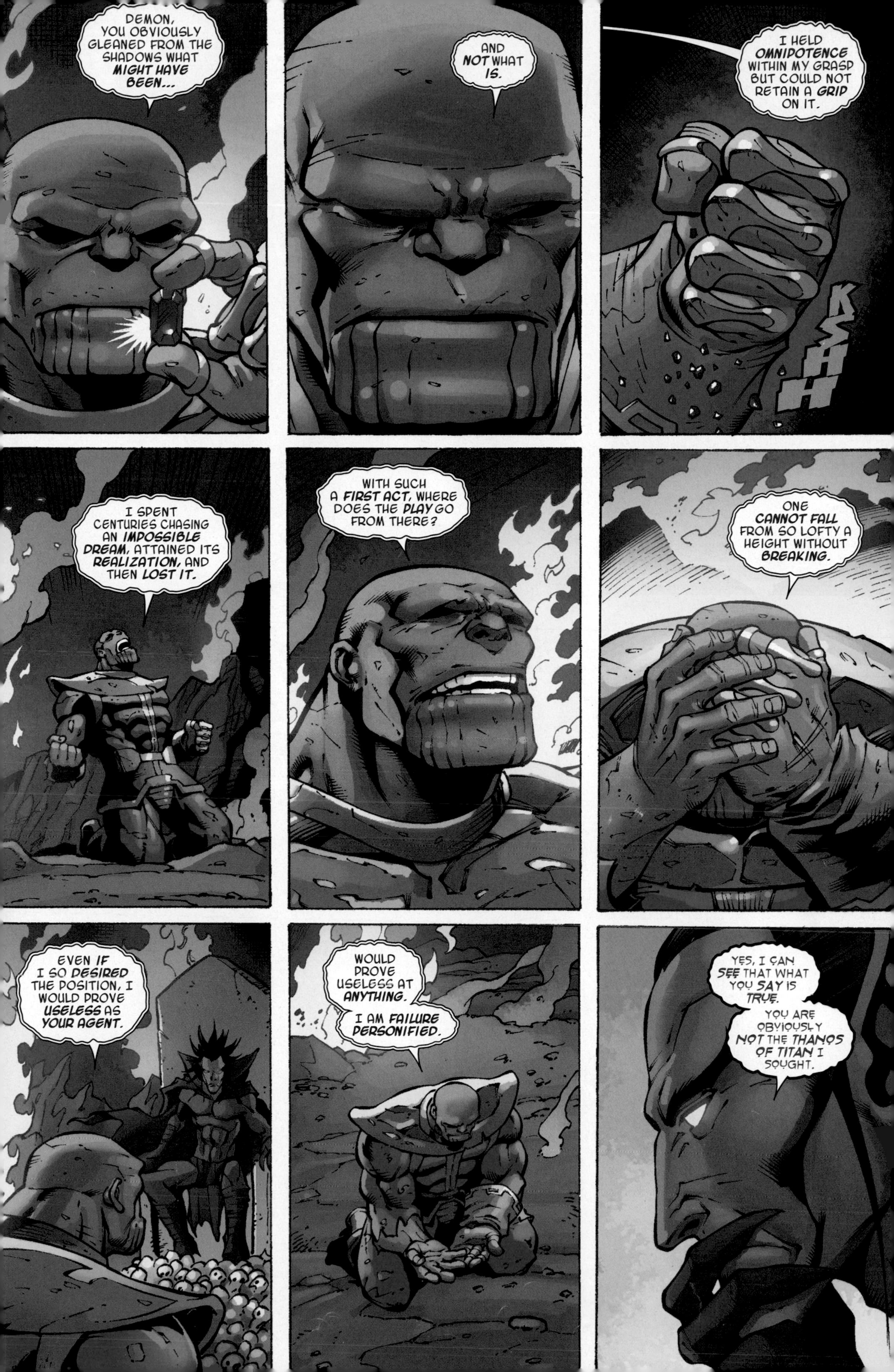
DEMON, YOU OBVIOUSLY GLEANED FROM THE SHADOWS WHAT MIGHT HAVE BEEN...
AND NOT WHAT IS.
I HELD OMNIPOTENCE WITHIN MY GRASP BUT COULD NOT RETAIN A GRIP ON IT.
KSHH
I SPENT CENTURIES CHASING AN IMPOSSIBLE DREAM, ATTAINED ITS REALIZATION, AND THEN LOST IT.
WITH SUCH A FIRST ACT, WHERE DOES THE PLAY GO FROM THERE?
ONE CANNOT FALL FROM SO LOFTY A HEIGHT WITHOUT BREAKING.
EVEN IF I SO DESIRED THE POSITION, I WOULD PROVE USELESS AS YOUR AGENT.
WOULD PROVE USELESS AT ANYTHING.
I AM FAILURE PERSONIFIED.
YES, I CAN SEE THAT WHAT YOU SAY IS TRUE.
YOU ARE OBVIOUSLY NOT THE THANOS OF TITAN I SOUGHT.

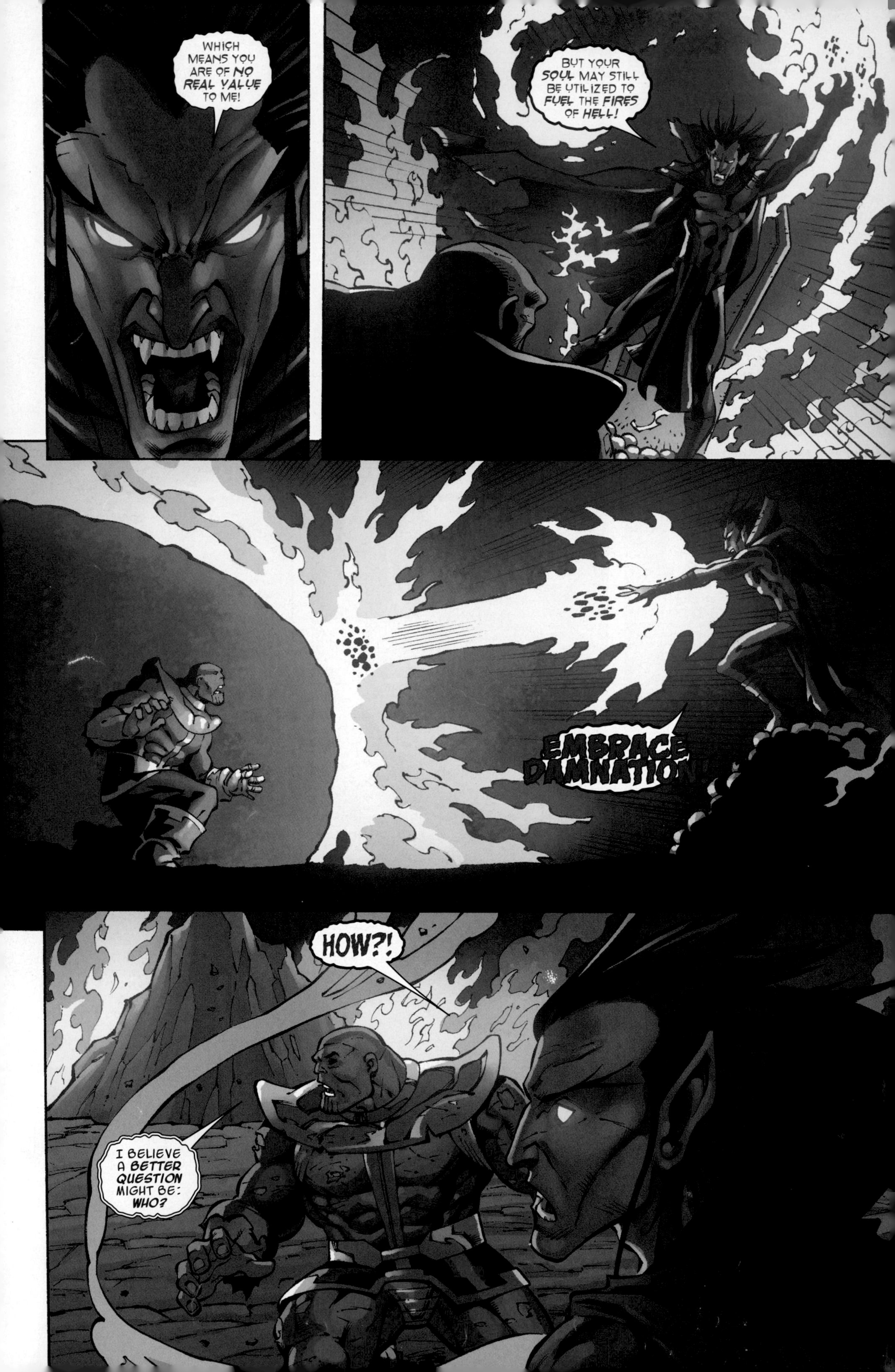
WHICH MEANS YOU ARE OF NO REAL VALUE TO ME!
BUT YOUR SOUL MAY STILL BE UTILIZED TO FUEL THE FIRES OF HELL!
EMBRACE DAMNATION!!
HOW?!
I BELIEVE A BETTER QUESTION MIGHT BE: WHO?

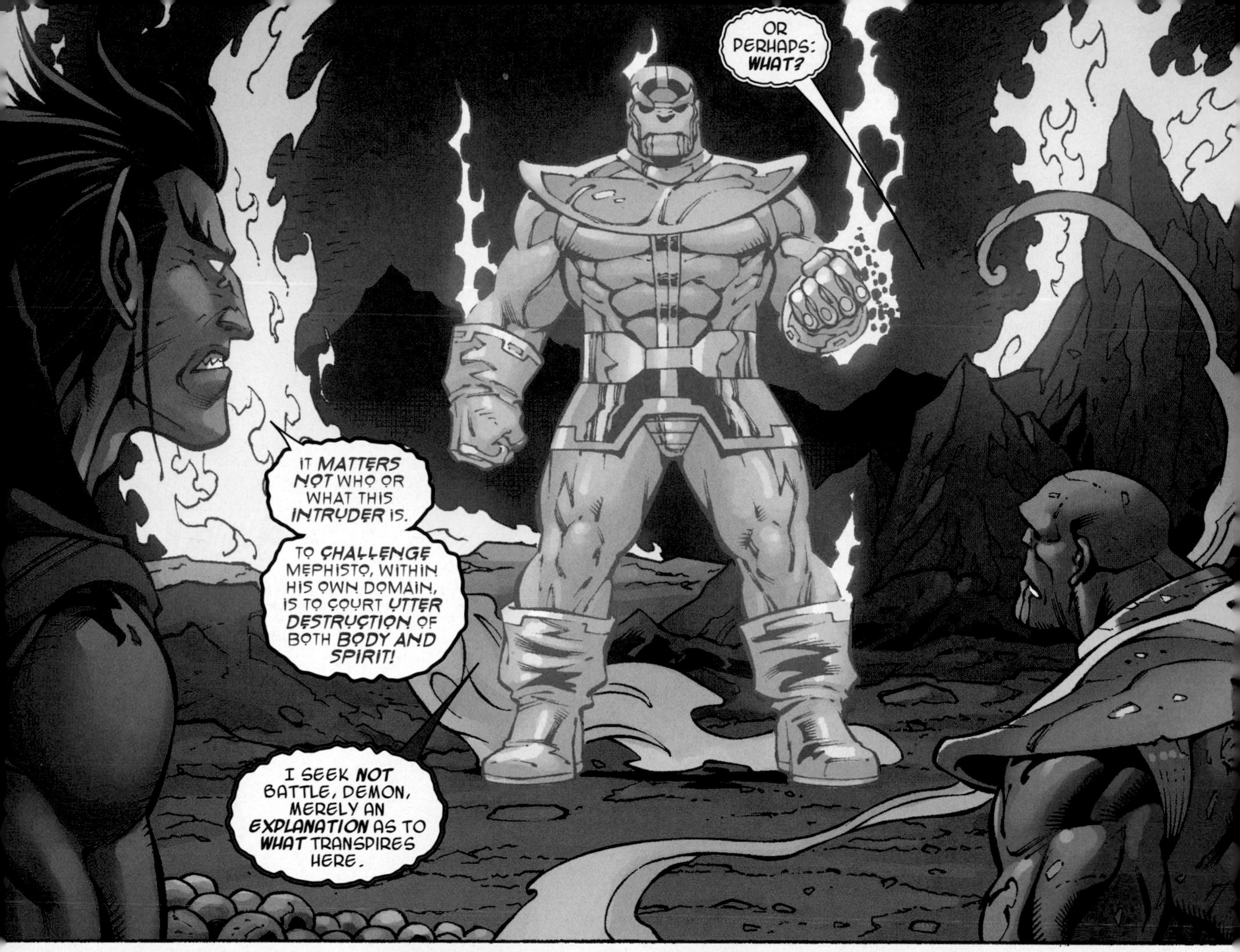
OR PERHAPS: WHAT?
IT MATTERS NOT WHO OR WHAT THIS INTRUDER IS.
TO CHALLENGE MEPHISTO, WITHIN HIS OWN DOMAIN, IS TO COURT UTTER DESTRUCTION OF BOTH BODY AND SPIRIT!
I SEEK NOT BATTLE, DEMON, MERELY AN EXPLANATION AS TO WHAT TRANSPIRES HERE.

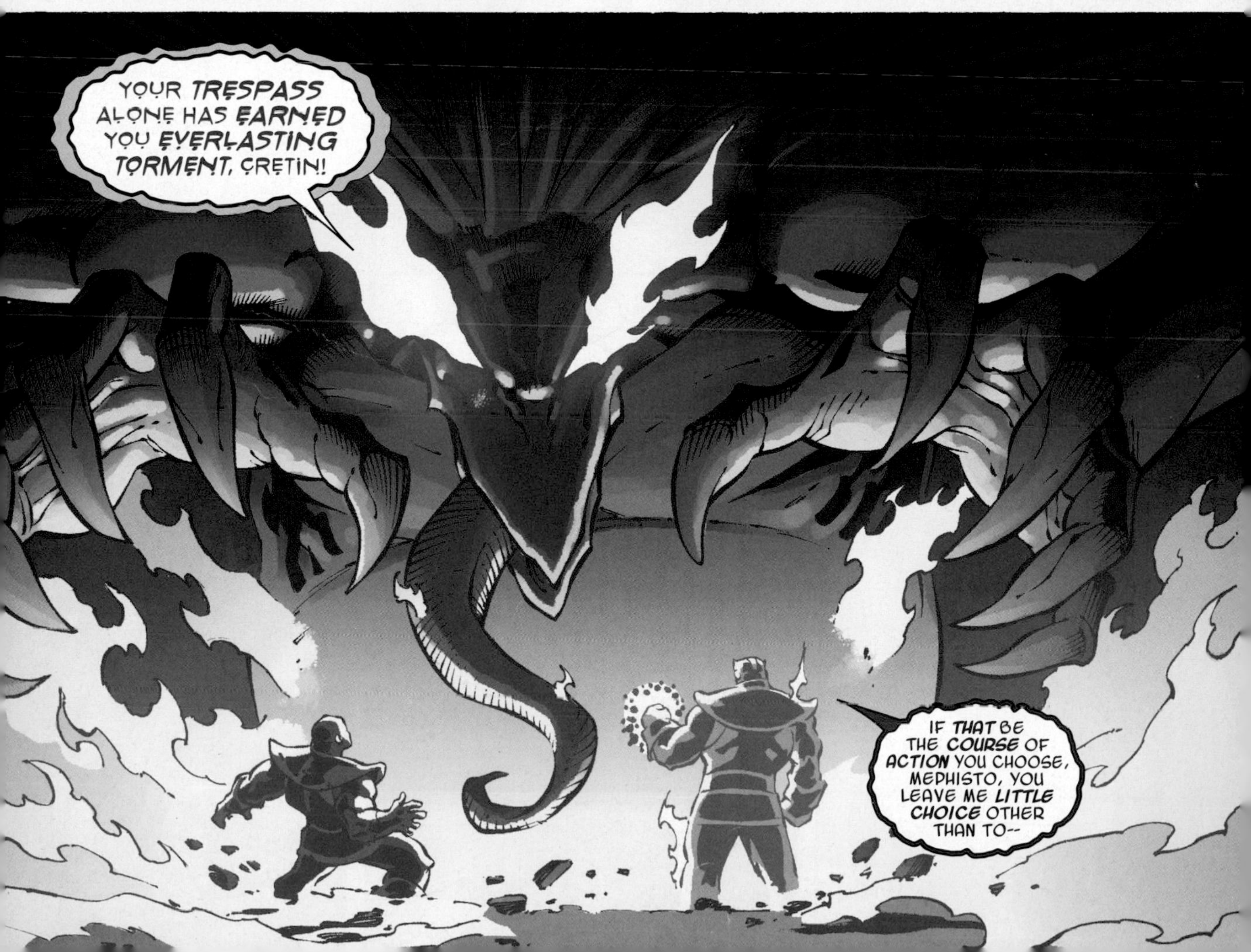
YOUR TRESPASS ALONE HAS EARNED YOU EVERLASTING TORMENT, CRETIN!
IF THAT BE THE COURSE OF ACTION YOU CHOOSE, MEPHISTO, YOU LEAVE ME LITTLE CHOICE OTHER THAN TO--

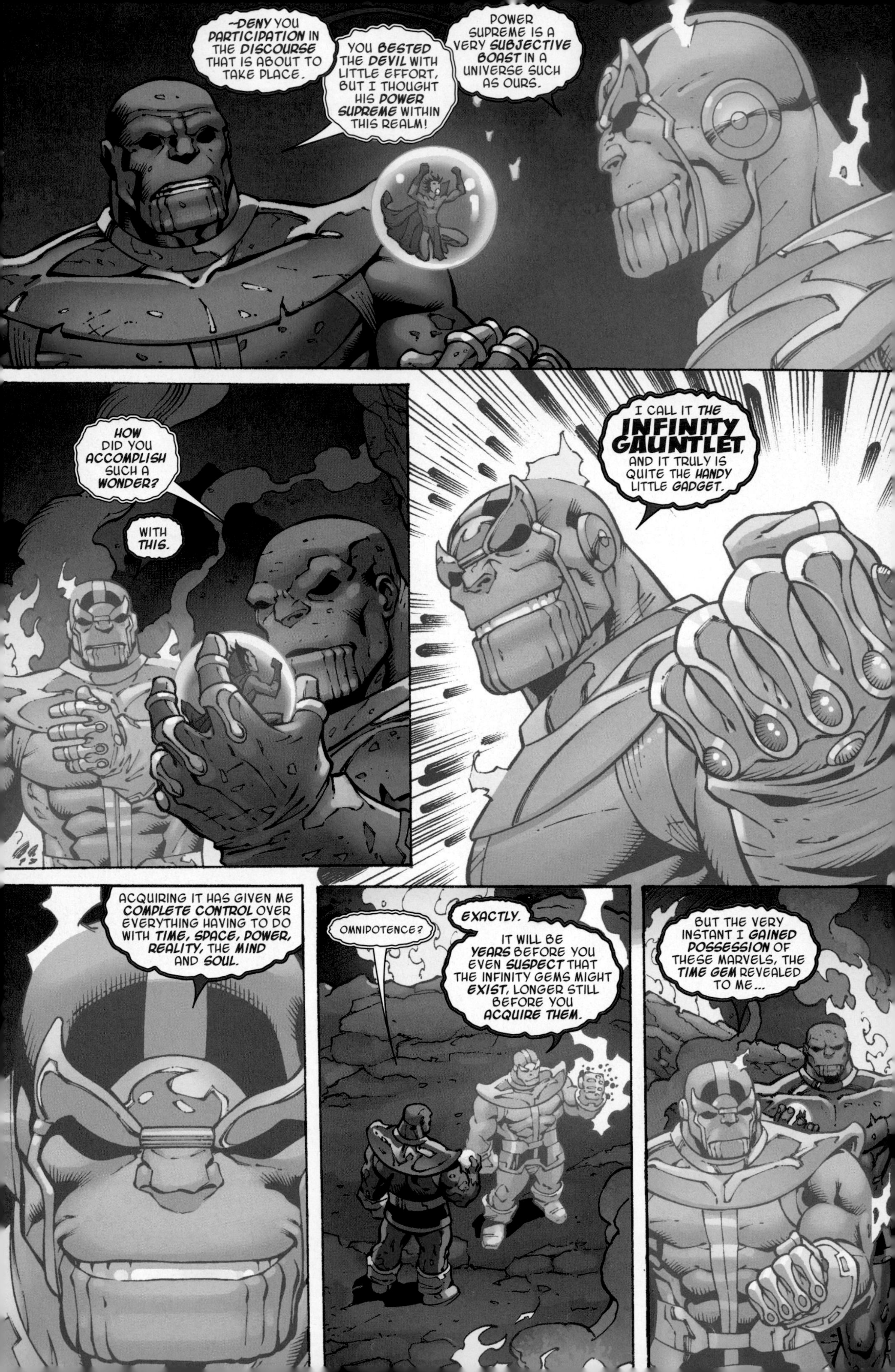

--DENY YOU PARTICIPATION IN THE DISCOURSE THAT IS ABOUT TO TAKE PLACE.
YOU BESTED THE DEVIL WITH LITTLE EFFORT, BUT I THOUGHT HIS POWER SUPREME WITHIN THIS REALM!
POWER SUPREME IS A VERY SUBJECTIVE BOAST IN A UNIVERSE SUCH AS OURS.
HOW DID YOU ACCOMPLISH SUCH A WONDER?
WITH THIS.
I CALL IT THE INFINITY GAUNTLET, AND IT TRULY IS QUITE THE HANDY LITTLE GADGET.
ACQUIRING IT HAS GIVEN ME COMPLETE CONTROL OVER EVERYTHING HAVING TO DO WITH TIME, SPACE, POWER, REALITY, THE MIND AND SOUL.
OMNIPOTENCE?
EXACTLY.
IT WILL BE YEARS BEFORE YOU EVEN SUSPECT THAT THE INFINITY GEMS MIGHT EXIST, LONGER STILL BEFORE YOU ACQUIRE THEM.
BUT THE VERY INSTANT I GAINED POSSESSION OF THESE MARVELS, THE TIME GEM REVEALED TO ME...

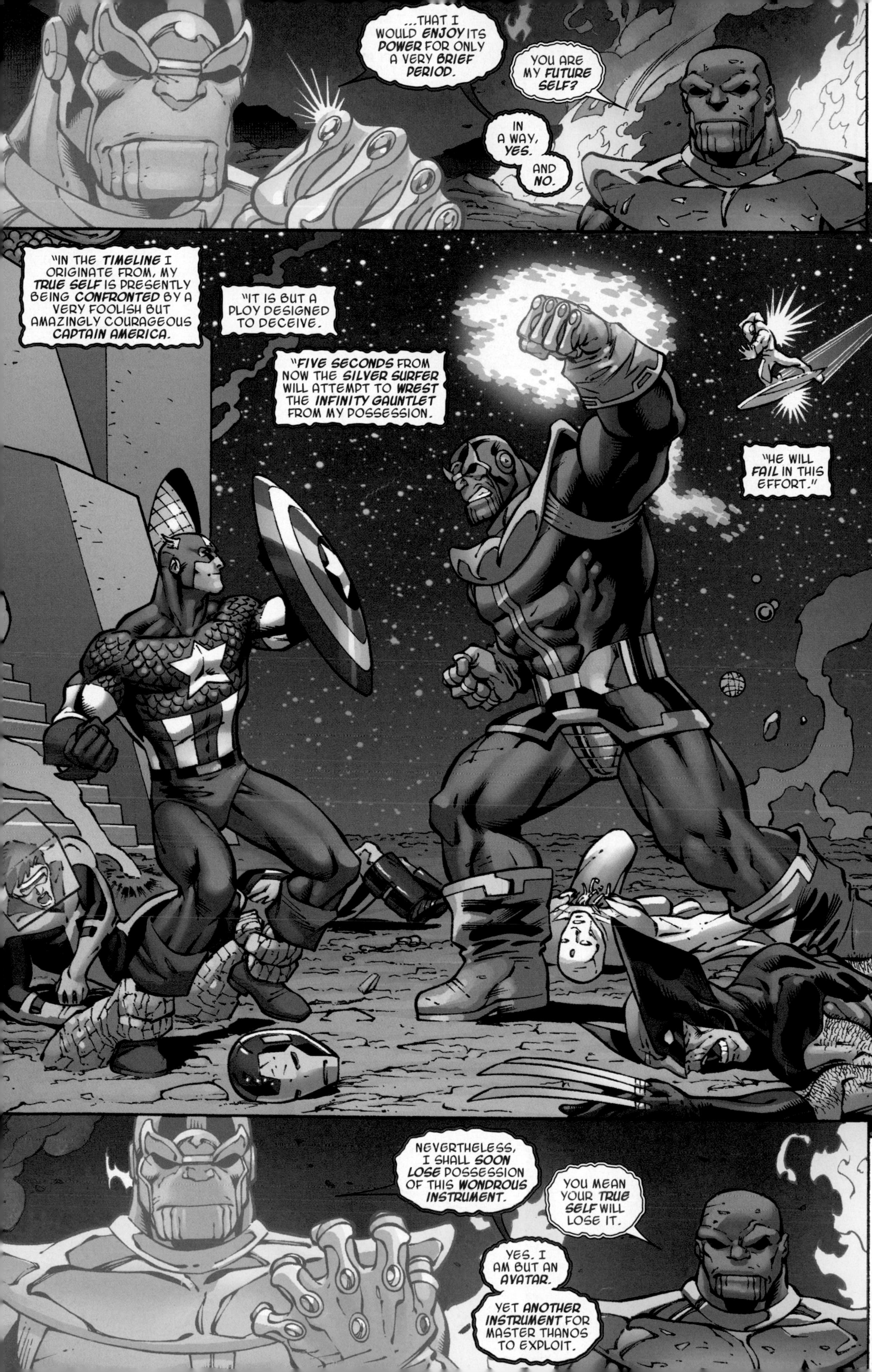

...THAT I WOULD ENJOY ITS POWER FOR ONLY A VERY BRIEF PERIOD.
YOU ARE MY FUTURE SELF?
IN A WAY, YES.
AND NO.
"IN THE TIMELINE I ORIGINATE FROM, MY TRUE SELF IS PRESENTLY BEING CONFRONTED BY A VERY FOOLISH BUT AMAZINGLY COURAGEOUS CAPTAIN AMERICA.
"IT IS BUT A PLOY DESIGNED TO DECEIVE.
"FIVE SECONDS FROM NOW THE SILVER SURFER WILL ATTEMPT TO WREST THE INFINITY GAUNTLET FROM MY POSSESSION.
"HE WILL FAIL IN THIS EFFORT."
NEVERTHELESS, I SHALL SOON LOSE POSSESSION OF THIS WONDROUS INSTRUMENT.
YOU MEAN YOUR TRUE SELF WILL LOSE IT.
YES. I AM BUT AN AVATAR.
YET ANOTHER INSTRUMENT FOR MASTER THANOS TO EXPLOIT.

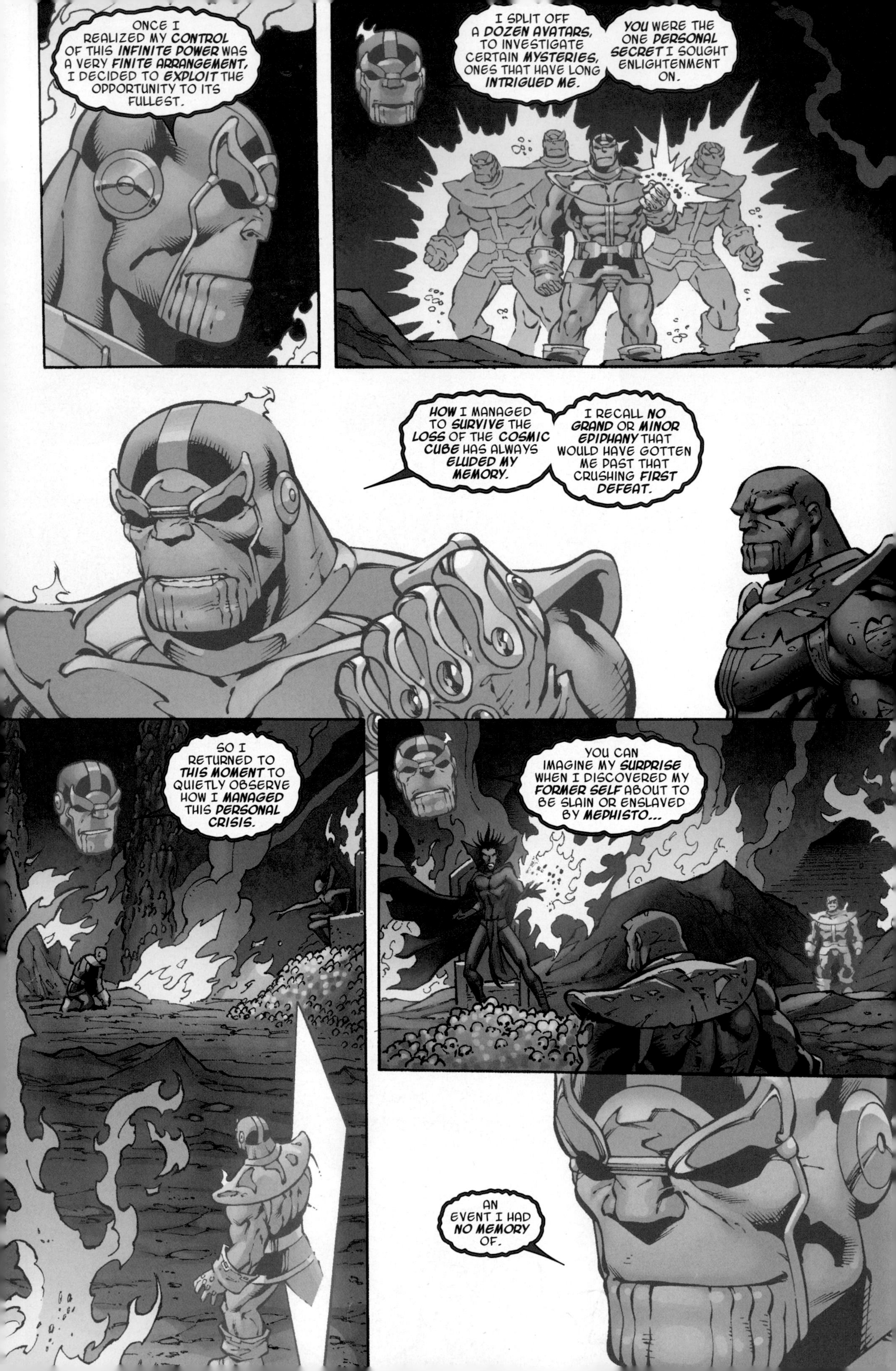
ONCE I REALIZED MY CONTROL OF THIS INFINITE POWER WAS A VERY FINITE ARRANGEMENT, I DECIDED TO EXPLOIT THE OPPORTUNITY TO ITS FULLEST.
I SPLIT OFF A DOZEN AVATARS, TO INVESTIGATE CERTAIN MYSTERIES, ONES THAT HAVE LONG INTRIGUED ME.
YOU WERE THE ONE PERSONAL SECRET I SOUGHT ENLIGHTENMENT ON.
HOW I MANAGED TO SURVIVE THE LOSS OF THE COSMIC CUBE HAS ALWAYS ELUDED MY MEMORY.
I RECALL NO GRAND OR MINOR EPIPHANY THAT WOULD HAVE GOTTEN ME PAST THAT CRUSHING FIRST DEFEAT.
SO I RETURNED TO THIS MOMENT TO QUIETLY OBSERVE HOW I MANAGED THIS PERSONAL CRISIS.
YOU CAN IMAGINE MY SURPRISE WHEN I DISCOVERED MY FORMER SELF ABOUT TO BE SLAIN OR ENSLAVED BY MEPHISTO...
AN EVENT I HAD NO MEMORY OF.

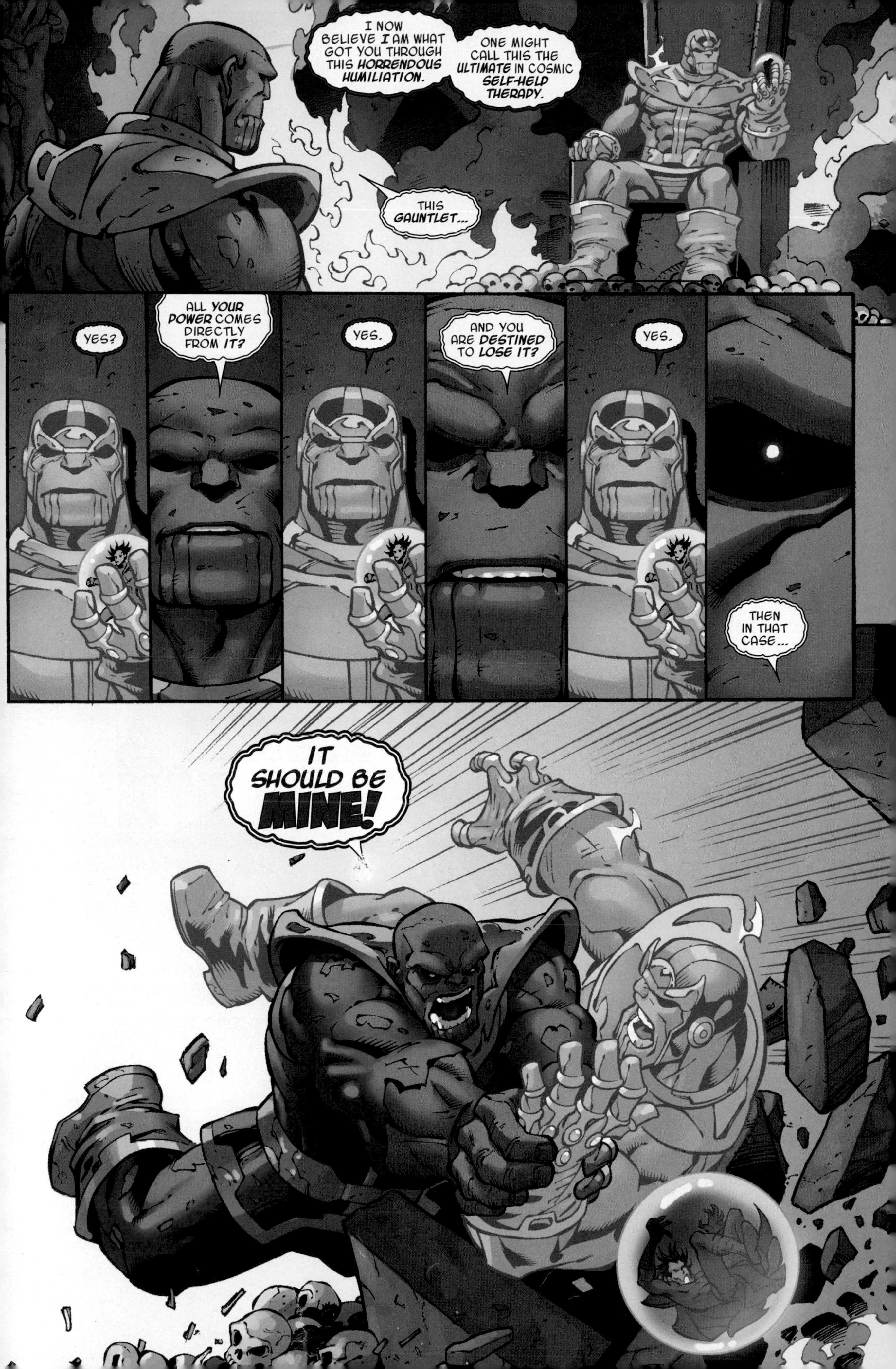

I NOW BELIEVE I AM WHAT GOT YOU THROUGH THIS HORRENDOUS HUMILIATION.
ONE MIGHT CALL THIS THE ULTIMATE IN COSMIC SELF-HELP THERAPY.
THIS GAUNTLET...
YES?
ALL YOUR POWER COMES DIRECTLY FROM IT?
YES.
AND YOU ARE DESTINED TO LOSE IT?
YES.
THEN IN THAT CASE...
IT SHOULD BE MINE!

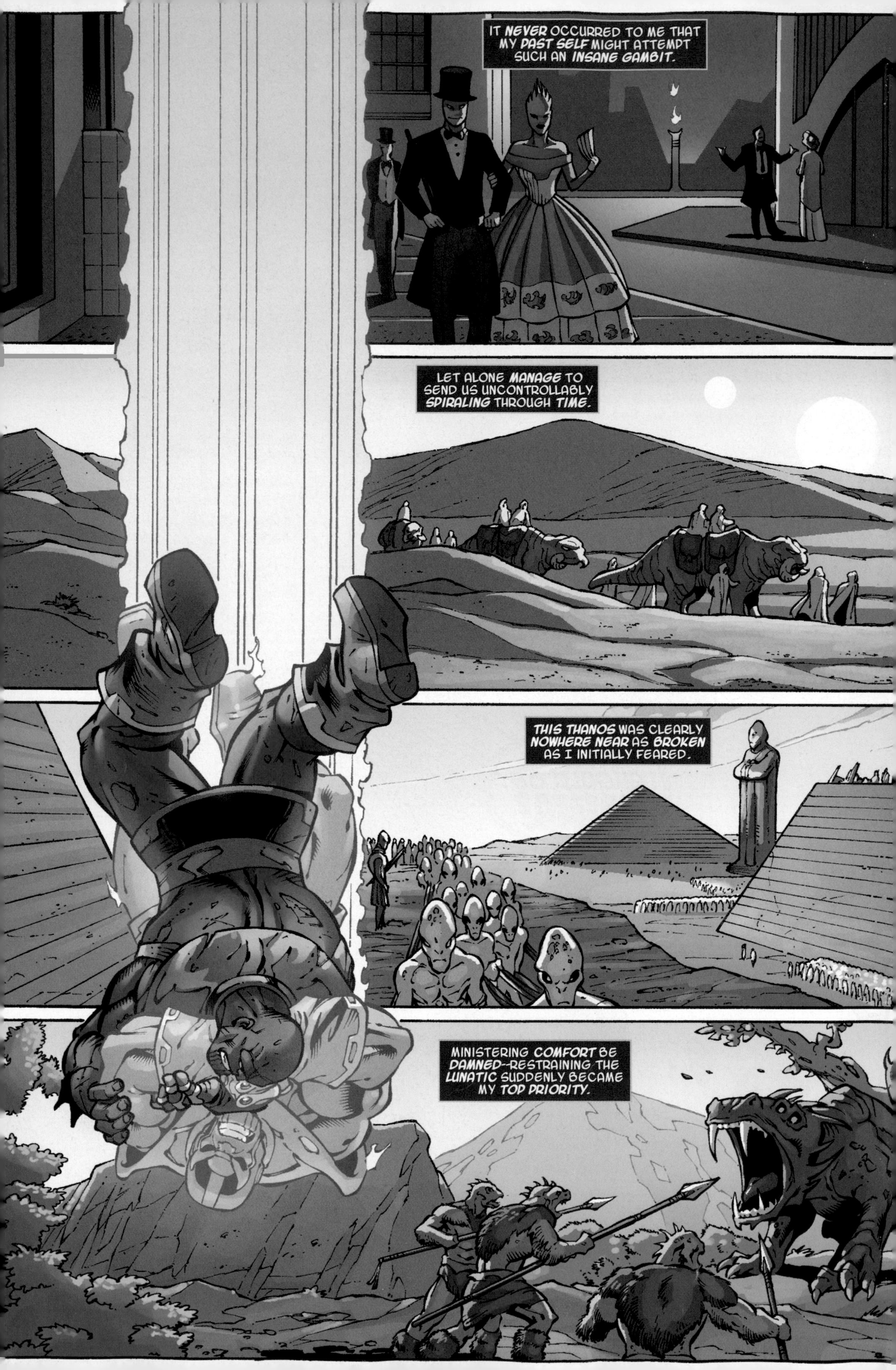
IT NEVER OCCURRED TO ME THAT MY PAST SELF MIGHT ATTEMPT SUCH AN INSANE GAMBIT.
LET ALONE MANAGE TO SEND US UNCONTROLLABLY SPIRALING THROUGH TIME.
THIS THANOS WAS CLEARLY NOWHERE NEAR AS BROKEN AS I INITIALLY FEARED.
MINISTERING COMFORT BE DAMNED--RESTRAINING THE LUNATIC SUDDENLY BECAME MY TOP PRIORITY.

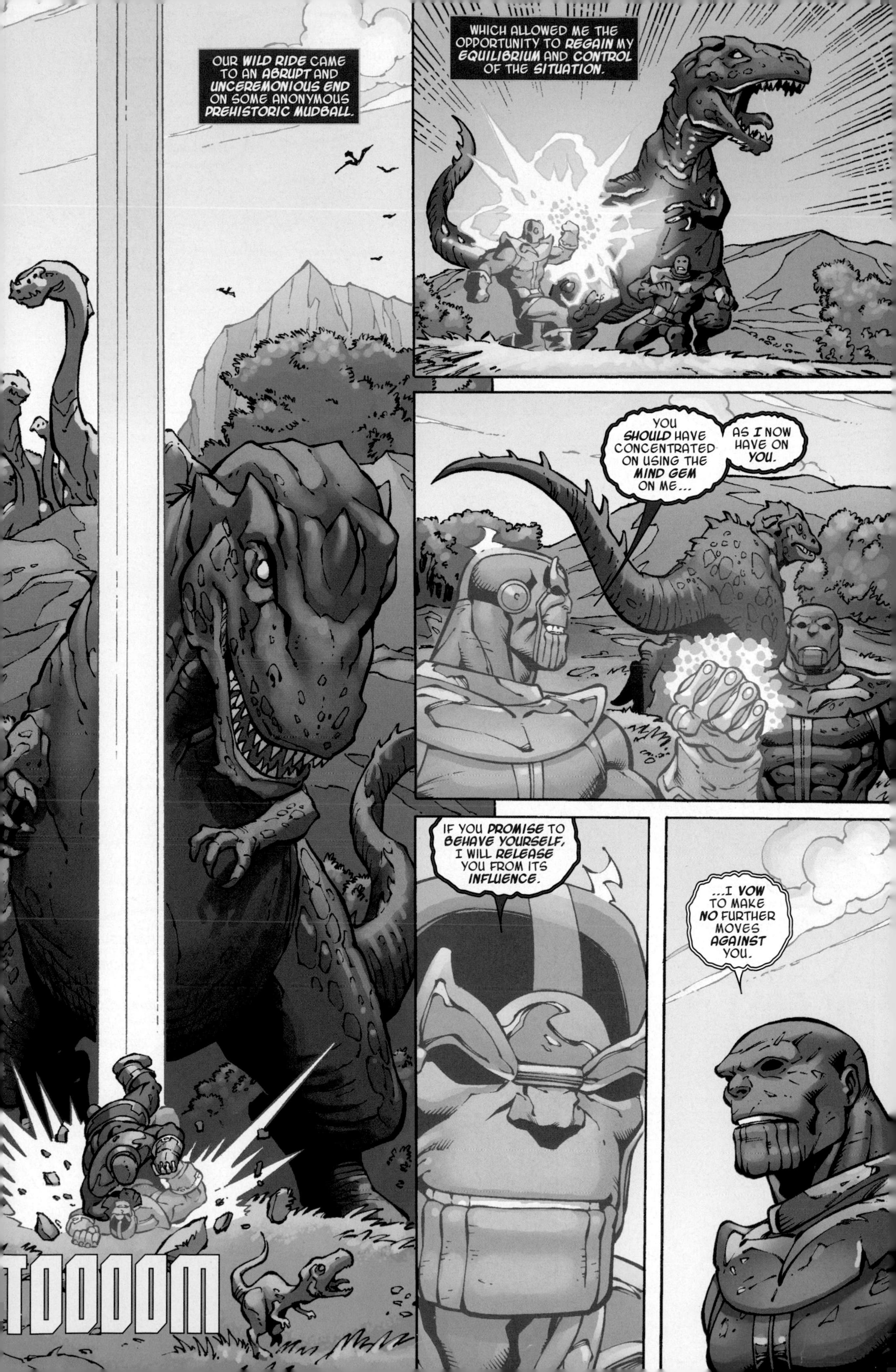
OUR WILD RIDE CAME TO AN ABRUPT AND UNCEREMONIOUS END ON SOME ANONYMOUS PREHISTORIC MUDBALL.
TOOOOM
WHICH ALLOWED ME THE OPPORTUNITY TO REGAIN MY EQUILIBRIUM AND CONTROL OF THE SITUATION.
YOU SHOULD HAVE CONCENTRATED ON USING THE MIND GEM ON ME...
AS I NOW HAVE ON YOU.
IF YOU PROMISE TO BEHAVE YOURSELF, I WILL RELEASE YOU FROM ITS INFLUENCE.
...I VOW TO MAKE NO FURTHER MOVES AGAINST YOU.

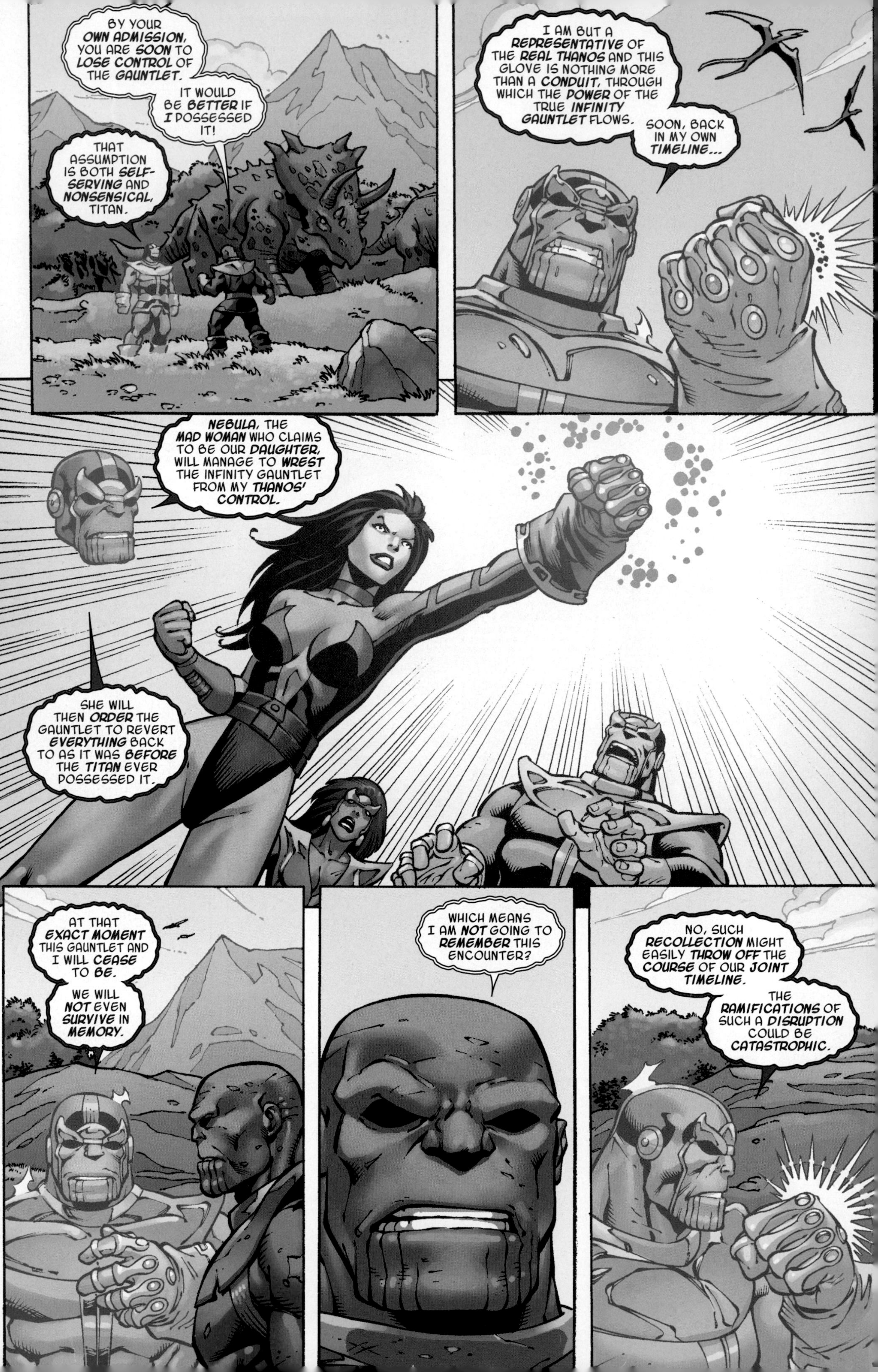

BY YOUR OWN ADMISSION, YOU ARE SOON TO LOSE CONTROL OF THE GAUNTLET.
IT WOULD BE BETTER IF I POSSESSED IT!
THAT ASSUMPTION IS BOTH SELF-SERVING AND NONSENSICAL, TITAN.
I AM BUT A REPRESENTATIVE OF THE REAL THANOS AND THIS GLOVE IS NOTHING MORE THAN A CONDUIT, THROUGH WHICH THE POWER OF THE TRUE INFINITY GAUNTLET FLOWS.
SOON, BACK IN MY OWN TIMELINE...
NEBULA, THE MAD WOMAN WHO CLAIMS TO BE OUR DAUGHTER, WILL MANAGE TO WREST THE INFINITY GAUNTLET FROM MY THANOS' CONTROL.
SHE WILL THEN ORDER THE GAUNTLET TO REVERT EVERYTHING BACK TO AS IT WAS BEFORE THE TITAN EVER POSSESSED IT.
AT THAT EXACT MOMENT THIS GAUNTLET AND I WILL CEASE TO BE.
WE WILL NOT EVEN SURVIVE IN MEMORY.
WHICH MEANS I AM NOT GOING TO REMEMBER THIS ENCOUNTER?
NO, SUCH RECOLLECTION MIGHT EASILY THROW OFF THE COURSE OF OUR JOINT TIMELINE.
THE RAMIFICATIONS OF SUCH A DISRUPTION COULD BE CATASTROPHIC.

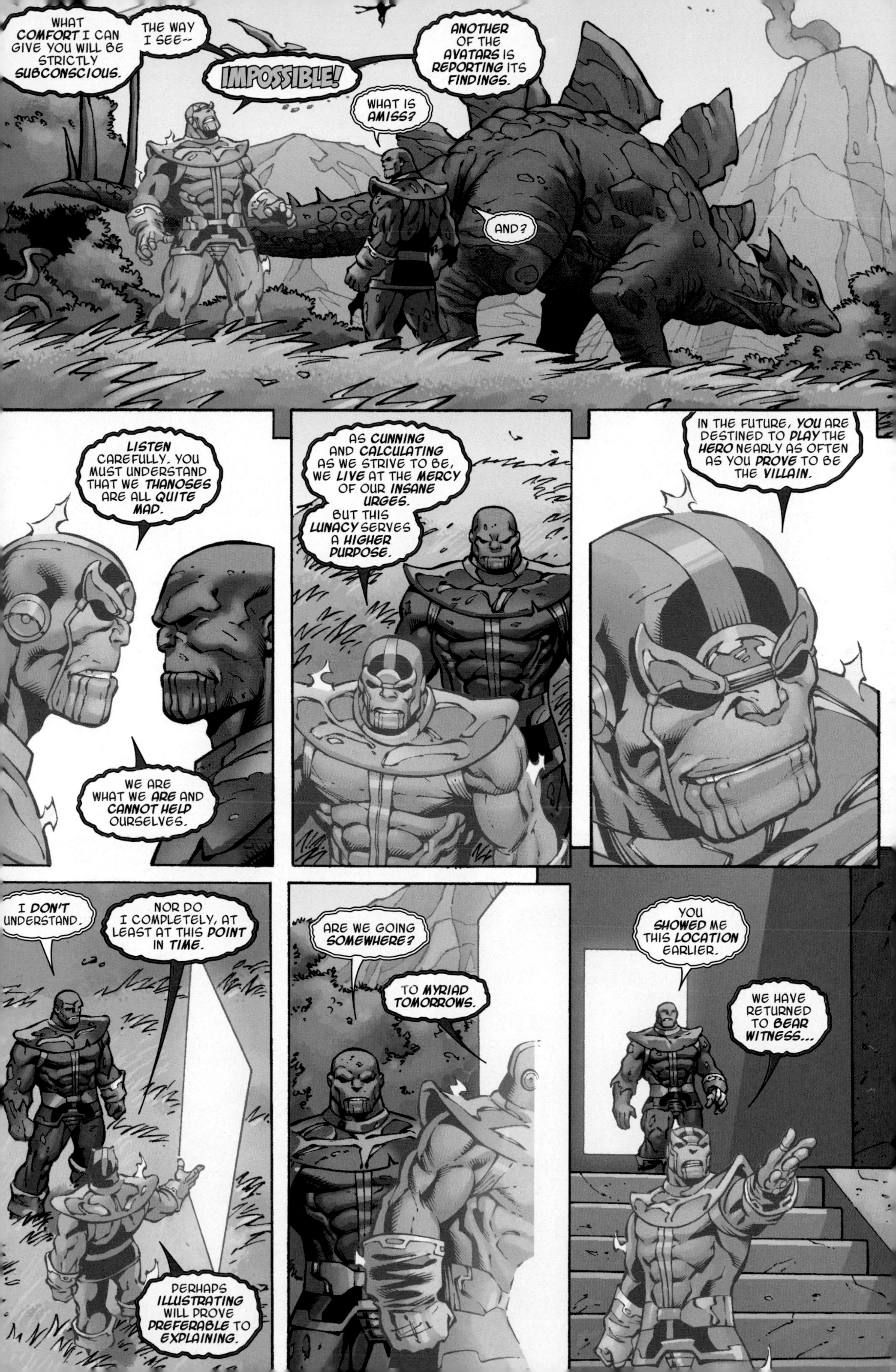

WHAT COMFORT I CAN GIVE YOU WILL BE STRICTLY SUBCONSCIOUS.
THE WAY I SEE--
IMPOSSIBLE!
ANOTHER OF THE AVATARS IS REPORTING ITS FINDINGS.
WHAT IS AMISS?
AND?
LISTEN CAREFULLY. YOU MUST UNDERSTAND THAT WE THANOSES ARE ALL QUITE MAD.
WE ARE WHAT WE ARE AND CANNOT HELP OURSELVES.
AS CUNNING AND CALCULATING AS WE STRIVE TO BE, WE LIVE AT THE MERCY OF OUR INSANE URGES.
BUT THIS LUNACY SERVES A HIGHER PURPOSE.
IN THE FUTURE, YOU ARE DESTINED TO PLAY THE HERO NEARLY AS OFTEN AS YOU PROVE TO BE THE VILLAIN.
I DON'T UNDERSTAND.
NOR DO I COMPLETELY, AT LEAST AT THIS POINT IN TIME.
PERHAPS ILLUSTRATING WILL PROVE PREFERABLE TO EXPLAINING.
ARE WE GOING SOMEWHERE?
TO MYRIAD TOMORROWS.
YOU SHOWED ME THIS LOCATION EARLIER.
WE HAVE RETURNED TO BEAR WITNESS...

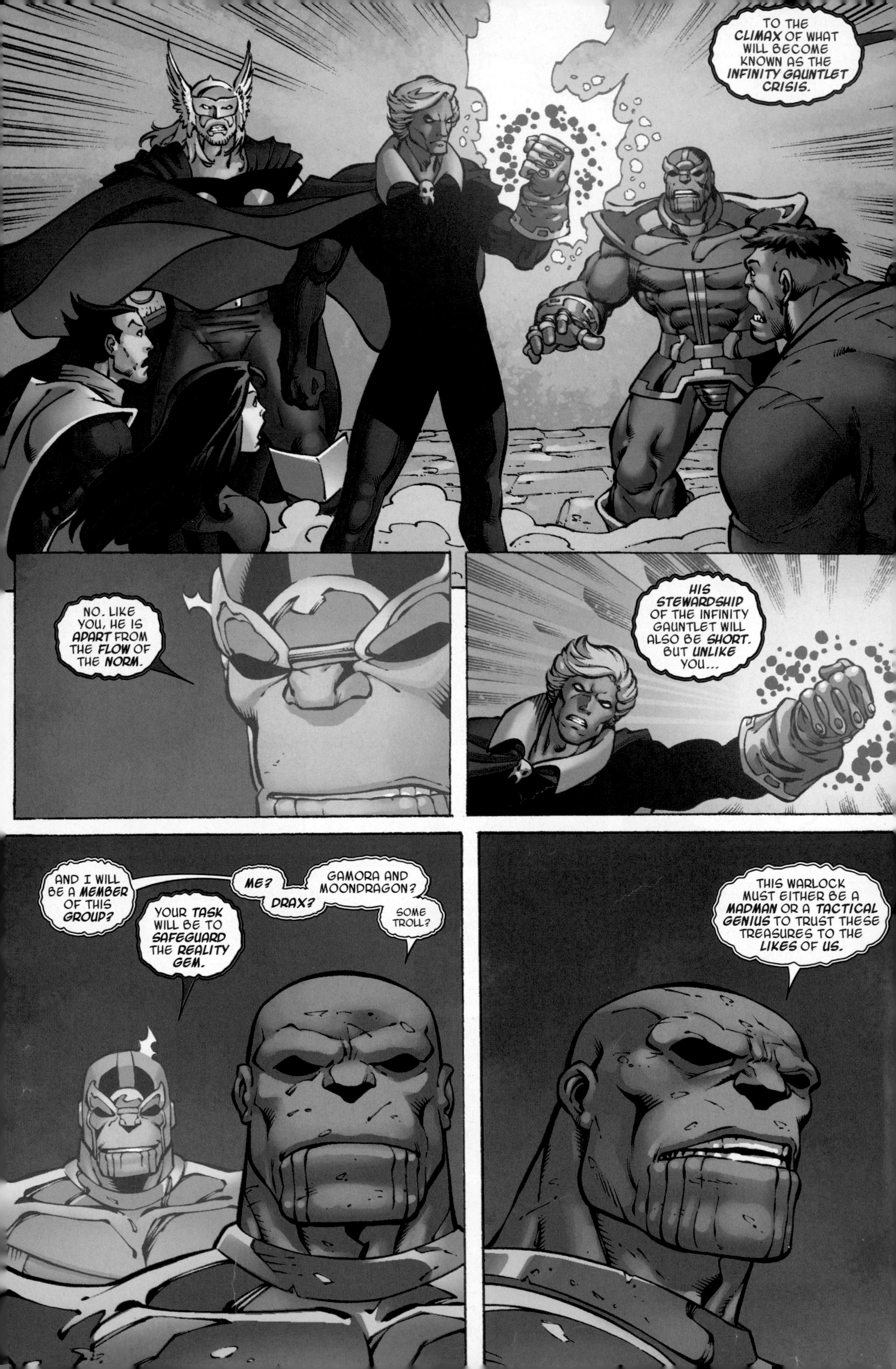
TO THE CLIMAX OF WHAT WILL BECOME KNOWN AS THE INFINITY GAUNTLET CRISIS.
NO. LIKE YOU, HE IS APART FROM THE FLOW OF THE NORM.
HIS STEWARDSHIP OF THE INFINITY GAUNTLET WILL ALSO BE SHORT. BUT UNLIKE YOU...
AND I WILL BE A MEMBER OF THIS GROUP?
YOUR TASK WILL BE TO SAFEGUARD THE REALITY GEM.
ME?
DRAX?
GAMORA AND MOONDRAGON?
SOME TROLL?
THIS WARLOCK MUST EITHER BE A MADMAN OR A TACTICAL GENIUS TO TRUST THESE TREASURES TO THE LIKES OF US.

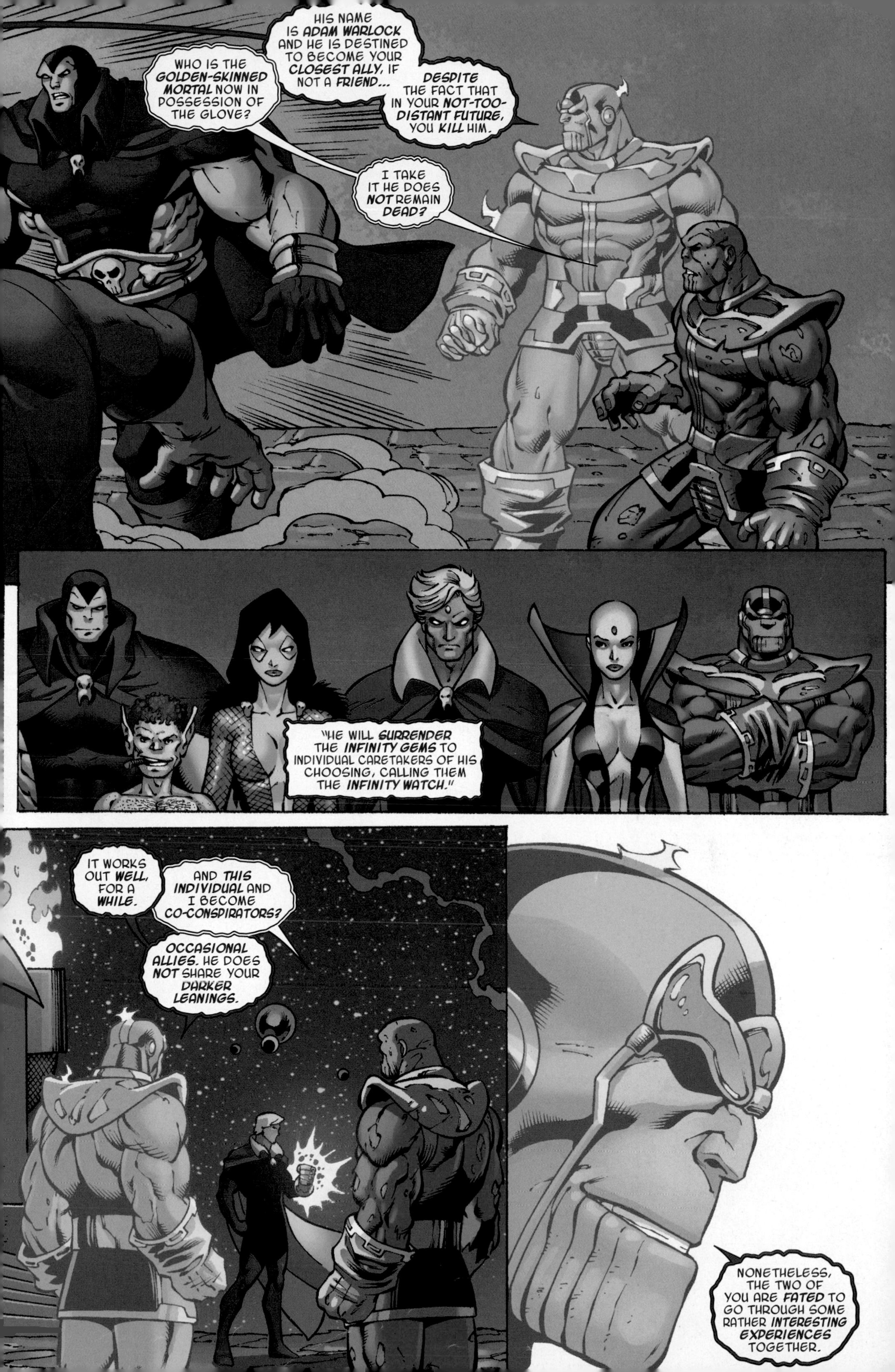
WHO IS THE GOLDEN-SKINNED MORTAL NOW IN POSSESSION OF THE GLOVE?
HIS NAME IS ADAM WARLOCK AND HE IS DESTINED TO BECOME YOUR CLOSEST ALLY, IF NOT A FRIEND...
DESPITE THE FACT THAT IN YOUR NOT-TOO-DISTANT FUTURE, YOU KILL HIM.
I TAKE IT HE DOES NOT REMAIN DEAD?
"HE WILL SURRENDER THE INFINITY GEMS TO INDIVIDUAL CARETAKERS OF HIS CHOOSING, CALLING THEM THE INFINITY WATCH."
IT WORKS OUT WELL, FOR A WHILE.
AND THIS INDIVIDUAL AND I BECOME CO-CONSPIRATORS?
OCCASIONAL ALLIES. HE DOES NOT SHARE YOUR DARKER LEANINGS.
NONETHELESS, THE TWO OF YOU ARE FATED TO GO THROUGH SOME RATHER INTERESTING EXPERIENCES TOGETHER.

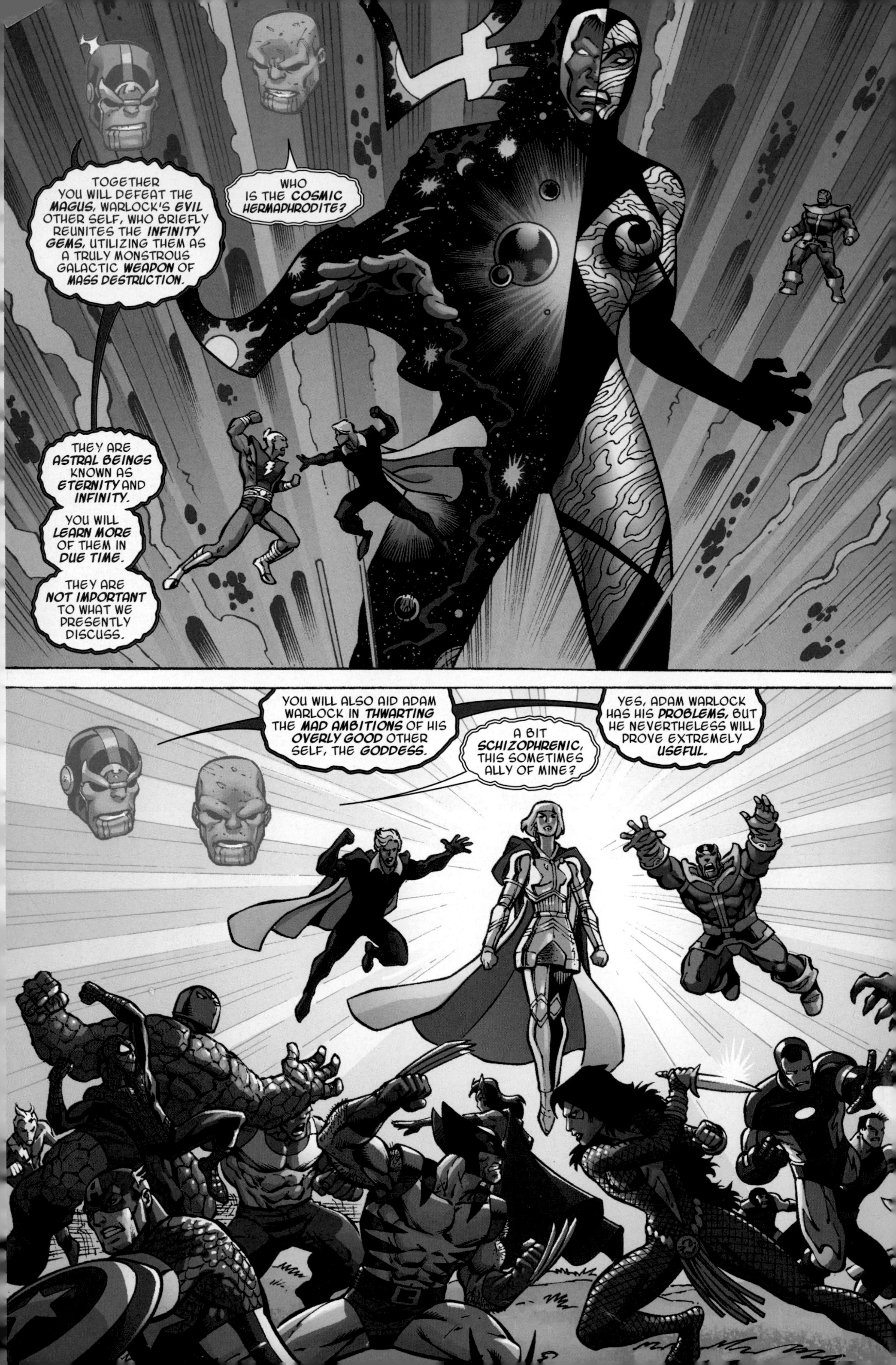
TOGETHER YOU WILL DEFEAT THE MAGUS, WARLOCK'S EVIL OTHER SELF, WHO BRIEFLY REUNITES THE INFINITY GEMS, UTILIZING THEM AS A TRULY MONSTROUS GALACTIC WEAPON OF MASS DESTRUCTION.
WHO IS THE COSMIC HERMAPHRODITE?
THEY ARE ASTRAL BEINGS KNOWN AS ETERNITY AND INFINITY.
YOU WILL LEARN MORE OF THEM IN DUE TIME.
THEY ARE NOT IMPORTANT TO WHAT WE PRESENTLY DISCUSS.
YOU WILL ALSO AID ADAM WARLOCK IN THWARTING THE MAD AMBITIONS OF HIS OVERLY GOOD OTHER SELF, THE GODDESS.
A BIT SCHIZOPHRENIC, THIS SOMETIMES ALLY OF MINE?
YES, ADAM WARLOCK HAS HIS PROBLEMS, BUT HE NEVERTHELESS WILL PROVE EXTREMELY USEFUL.

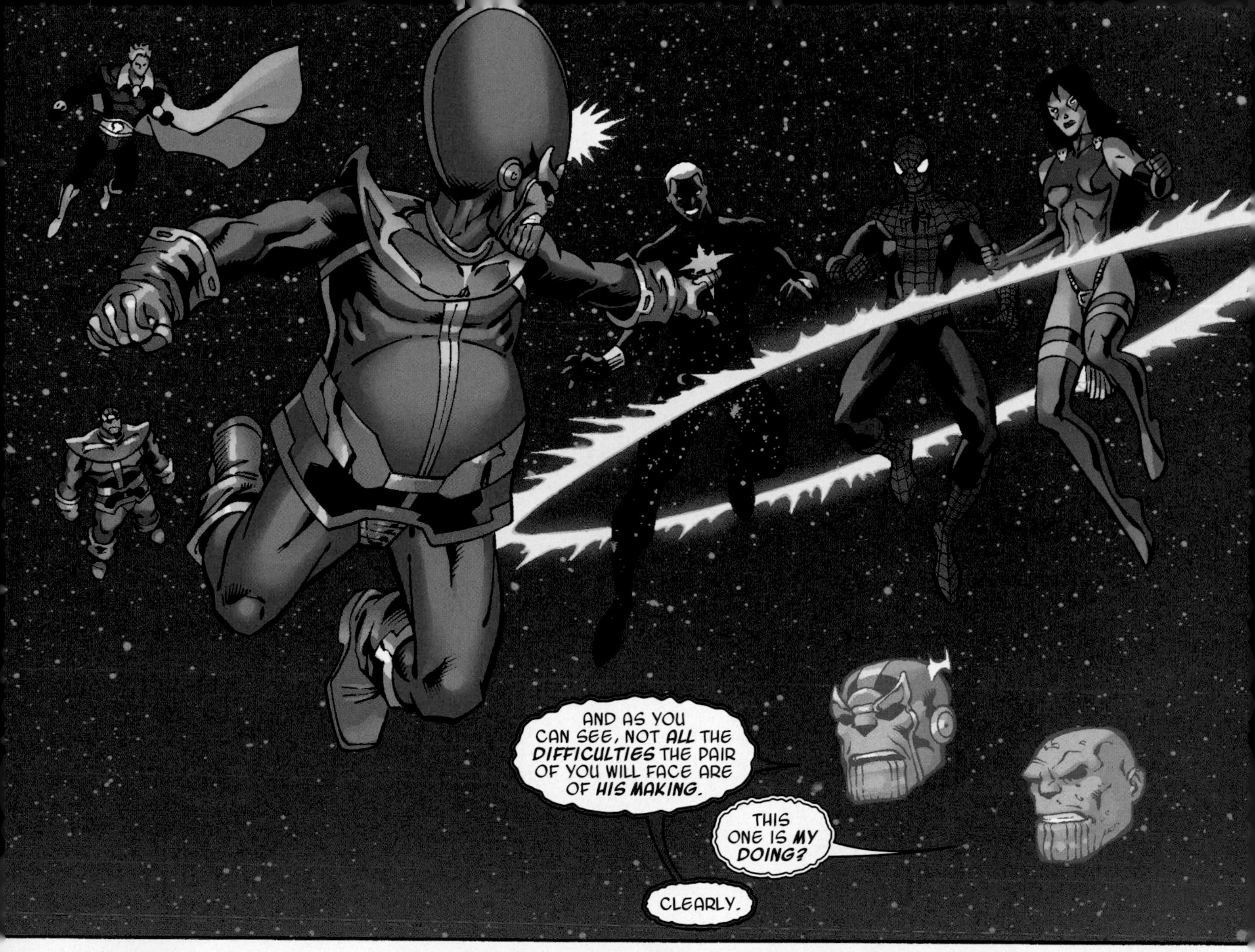
AND AS YOU CAN SEE, NOT ALL THE DIFFICULTIES THE PAIR OF YOU WILL FACE ARE OF HIS MAKING.
THIS ONE IS MY DOING?
CLEARLY.

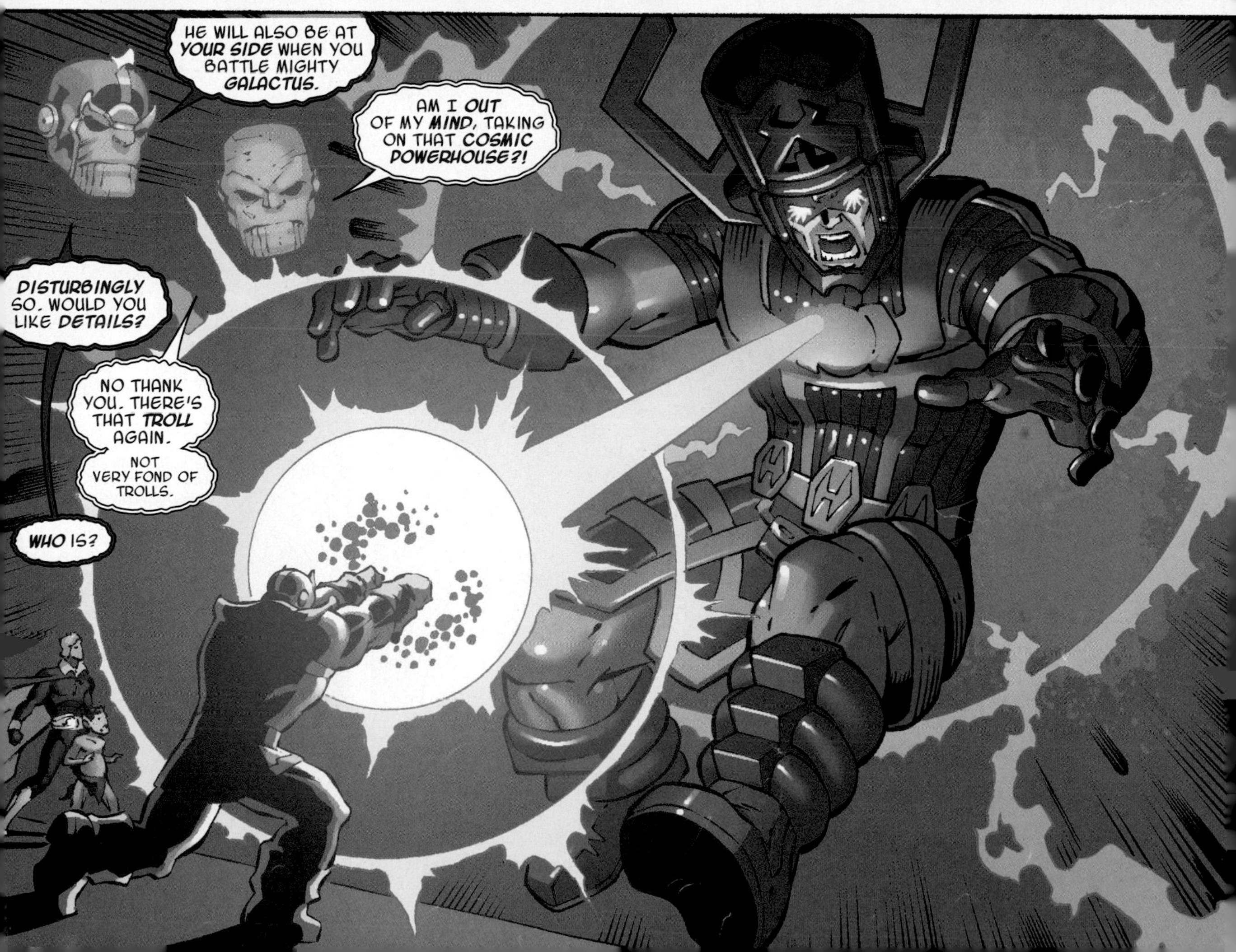
HE WILL ALSO BE AT YOUR SIDE WHEN YOU BATTLE MIGHTY GALACTUS.
AM I OUT OF MY MIND, TAKING ON THAT COSMIC POWERHOUSE?!
DISTURBINGLY SO. WOULD YOU LIKE DETAILS?
NO THANK YOU. THERE'S THAT TROLL AGAIN.
NOT VERY FOND OF TROLLS.
WHO IS?

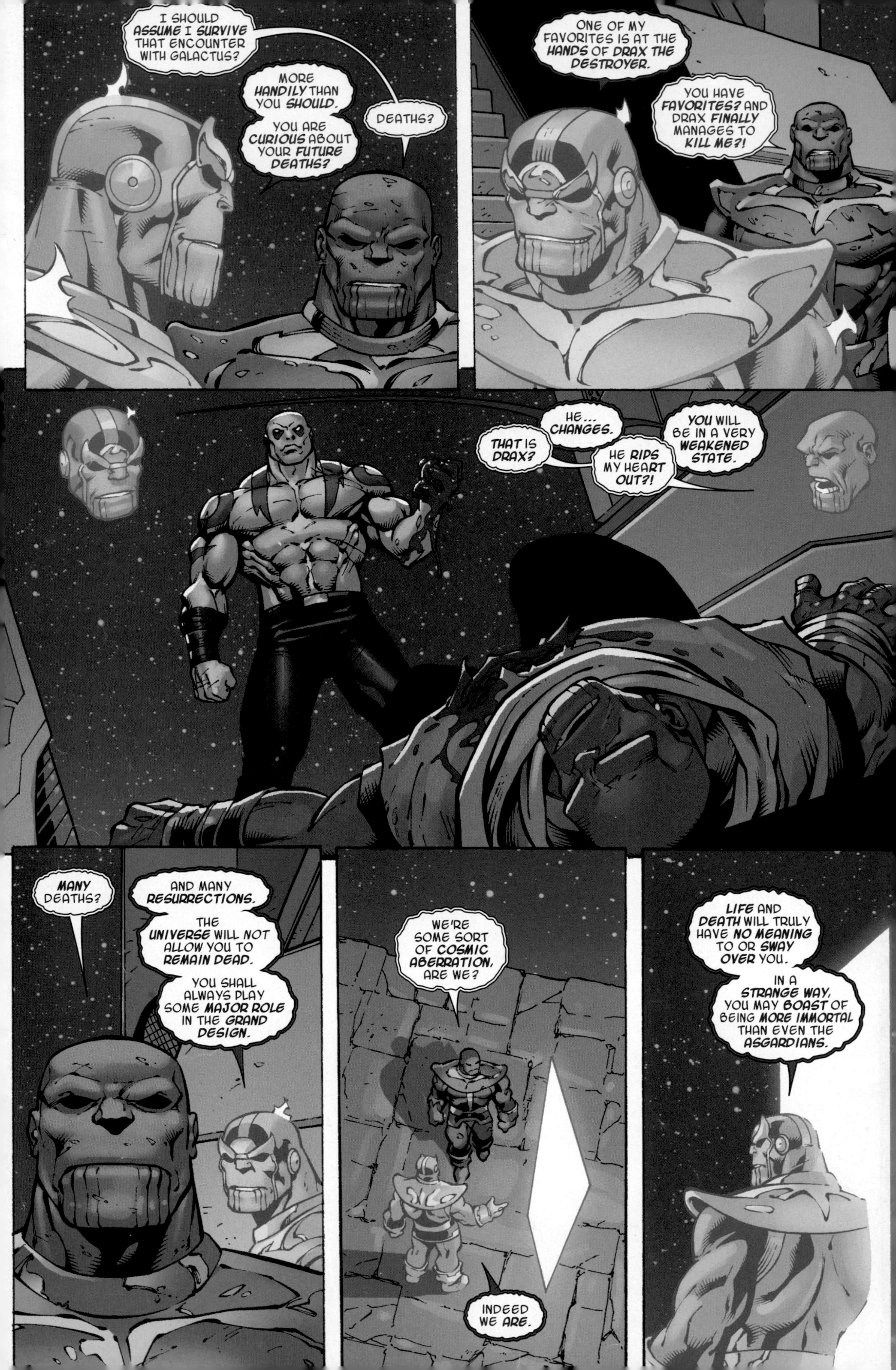

I SHOULD ASSUME I SURVIVE THAT ENCOUNTER WITH GALACTUS?
MORE HANDILY THAN YOU SHOULD.
YOU ARE CURIOUS ABOUT YOUR FUTURE DEATHS?
DEATHS?
ONE OF MY FAVORITES IS AT THE HANDS OF DRAX THE DESTROYER.
YOU HAVE FAVORITES? AND DRAX FINALLY MANAGES TO KILL ME?!
THAT IS DRAX?
HE... CHANGES.
HE RIPS MY HEART OUT?!
YOU WILL BE IN A VERY WEAKENED STATE.
MANY DEATHS?
AND MANY RESURRECTIONS.
THE UNIVERSE WILL NOT ALLOW YOU TO REMAIN DEAD.
YOU SHALL ALWAYS PLAY SOME MAJOR ROLE IN THE GRAND DESIGN.
WE'RE SOME SORT OF COSMIC ABERRATION, ARE WE?
INDEED WE ARE.
LIFE AND DEATH WILL TRULY HAVE NO MEANING TO OR SWAY OVER YOU.
IN A STRANGE WAY, YOU MAY BOAST OF BEING MORE IMMORTAL THAN EVEN THE ASGARDIANS.

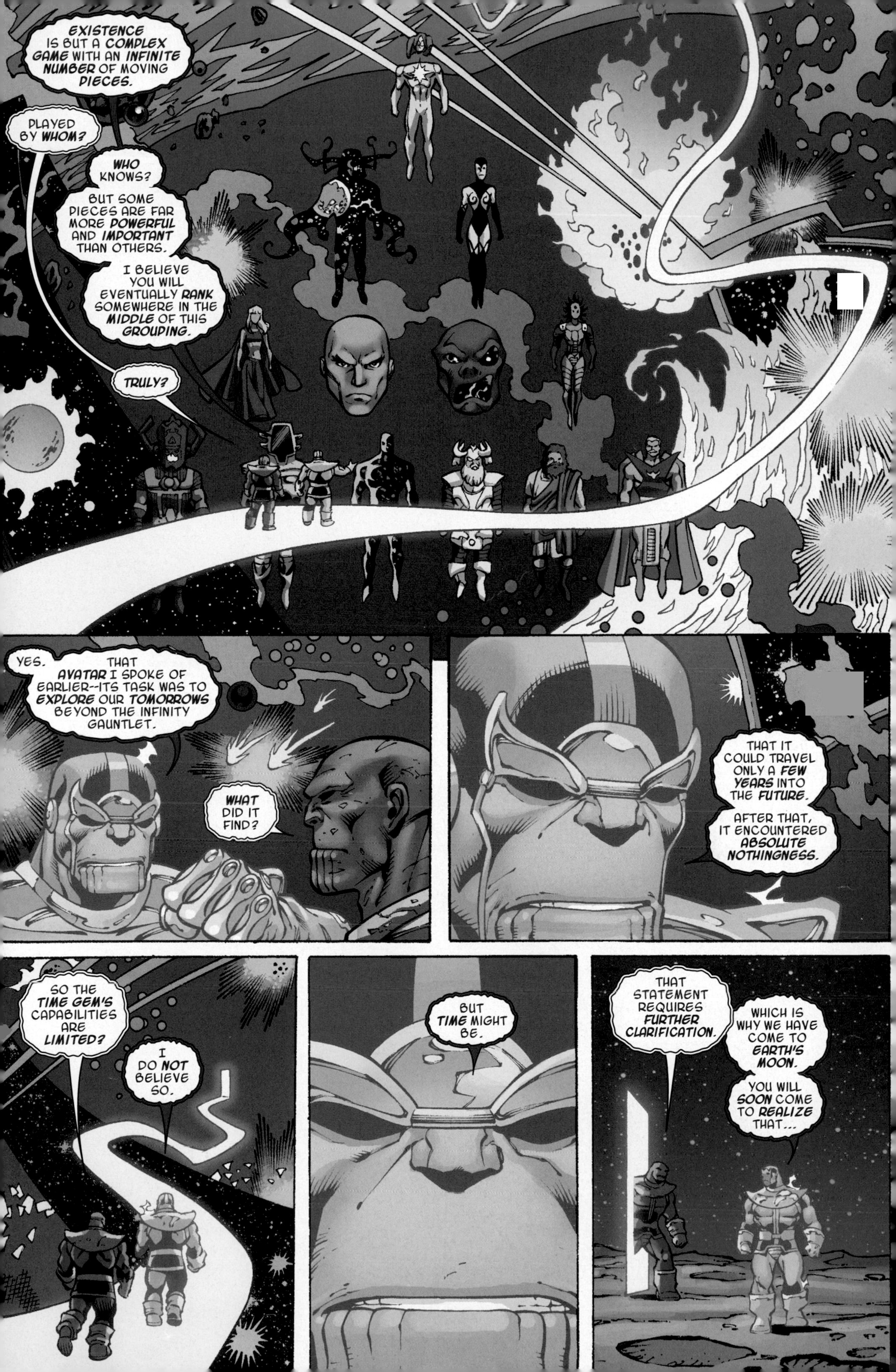
EXISTENCE IS BUT A COMPLEX GAME WITH AN INFINITE NUMBER OF MOVING PIECES.
PLAYED BY WHOM?
WHO KNOWS?
BUT SOME PIECES ARE FAR MORE POWERFUL AND IMPORTANT THAN OTHERS.
I BELIEVE YOU WILL EVENTUALLY RANK SOMEWHERE IN THE MIDDLE OF THIS GROUPING.
TRULY?
YES.
THAT AVATAR I SPOKE OF EARLIER--ITS TASK WAS TO EXPLORE OUR TOMORROWS BEYOND THE INFINITY GAUNTLET.
WHAT DID IT FIND?
THAT IT COULD TRAVEL ONLY A FEW YEARS INTO THE FUTURE.
AFTER THAT, IT ENCOUNTERED ABSOLUTE NOTHINGNESS.
SO THE TIME GEM'S CAPABILITIES ARE LIMITED?
I DO NOT BELIEVE SO.
BUT TIME MIGHT BE.
THAT STATEMENT REQUIRES FURTHER CLARIFICATION.
WHICH IS WHY WE HAVE COME TO EARTH'S MOON.
YOU WILL SOON COME TO REALIZE THAT...

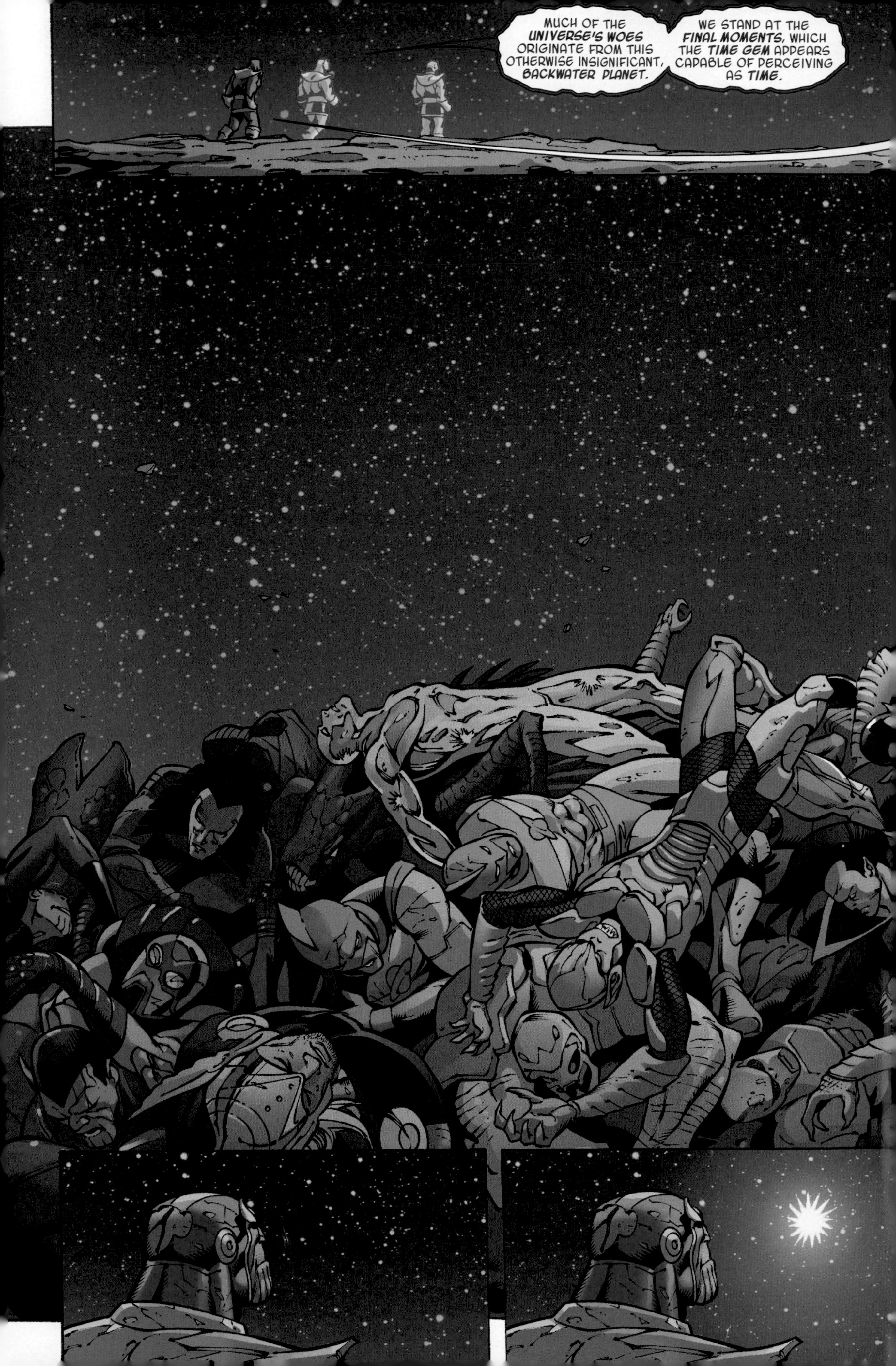
MUCH OF THE UNIVERSE'S WOES ORIGINATE FROM THIS OTHERWISE INSIGNIFICANT, BACKWATER PLANET.
WE STAND AT THE FINAL MOMENTS, WHICH THE TIME GEM APPEARS CAPABLE OF PERCEIVING AS TIME.

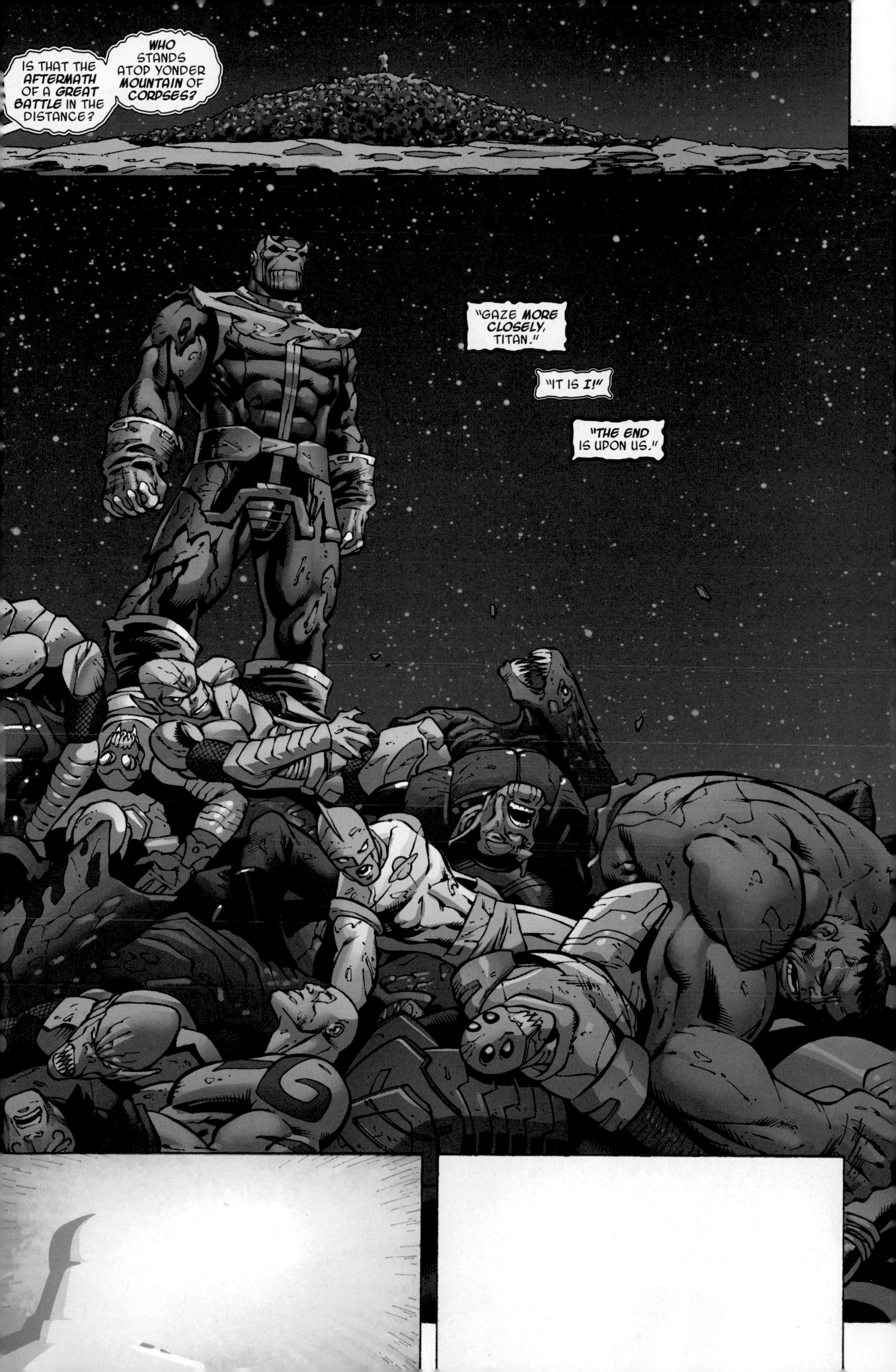
IS THAT THE AFTERMATH OF A GREAT BATTLE IN THE DISTANCE?
WHO STANDS ATOP YONDER MOUNTAIN OF CORPSES?
"GAZE MORE CLOSELY, TITAN."
"IT IS I!"
"THE END IS UPON US."

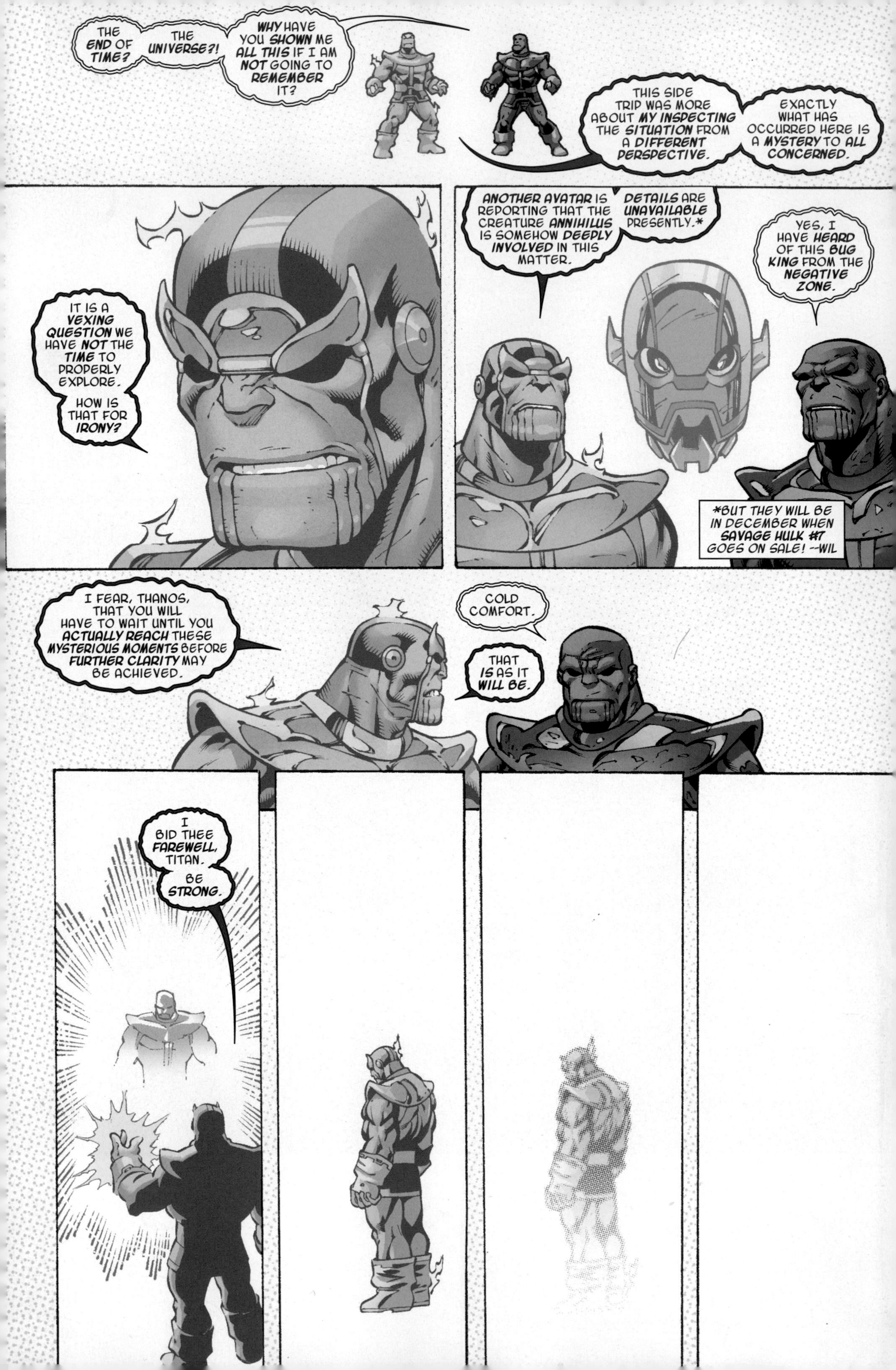
THE END OF TIME?
THE UNIVERSE?!
WHY HAVE YOU SHOWN ME ALL THIS IF I AM NOT GOING TO REMEMBER IT?
THIS SIDE TRIP WAS MORE ABOUT MY INSPECTING THE SITUATION FROM A DIFFERENT PERSPECTIVE.
EXACTLY WHAT HAS OCCURRED HERE IS A MYSTERY TO ALL CONCERNED.
IT IS A VEXING QUESTION WE HAVE NOT THE TIME TO PROPERLY EXPLORE.
HOW IS THAT FOR IRONY?
ANOTHER AVATAR IS REPORTING THAT THE CREATURE ANNIHILUS IS SOMEHOW DEEPLY INVOLVED IN THIS MATTER.
DETAILS ARE UNAVAILABLE PRESENTLY.*
YES, I HAVE HEARD OF THIS BUG KING FROM THE NEGATIVE ZONE.
*BUT THEY WILL BE IN DECEMBER WHEN SAVAGE HULK #7 GOES ON SALE! --WIL
I FEAR, THANOS, THAT YOU WILL HAVE TO WAIT UNTIL YOU ACTUALLY REACH THESE MYSTERIOUS MOMENTS BEFORE FURTHER CLARITY MAY BE ACHIEVED.
COLD COMFORT.
THAT IS AS IT WILL BE.
I BID THEE FAREWELL, TITAN.
BE STRONG.

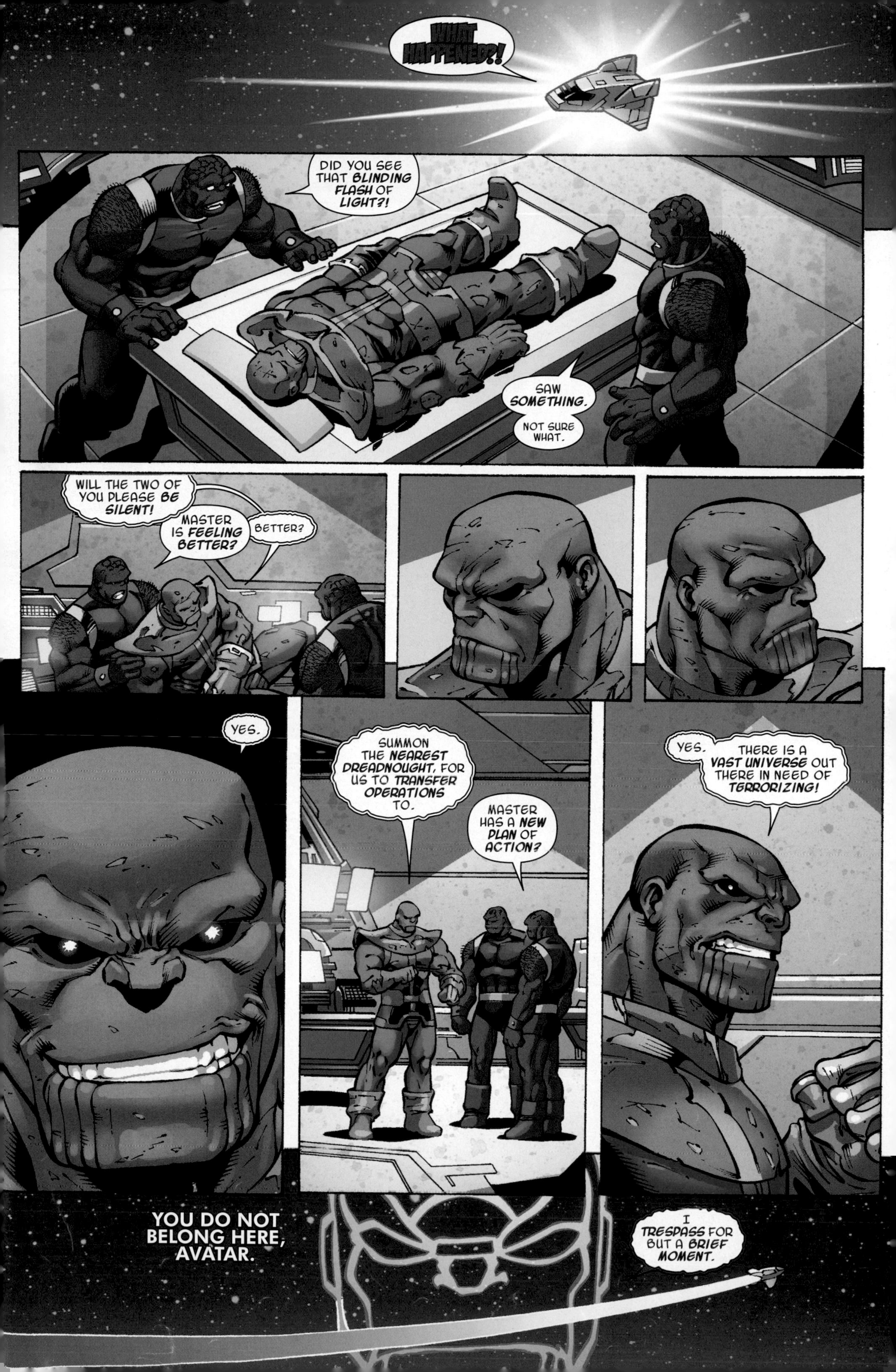
WHAT HAPPENED?!
DID YOU SEE THAT BLINDING FLASH OF LIGHT?!
SAW SOMETHING.
NOT SURE WHAT.
WILL THE TWO OF YOU PLEASE BE SILENT!
MASTER IS FEELING BETTER?
BETTER?
YES.
SUMMON THE NEAREST DREADNOUGHT, FOR US TO TRANSFER OPERATIONS TO.
MASTER HAS A NEW PLAN OF ACTION?
YES.
THERE IS A VAST UNIVERSE OUT THERE IN NEED OF TERRORIZING!
YOU DO NOT BELONG HERE, AVATAR.
I TRESPASS FOR BUT A BRIEF MOMENT.

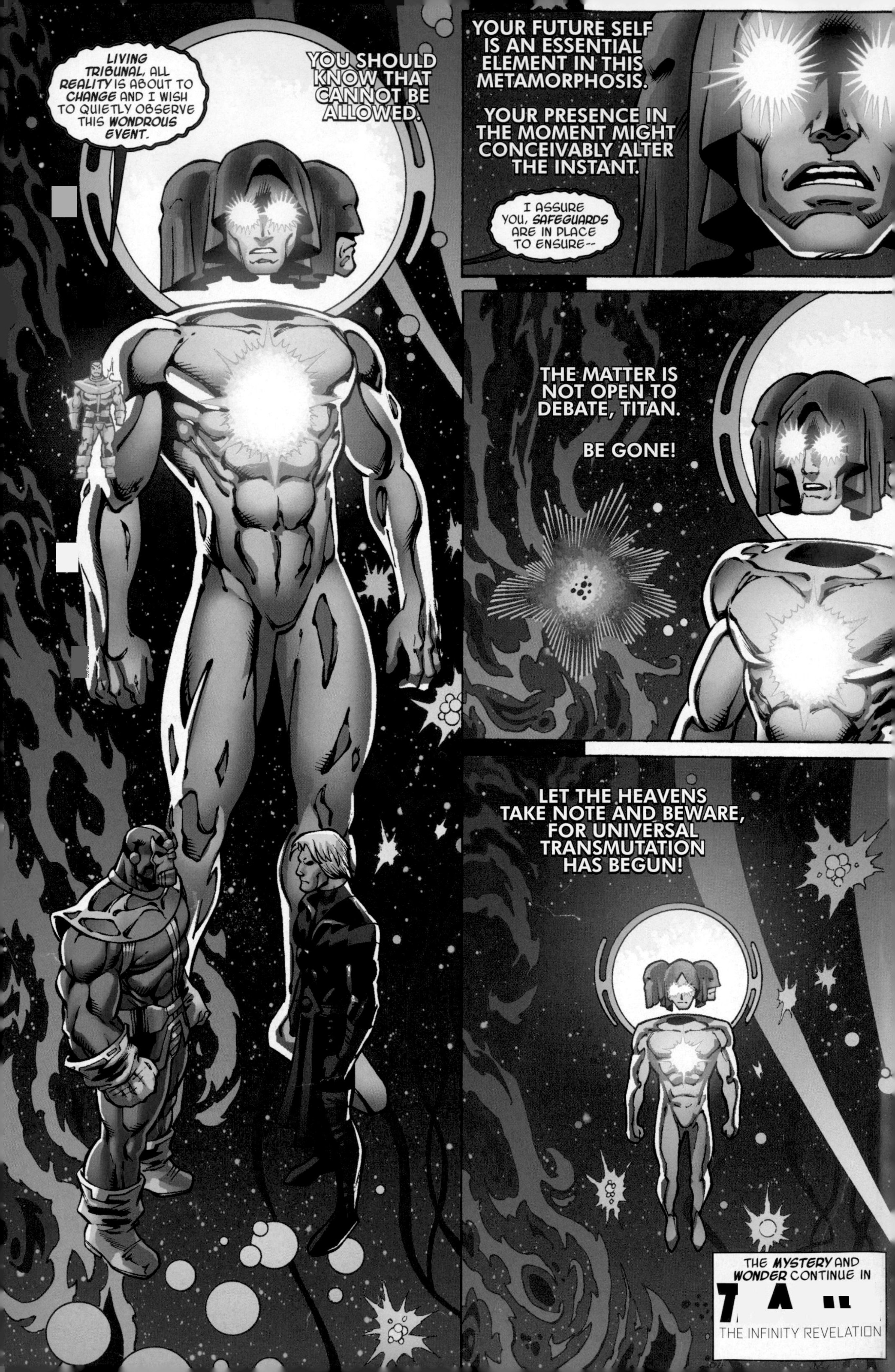
LIVING TRIBUNAL, ALL REALITY IS ABOUT TO CHANGE AND I WISH TO QUIETLY OBSERVE THIS WONDROUS EVENT.
YOU SHOULD KNOW THAT CANNOT BE ALLOWED.
YOUR FUTURE SELF IS AN ESSENTIAL ELEMENT IN THIS METAMORPHOSIS.
YOUR PRESENCE IN THE MOMENT MIGHT CONCEIVABLY ALTER THE INSTANT.
I ASSURE YOU, SAFEGUARDS ARE IN PLACE TO ENSURE--
THE MATTER IS NOT OPEN TO DEBATE, TITAN.
BE GONE!
LET THE HEAVENS TAKE NOTE AND BEWARE, FOR UNIVERSAL TRANSMUTATION HAS BEGUN!
THE MYSTERY AND WONDER CONTINUE IN
THE INFINITY REVELATION

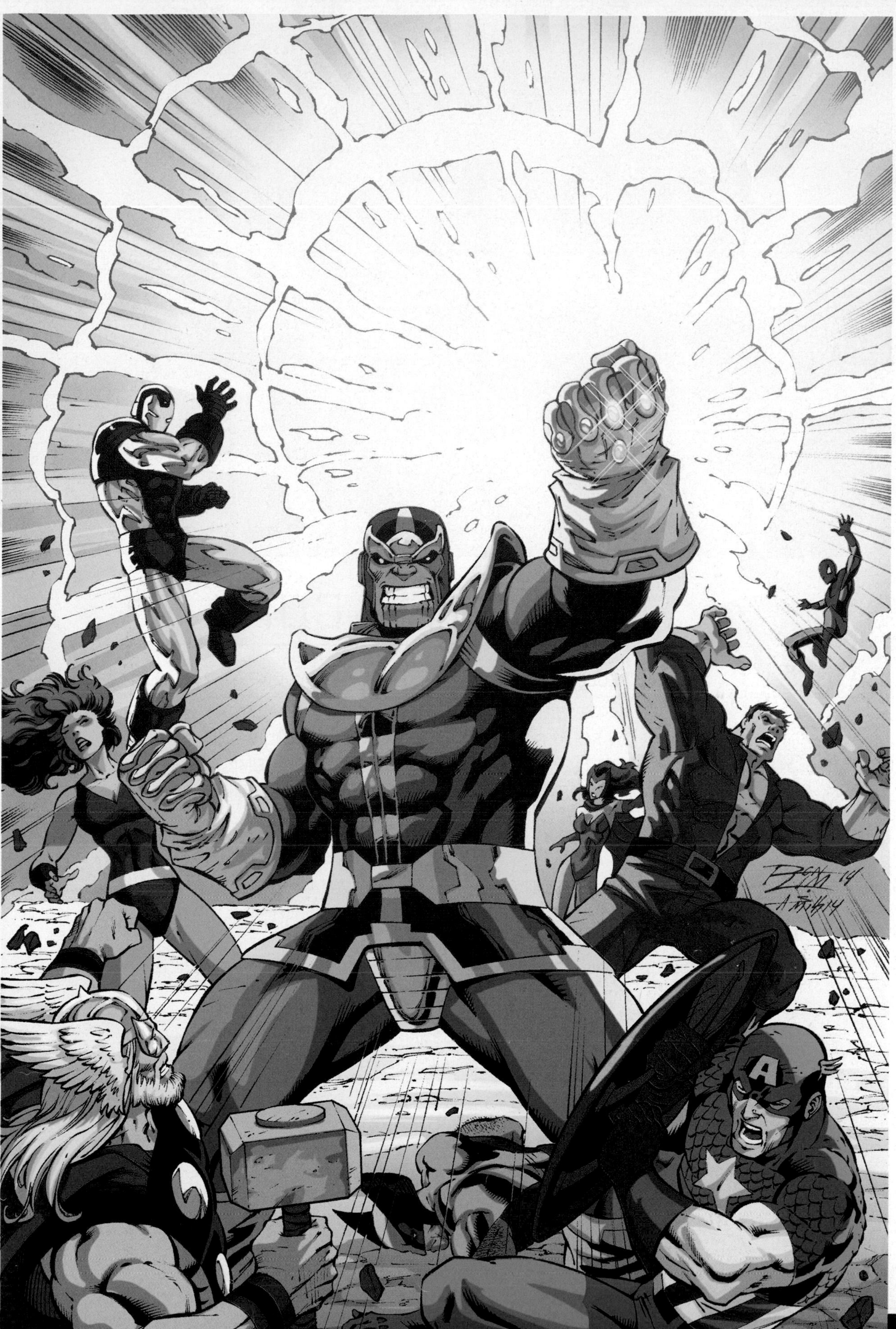

ANNUAL #1 VARIANT
BY RON LIM, ANDY SMITH & BRAD ANDERSON

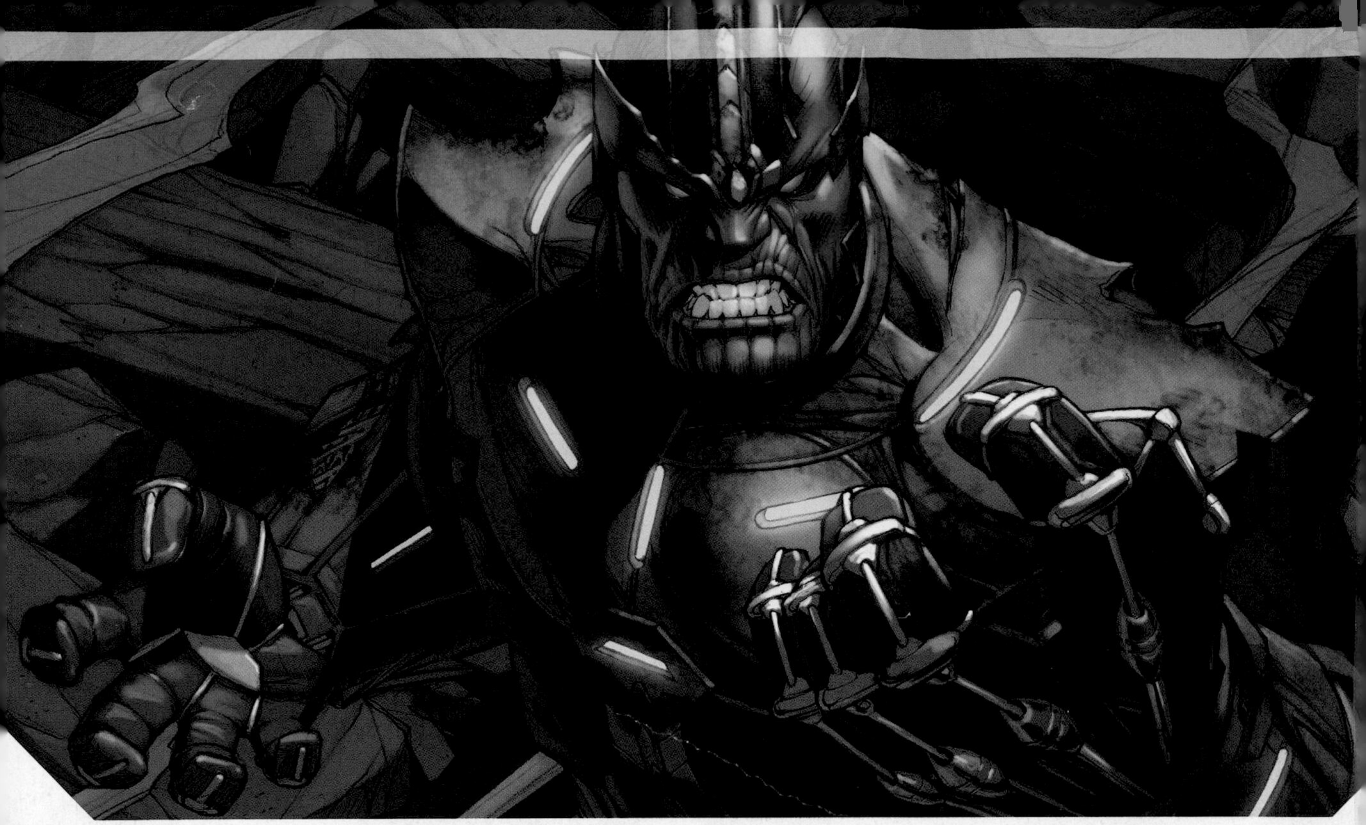

FREE DIGITAL COPY

TO REDEEM YOUR CODE FOR A FREE DIGITAL COPY:

1 GO TO MARVEL.COM/REDEEM. OFFER EXPIRES ON 12/03/16.
2 FOLLOW THE ON-SCREEN INSTRUCTIONS TO REDEEM YOUR DIGITAL COPY.
3 LAUNCH THE MARVEL COMICS APP TO READ YOUR COMIC NOW.
4 YOUR DIGITAL COPY WILL BE FOUND UNDER THE 'MY COMICS' TAB.
5 READ AND ENJOY.

YOUR FREE DIGITAL COPY WILL BE AVAILABLE ON:

MARVEL COMICS APP FOR APPLE IOS® DEVICES

MARVEL COMICS APP FOR ANDROID™ DEVICES

MTML168N0VFF

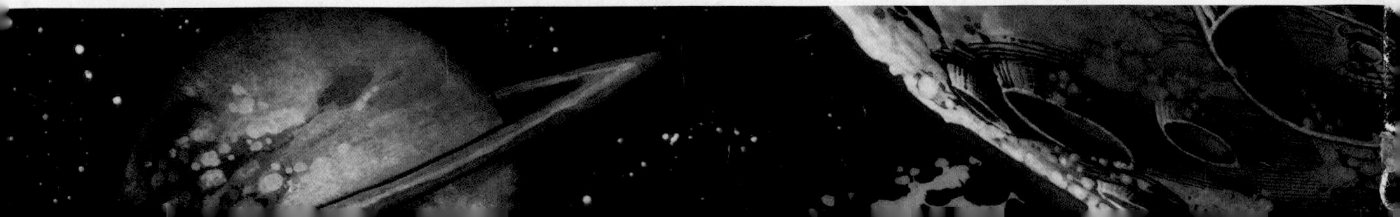